GEOMETRY AND JEAN GENET
SHAPING THE SUBJECT

LEGENDA

LEGENDA is the Modern Humanities Research Association's book imprint for new research in the Humanities. Founded in 1995 by Malcolm Bowie and others within the University of Oxford, Legenda has always been a collaborative publishing enterprise, directly governed by scholars. The Modern Humanities Research Association (MHRA) joined this collaboration in 1998, became half-owner in 2004, in partnership with Maney Publishing and then Routledge, and has since 2016 been sole owner. Titles range from medieval texts to contemporary cinema and form a widely comparative view of the modern humanities, including works on Arabic, Catalan, English, French, German, Greek, Italian, Portuguese, Russian, Spanish, and Yiddish literature. Editorial boards and committees of more than 60 leading academic specialists work in collaboration with bodies such as the Society for French Studies, the British Comparative Literature Association and the Association of Hispanists of Great Britain & Ireland.

The MHRA encourages and promotes advanced study and research in the field of the modern humanities, especially modern European languages and literature, including English, and also cinema. It aims to break down the barriers between scholars working in different disciplines and to maintain the unity of humanistic scholarship. The Association fulfils this purpose through the publication of journals, bibliographies, monographs, critical editions, and the MHRA Style Guide, and by making grants in support of research. Membership is open to all who work in the Humanities, whether independent or in a University post, and the participation of younger colleagues entering the field is especially welcomed.

RESEARCH MONOGRAPHS IN FRENCH STUDIES

The *Research Monographs in French Studies* (RMFS) are selected, edited and supported by the Society for French Studies. The series seeks to publish the best new work in all areas of the literature, language, thought, history, politics, culture and film of the French-speaking world and to cover the full chronological range from the medieval period to the present day. Proposals are accepted for monographs of up to 85,000 words, while proposals for 'short' monographs (50,000–60,000 words), a traditional strength of the series, are still welcomed.

❖

PUBLISHED IN THIS SERIES

www.rmfs.mhra.org.uk

Geometry and Jean Genet

Shaping the Subject

❖

JOANNE BRUETON

l

LEGENDA

Research Monographs in French Studies 61
Modern Humanities Research Association
2022

Published by Legenda
an imprint of the Modern Humanities Research Association
Salisbury House, Station Road, Cambridge CB1 2LA

ISBN 978-1-78188-452-2 (HB)
ISBN 978-1-78188-456-0 (PB)

First published 2022

Copy-Editor: Charlotte Brown

CONTENTS

❖

ACKNOWLEDGEMENTS

❖

Travaille bien ton Genet, c'est important.
Amitiés
        Christian.

30 March 2020 at 13:38

I received this email from Christian Biet shortly before he died last year. Ever a magnanimous mentor, Christian may not have realized how vital these words have been in bringing this book to fruition. I think of them often, as a reminder that the work we do on dissident thinkers like Genet carries importance beyond the purely academic. This book is a product of the intellectual guidance, support, friendships and shared ambition of the community that has helped to forge my own academic journey. It is with profound gratitude that I thank the following people for their invaluable help on a project that has shaped my academic journey.

This monograph grew out of my doctoral thesis at University College London, during which time I had the good fortune to be supervised by Mairéad Hanrahan and Timothy Mathews. Mairéad taught me how to read Genet atomistically, balletically and with a poetic intuition that has inspired so much of how I approach literary analysis more generally. Her seminal scholarship on Genet, Cixous and Derrida has stimulated so much of my own, and hers is the empowering voice to which I turn when most stretching myself. Tim's way of seeing the world and its impact on why and how we produce art has been central to expanding my own ideas. Any conversation with him is a gift that galvanizes a more dynamic approach to the intellectual endeavour, and I am always grateful for his guidance and friendship.

The generosity of my thesis examiners, Clare Finburgh and Katherine Ibbett, has driven much of my postdoctoral work. It is to them that I owe perhaps the greatest thanks, since their report not only provided the confidence to produce this book, but it lent direction to the bigger questions a monograph should pose. Clare's unwavering belief in me as a researcher has yielded collaborative projects with colleagues including Carl Lavery, Christian Biet and Agnès Vannouvong, and encouraged me to pursue publication projects that otherwise I could have only hoped to achieve. Katherine has been an effusive and magnanimous reader of my work, encouraging me and a whole generation of scholars to change the field in which we work.

The institutional support I have received throughout my academic journey — at Cambridge under the tutelage of Martin Crowley, Bill Burgwinkle and Victoria Best, at UCL as a recipient of an AHRC doctoral award, at the École normale supérieure with an ASMCF early career research award, and now as a lecturer at the University of London Institute in Paris — has shaped and embedded ways of thinking that I can only hope to pass on as a teacher. Special thanks to Anna-Louise Milne whose brilliant insights and generative readings nudged this manuscript to submission. I extend my appreciation to Albert Dichy, curator of Genet's estate at the Institut mémoires de l'édition contemporaine (IMEC), for permitting me to consult four of Genet's drawings held in his archive. I am grateful to Taylor & Francis for granting me the copyright license to revisit a newer version of an article published in *Performance Research* (2017) in my chapter 'Obliques' (Part 2.II). Most gratitude, however, is due to Diana Knight, Graham Nelson, Charlotte Wathey and the readers at Legenda, whose editorial intuitions, attentiveness and patience have brought this book to publication.

Undoubtedly, this journey would have been too arduous without the support of my family — Jacqui, David and Gina — who have lent perspective, kindness and an inquisitive ear, and to the forbearance of my husband, Richard. I cannot count the times you have listened, nor measure the depth of your understanding; when I have been going around in circles, you have helped me get straight to the point. In the spirit of exciting new ways of seeing that I hope this book inspires, I dedicate it to the widest eyes of our family: to B. and A.S.

NOTE ON TRANSLATIONS

❖

Sources have been primarily quoted in their original language. Where English translations exist, published versions have been cited in square brackets after the French reference and in the bibliography. However, much of the archival material from IMEC or recent Francophone publications on Genet are yet to be translated, in which case all translations are my own.

Where two published translations exist, I have opted to either use the most recent or the most well-known depending on the context. For the translation of *L'Atelier d'Alberto Giacometti*, I have used the translation in *Fragments of the Artwork* (2013). For *Le Funambule*, I have used a more recent translation in the 2020 publication of *The Criminal Child* as I felt the translation decisions were more faithful to the original.

LIST OF ABBREVIATIONS

❖

Primary works by Genet that recur frequently in the text are abbreviated as below. Less well-known Genet texts, including *La Sentence*, *Le Bagne* and *Elle*, or material from Genet's archives are cited in full for maximum clarity.

AAG *L'Atelier d'Alberto Giacometti*, in *OC*, v, 41–73
     The Studio of Alberto Giacometti, in *Fragments of the Artwork*, trans. by Charlotte Mendell (Stanford, CA: Stanford University Press, 2003)
B   *Le Bagne* (Paris: L'Arbalète, 1994)
CA   *Un captif amoureux* (Paris: Gallimard, 1986)
     Prisoner of Love, trans. by Barbara Bray, intro. by Ahdaf Soueif (New York: New York Review of Books, 1986)
ED   *L'Ennemi déclaré: textes et entretiens*, ed. by Albert Dichy (Paris: Gallimard, 1991)
F   *Le Funambule*, in *OC*, v, 8–27
     The Tightrope Walker, in *The Criminal Child*, trans. by Charlotte Mendell and Jeffrey Zuckerman (New York: New York Review of Books, 2020), pp. 98–117
JV   *Journal du voleur* (Paris: Gallimard, 1986)
LMOB *Lettres à Marc et Olga Barbezat* (Décines: L'Arbalète, 1988)
MR   *Miracle de la rose*, in *OC*, ii, 261–469
     Miracle of the Rose, trans. by Bernard Frechtman, intro. by Jean-Paul Sartre (New York: Grove Press, 1966)
NDF *Notre-Dame-des-Fleurs*, in *OC*, ii, 7–207
     Our Lady of the Flowers, trans. by Bernard Frechtman (London: Faber & Faber, 1973)
OC   *Œuvres complètes*, 6 vols (Paris: Gallimard, 1952–79)
PF   *Pompes funèbres*, in *OC*, iii, 7–162
     Funeral Rites, trans. by Bernard Frechtman (London: Grove Press, 1994)
S   *La Sentence, suivi de J'étais et je n'étais pas* (Paris: Gallimard, 2010)
TC   *Théâtre complet*, ed. by Michel Corvin and Albert Dichy (Paris: Gallimard, 2002)

Two other frequently-cited works are also abbreviated:

G   Jacques Derrida, *Glas* (Paris: Galilée, 1974)
     Glas, trans. by John P. Leavey, Jr. and Richard Rand (Lincoln & London: University of Nebraska Press, 1986)
SG   Jean-Paul Sartre, *Saint Genet: comédien et martyr* (Paris: Gallimard, 1952)
     Saint Genet: Actor & Martyr, trans. by Bernard Frechtman (London: Heinemann, 1988)

Si l'ordre du cosmos exige des soleils autour desquels gravitent des astres, l'ordre social alors me parut semblable; tout soleil garde ses distances au sens géométrique de ce terme.

[It seems to me that the social as well as cosmic order calls for suns with stars revolving around them, and every sun keeping its distance [in the geometric sense of the term.] — JEAN GENET

What sort of morning was Euclid having
when he first considered parallel lines?
Or that business about how things equal
to the same thing are equal to each other?
                    [...] how distance
from a centre point can be both increased
endlessly and endlessly split — a mystery
where the local and the global share
the same vexations and geometry?
                    — THOMAS LYNCH[1]

INTRODUCTION

❖

Genet the Geometer

Se connaître — où est notre etalon?
[To know each other. By what measure?]
— Jean Genet[2]

In April 1986, days before his death, Jean Genet gave his lawyer Roland Dumas two briefcases of manuscripts. Without any fixed abode, this travelling archive of personal notes, press cuttings, reworked versions of existing texts or drafts of new ones charts a trajectory not only through Genet's literary and political life from 1967 to 1982, but through the words and worlds he held close for the final fifteen years of his life. These portable annals are being commemorated in an exhibition at IMEC as I write, just prior to Genet's consecration on the hallowed pages of the Pléiade with their uncensored edition of his early novels and poems.[3] Interest has burgeoned in the unpublished Genet; in the little-known fragments of a now canonical, albeit seditious, anti-French writer whose reckoning with the plight of the dispossessed, the violence of a verdict, the yoke of territory and its colonial appetite, and the Western mechanisms of power that structure and entrench oppression speaks presciently to the political crises that demand a language of resistance today. Yet, within this 'atelier portatif et permanent' [permanent and portable studio] — where Genet creatively reworked the revolutionary justice of May '68 into his advocacy for the Palestinians, the Black Panthers and Moroccan immigrant workers in France — lies a more abstract, more self-reflective trope that this book argues is a central tenet of Genet's anti-identitarian epistemology.[4] How to navigate a subjectivity that ruptures calculation, but which endlessly seeks form?

Perhaps unexpectedly, Genet turns to the language of geometry to address this question. These archives contain drafts of two intertwined texts, *La Sentence* and *J'étais et je n'étais pas*, first conceived in 1956 and likely written in Tangiers in 1969, both of which offer a lacerating meditation on crime, punishment and the space and time of the condemned subject. The first is composed of a gridded series of unequal red and black blocks, whose form is anathema to the monolithic structures of discipline and sentencing excoriated by Genet. The second is a prose poem, which riffs on the ontological leitmotif of being (*j'étais*) and non-being (*je n'étais pas*), as Genet asks where to draw the borders of a self who is judged for eternity. Both are inspired by what Albert Dichy calls 'l'influence de Mallarmé' since 'ce livre poursuit un projet d'œuvre fondée sur le calcul et le nombre' [Mallarmé's influence, since this book is based on calculation and numbers], as Genet strives to measure a subjectivity that is not pinned to the static, essentialising metrics of judgement.[5] Instead, he looks for a vocabulary able to articulate a *je* who is both aggressively bordered by the taxonomies of the magistrate, but who also dances around those spatial, temporal and discursive frames in an irrecuperable form. 'Non rattrapable' [uncatchable], he proclaims in an unnamed note in the pocket of the briefcase.[6] Turning inwards, he looks to the paradoxes of his own selfhood, which he situates in the torsion between the materiality of form, land, rootedness ('les divers accidents de ma vie hors du ventre maternel qui donnent à mon aventure sur Terre la forme que j'avais choisie de toute éternité' [the various accidents of my life outside the maternal womb that gave my adventure on Earth the form I had chosen for all eternity]), and the abstraction of being separated from spatiotemporal experience, unanchored to 'l'espace puisque *je* n'occupais aucun espace, *je* n'étais nulle part' [space since *I* didn't occupy any space, *I* was nowhere].[7] Genet's subject is caught between the telluric and the imaginary, between realisation and idealisation. And rather than seeking to solve these ontological paradoxes through the well-worn philosophical routes of Cartesian metaphysics, Foucauldian subjectivation (where the subject is produced through obedience to power) or Lacanian misrecognition in which subjectivity is founded on illusion, Genet turns to the metaphor of the geometer as a figure who both measures the land and conceives of idealised shapes, to articulate his elusive vision of subjectivity.[8] In a concluding remark in the 2010 version of *J'étais et je n'étais pas*, Genet asks:

> Doit-on parcourir, vite ou lentement, notre seule individualité, en la mesurant, comme ferait un arpenteur, en l'évaluant selon ce que chacun peut apercevoir chez les autres, c'est-à-dire que notre connaissance de nous-même se bornerait à des 'rapports' et que nous ne pouvons nous connaître que par l'évaluation de ces 'rapports', ou l'apprécier seulement dans nos principales ressources, ou bien doit-on chercher ailleurs? Ailleurs, le mot servirait à désigner non une vague et imprécise direction, mais quelque chose — état, possibilité ou potentiel — qui est là, et là seulement, enfermé dans le mot ailleurs, ou peut-être désigné par lui.[9]

> [Must we navigate our own individuality by measuring it like a geometer/ surveyor? Pacing around it quickly or slowly, and evaluating it according to what each person perceives in the other? That means our self-understanding would be constrained by 'relations', such that we would only know ourselves through the evaluation of these relations, or that we would only gauge it via our primary resources. Or must we look elsewhere? Elsewhere: the word signifies not a vague and imprecise direction, but something that is there — a state, a possibility or a potential — and there only, enclosed in the word elsewhere, or perhaps named by it.]

In seeking a metaphor that navigates subjectivity from the outside, projecting it beyond the realms of what is internally known, Genet considers the consequences of being bound in form. On the one hand, all his texts are in dogged pursuit of new ways to figure the idiosyncrasy of human experience; on the other, they are in absolute flight from any immutable, definable property that may diminish that irretrievable uniqueness. Here, in this uncommented archival scrap, Genet emulates an *arpenteur*, a word whose prima facie meaning points both to a land surveyor who measures the earth, replete with the colonial connotations of possessing, mastering or marking out for commercial purposes; and to a rambler, who paces, stalks the land and traverses the surface of the earth without mapping.[10] The cartographer and the walker: the two postures are radically opposed. The former calls on the historic roots of geometry as a way to apportion land, which Herodotus tells us first originated in Egypt as King Sesostris divided the terrain equally between citizens who paid dividends and any erosion of that land by the river was then subtracted from the amount owed.[11] Geometry thus yielded a form of economic servility, and later became a colonial practice that politicised the boundaries of space as European cartographers carved up territory in the expansion of empire. But the *arpenteur* as walker resists that spatial domination, their errancy tapping into an urban poetics of perambulation that has long been a topos in French thought. For Baudelaire, Benjamin, de Certeau, even the Situationist International (SI), the aimless drifter resists the hegemony of geographic borders to move freely between the structures, patterns and boundaries that over-determine daily life.[12] Genet plays with these polarities in his attempt to shape a nimble vision of subjectivity that is not pinned to essentialism, but that still has form, place and position: 'qui est là', however unassailably.

His geometer-*arpenteur* does not offer a flat or vapid representation of space. Rather, it becomes a dynamic form deeply rooted in his core questions about how the self exists in space, how the self relates to the other without ligature, and how to begin measuring our subjective experience without the yoke of 'evaluation', metrics or measurability that have taken on almost axiomatic status in a neo-liberal world. While the *arpenteur* seems to leave little room for the autonomous play of Genet's irrepressible, self-shattering subjects who are forged from points of change, perennial displacement and the transgression of their own limits, this book will argue that Genet uses the language of geometry to figure a mobile cartography of selfhood that inscribes the very border it uproots.[13] In asking whether to measure individuality like a geometer does the earth, Genet echoes Euclid's original definition of geometry in *The Elements* in which the 'object of Geometry is the properties of the figure, and figure is to be defined as the relation which subsists between the boundaries of space'.[14] In his commentary on the text, the philosopher of classical antiquity, Proclus, explains that the figure is predominantly conceived in the mind of the geometer, joined with matter and extended in the imagination as a form whose boundary will always contain it from the outside. A 'figure is thus not a limit, but is limit*ed*; it is not its own boundary (the bounding is other than that which is bounded), nor is it *in* it, it is simply contained by it'.[15] The geometric figure is thus never total, it is delimited by borders that hem it in, but whose enclosure never defines nor essentialises it. Grafted onto Genet's embodied image of 'notre seule individualité', geometry starts to offer the material and conceptual terrain in which to plot a subjectivity that is salvaged from the totalising discourses of identity.

Rather than being a technically sophisticated geometer, Genet thus treats geometry democratically: borrowing from a language extrapolated from the real, material or physical world to imagine an individuality at its liminal edge, and navigating a self-understanding forged from negation, as that which is left over from the boundary that demarcates it. The metaphor of the *arpenteur* allows him to avoid the ontologising vocabulary of self-mastery to expose instead the lines that constrain all individuals, the reterritorialising frontiers that beckon for their own transgression. It is *se borner à* that Genet emphasises here, but he plays with the paronomasia of the term as meaning both to be limited to (the negativity of the barrier, or *schranke* to use Kantian terminology) and to settle for (the positivity of the boundary or threshold, *grenze*, as that which can be transgressed), in order to complicate the relationship between defining and restraining our individuality.[16] In an almost Sartrean outburst against *mauvaise foi*, Genet seems to warn against determining the self through the estimation of the other. He berates the modes of quantification — 'évaluation', 'apprécier', 'principales ressources' — that reduce the human relation to static, empirical metrics or that hold the subject hostage to the ethical demand or appraisal of the other (in the Levinasian sense).

But while he seems to be anticipating the anti-communitarian commentary of his critics, Genet is careful to couch these relations not in the language of ethics, but in the language of geometry.[17] The agency of *se borner à* thus changes, such that the individual is not barricaded by the evaluative measurement of the other, but is brought to the threshold of the spaces that demarcate their subjectivity and nudged to cross that limit, to walk around the periphery of a selfhood whose borders are endlessly shifting. In 'settling for' a geometric subjectivity, Genet plots a selfhood that cannot be dominated because it is forever on the horizon of an elsewhere, an 'ailleurs' that exists only in the poetics of space. His 'elsewhere' thus uses the cartographic logic of geometry against itself. This is not a direction that can be charted or colonised; it is a language of deterritorialisation that beckons the subject's becoming, not being. Like Badiou's notion of the 'Event' — expressed as a mathematical equation that breaks through the normal structures of social control to stage the emergence of something radically new — so Genet plots a locus of selfhood that is kinetic, catalysing the unbridled and the new: a possibility, a potential, a state, which vibrates with the energy of that which is finding form, but which constitutively transgresses any barrier that seeks to control it. Such shape-shifting disavows any of the fixed relations that might formalise an identity, and it is Genet's insistence on using a symbol of measurement that refuses to ontologise the subject that makes his geometric practice so productive.

Perhaps it is not incidental that Genet's geometric sensibility is articulated so explicitly in a text that excoriates the linguistic barriers of the verdict, which annex the subject, and ousts them from the frames of social cohesion. Taking refuge in the abstraction of the geometer, Genet transforms the injunctive perimeter and its totalising ambition to measure and classify, into a liminality that positions the self at the very limit of what can be quantified. We might recall how Moroccan deconstructionist and Genet admirer, Abdelkébir Khatibi, also draws on the *arpenteur* to symbolise the illegibility of those condemned to non-assimilation. In dialogue with Derrida in 2007, Khatibi argues, 'dès qu'on est rejeté dans le monde de l'illisibilité, on devient un étranger professionnel, c'est-à-dire un arpenteur des passages, des frontières' [as soon as one is thrown back into the world of illegibility, one becomes a professional foreigner, that is to say a surveyor/geometer of crossings, borders].[18] Khatibi's image of unauthorised wandering refers to the interstitial state of inhabiting two languages, yet his terms evoke the precarious perch of Genet's geometer who looks not for the 'vague et imprécise direction' of an ontological telos, but to demarcate the gates of escape from belonging or settlement. Genet the outcast becomes a geometer without a ruler, an *arpenteur* who crosses the frontiers of a selfhood inscribed in the pure ideal of an exit.

Unlike Khatibi's spatial topography of the peripheralised migrant, Genet conceives of a more universal, plural singular subject — 'notre seule individualité' — who shares the experience of being born on the frontier, in communication with an outside that has no geographic bearings but is etched in the coordinates of geometric figures written on the map of the page. Enclosed in the word *ailleurs*, in a space without place, Genet inscribes his subjects into the spatial signifiers of points, lines, obliques, squares, circles and grids that abound in his prose. From a language of measurement emerges a poetics of perennial movement as these figures never lead us to one totalisable picture of a stable self. Genet seeks to liberate subjectivity from the petrification of such psychological, moral or transcendental revelations that might unveil a hidden identity struggling to come to the fore.[19] His geometric constellations offer a new set of ideas about how to negotiate the human relation beyond the ethical vantage point that Leo Bersani, Éric Marty, Ivan Jablonka, even Sartre, have institutionalised in the reception of his work.[20] His kaleidoscopic shapes trace material patterns of being in the world not reducible to one political teleology, but, like a cubist painting fragmenting our ways of seeing, demand we learn from the subject's mobile positions towards the world, to the other and even to meaning itself.

This book is the first to explore how Genet's poetics are marked by a language of geometry, which, I argue, both structures his radical anti-identitarian epistemology and galvanises the possibility for social transformation. By tracing the geometric figures strewn across almost every one of his texts, I read the points, lines, diagonals, grids and circles as figures that not only symbolise Genet's unique means of relating to the world, but as shapes that provide a spatial map to navigate subjectivity in his writing. Despite the apparent incongruity of bringing together the abstract logic of geometry with the fleshy, affective and politicised world of Genet's texts, this book aims to show that geometry offers both a prism for reading and a recurrent pattern in Genet's writing that underlies his representation of selfhood. In a typically Genetian reversal of expected discursive norms, it is through his mathematic metaphors that we gain an insight into aspects of subjectivity that remain otherwise ineffable.

Genet wildly displaces the objective, rational pursuit of axiomatic truth that has long characterised philosophical engagements with geometry, such as in Pascal's *L'Esprit géometrique* or Descartes's appendix to his *Discours de la méthode, La Géometrie*.[21] Selfhood could not feel further from the agricultural surfaces that Egyptian geometers sought to map; yet, interpreting the human impression on those surfaces has long been at the heart of why geometry matters. Consider Vitruvius's treatise *De architectura*, which recounts how when the philosopher Aristippus discovered the traces of geometric figures on the island of Rhodes, he felt immediately reassured:

not because humans had been physically present, but because in their absence, the projection of forms signalled the ethical promise of some *humanitas*.[22] At its very genesis, then, geometry brings what is most incalculable about being human into relief, gesturing to an ineffability that is firmly set apart from the axiomatic truths of abstract and universal logic.

Philosophers and poets have nevertheless sought to set the computational drive of the mathematic in opposition to the orphic idiosyncrasy of the self. Aimé Césaire frames the debate in anti-colonial terms, as he famously opens his 1944 treatise *Poésie et connaissance*, by associating quantification with dehumanisation: 'la connaissance poétique naît dans le grand silence de la connaissance scientifique [...] la connaissance scientifique nombre, mesure, classe et tue [...]. Pour acquérir cette connaissance impersonnelle qu'est la connaissance scientifique, l'homme s'est *dépersonnalisé*, s'est *désindividualisé*' [Poetic knowledge is born in the great silence of scientific knowledge [...] scientific knowledge enumerates, measures, classifies, and kills [...]. To acquire this impersonal knowledge that is scientific knowledge, man has *depersonalised* and *deindividualized* himself].[23] For Césaire, writing in the anti-imperial context of a then-still colonised Martinique, poetry offers a clairvoyance drowned out by the epistemic brutality of measurements, taxonomies and calculations that strip the individual of any humanity. He rails against the rationalism of a European Enlightenment that coincided with the growth of empires, linking the abstract logic of mathematics to the brutalising violence of systemic classification that cleaved between citizen and slave. Objectivity has subjective consequences here, as Césaire suggests that the hegemony of axiomatic knowledge not only replaces individual thought — perversely empowering those who acquire given truths — but is weaponised to reify and eradicate some individuals, counting some subjects as those who do not count. Amidst an ongoing French domination of lands and people, only textual spaces are freed from the expendable processes of measurement that erode the self. Poetry speaks into the uncharted terrain left over from the objectively knowable that is exhausted by European cartography, peering into a human reality that sits contiguous to the impersonal mechanics of science. However, for the phenomenologist Edmund Husserl, this depersonalisation is what makes collective intuition possible. He depoliticises geometry to argue that in its pure form, it becomes the great equaliser: 'geometric existence is not psychic existence; it does not exist as something personal within the personal sphere of consciousness; it is the existence of what is objectively there for everyone'.[24] The ideal emerges out of the real here, as Husserl suggests that geometry draws on embodied spatio-temporal experience in order to produce a transcendental understanding shared by all; these abstract processes of measurement are salvaged from political partisanship or individual fallibility such that geometric knowledge rises above selfhood, as profoundly incompatible with it.

Susan Sontag's 1963 essay 'Sartre's *Saint Genet*' certainly confirms these dialectical responses to geometry and humanity. Identifying two traditions of French literary thought in the twentieth century, she argues that the ornate effect of the first is embodied by Genet as a 'baroque and didactic and insolent writer whose ego effaces all objective narrative; who is the master of games and artifices, of a rich, overrich style stuffed with metaphors and conceits'. The second tradition, she claims, is:

> The cult of aloofness, *l'esprit géometrique*. This tradition is represented among the new novelists, by Nathalie Sarraute, Alain Robbe-Grillet, and Michel Butor, so different from Genet in their search for an infinite precision, their narrow dehydrated subject-matter and cool microscopic styles.[25]

Sontag reads Genet's attention to the self, his embodied, visceral, quasi-masturbatory prose as incongruous to the logical restraint of his contemporaries seeking to reinvent the complex operation of fiction and its relation to reality.

The claim of this book is not only that Genet muddies such dialectical distinctions — deploying an *esprit géometrique* as the very idiom of his subjective poetics — but that geometry provides the fertile stage on which to collapse the bombastic humanism that posits the self as the sovereign of knowledge, logic, rationality or understanding. As Sartre argues through an uncannily prescient geometric metaphor, the poetic experience in Genet navigates between the human and the inhuman, between what Christina Howells existentially reads as the '*néant* of consciousness and the *être* of things', in order to expose the artifice of those idealising procedures that result in axiomatic truths.[26] Sartre remarks that 'la géometrie est une invention de l'homme et pourtant il n'y a rien de plus inhumain' [geometry is an invention of man, and yet there is nothing that is more inhuman] (*SG*, pp. 256; 274). Genet revels in highlighting the contrived nature of his geometric figures, ladening his shapes with a word-play that irreverently refuses for these signifiers to become reified into concepts from which a dominant truth might be gleaned. Geometry is never identical to itself in any of his texts, and thus rather than being yoked to the inhuman historic processes of enumeration and mensuration that turned space into capital, Genet uses measurement against itself, using order against order to shape a subject who is not retrievable in any stable form.

Genet's geometry thus offers a way to negotiate — rather than consolidate — a subjectivity that ruptures calculation and yet endlessly seeks form. Echoing the playful deterritorialised structures of existence we find in the thinking of Gilles Deleuze and Félix Guattari, Genet's geometry situates him as a thinker of his time, bringing him into contact with contemporary post-structuralist discourses (in particular Jacques Derrida, Hélène Cixous, Michel Foucault, Roland Barthes, Jean-Luc Nancy, Gilles Deleuze, Edward Said) also wrestling with how to signify the indeterminacy of subjectivity in the twentieth century. Faced with the conceptual constraints of a structuralist outlook that is organised by oppositional positions and relations in set cultural (Claude Lévi-Strauss) and semiotic (Ferdinand de Saussure) systems, post-structuralism seems to seek refuge in geometric figurations that enable a more asymmetrical cartography of being in the world.

Geometry and Jean Genet thus takes us on a journey around post-structuralist geometries refracted by Genet's poetics: singular points (Barthes, Cixous); rhizomatic lines of identity (Deleuze and Guattari); labyrinthine forms of affiliation rather than problematic notions of lineage (Derrida, Nancy); transversal sexualities (Foucault, Guattari); and elliptical approaches to meaning that explode the promise of any self-evident signification (Derrida, Cixous). Genet is foregrounded as a unique interlocutor in the debate about how to quantify and materialise subjective experience: his joyously prismatic geometry is not merely a post-structuralist example that displaces the totalising or definite propositions we would expect to find in mathematic discourse, but a balletic resistance to the unity of any form, space or logic that seeks to immobilise the self. This book paints a picture of the modulations, fragmentations and constellations that a geometric imagination might bring to the untotalisable nature of subjectivity.

Each part concentrates on a different geometric figure, coupling close analysis with comparisons from other theoretical and visual references. Part One, 'Points', examines the presence of the point in Genet's writing, examining how its symbolism of puncture, atomistic singularity and ellipsis evokes the radical solitude of Genet's selves. I read the point as a profoundly affective signifier: driving its way into Genet's text to evoke the figural violence of trying to pin down meaning, an experience that Wassily Kandinsky, Cixous and Deleuze also explore; as well as existing within his texts like a *punctum* (Barthes), or poignant wound at the origin of his representation of subjectivity. Rather than reading the point as an empty value of solitude, as Bersani presents Genet's ethical position, I argue that these points construct a vision of relation based on our shared solitude. They crystallise the irretrievable singularity of being as the very condition of engaging with the other, and thus atomise the very language of relation as founded on any kind of continuity.

This perforated relation is developed in Part Two, 'Vectors', which is divided between straight and oblique lines. First, in 'Lines', I analyse the linear figures that Genet reifies in Alberto Giacometti's artworks, in the cord of *Le Funambule*, as well as in his ubiquitous motif of the thread, as deeply evocative of the status of lineage and filiation in his writing. Lines in Genet's texts never tie his subjects down to any rooted form of legacy. Instead, he plays on the paranomasia of the *fils*, as both threads and a son, to fabricate new lines of relation with the world and its subjects in order to free him from any form of ligature. Yet there is a tension implicit in this nomadic desire to suspend any relation that might bind the subject: lines often bring us back to a filial nostalgia in his writing, and their symbolic presence allows him to materialise new filiations within the text that will never exist outside it. Set against Derrida's reading of the silkworm, Jean-Luc Nancy's *Être singulier pluriel* and Deleuze and Guattari's lines of flight, I am interested here in how Genet's linear geometries help us better to understand a subjectivity that seeks to break the very tie that is endlessly being constructed in his texts.

The second section, 'Obliques', explores the geometry of perspective and offers a study of Genet's self-professed oblique outlook. The indirect play of the oblique angle challenges the straight axes on which Maurice Merleau-Ponty bases his *Phénoménologie de la perception*, and, by harnessing the subversive potential of transversal lines, Genet can be situated amidst wider scholarship on queer orientations (Sara Ahmed, Lee Edelman, Foucault).[27] This chapter considers the obliquity in and of Genet's theatre: a privileged medium that intersects with the performative practices of the SI to dramatise the displaced, the virtual and the deviant in three dimensions. I analyse the errant choreography of diagonals in *Les

Bonnes, the slanted scenography of *Les Paravents*, the decentred obliquity in *L'Étrange mot d'...*, while considering more widely how his paratexts on theatre become oblique forms themselves (Genette). Conscious of the *limus*, or waste, that haunts the etymology of the oblique, I consider how Genet's oblique stance collapses political, social and epistemic norms by being positioned as a remnant not recuperated by any system. For Genet's representation of subjectivity, the power of the *démarche oblique* is found in a reckless pursuit of freedom: refusing to inscribe itself in any one stable direction, it becomes as an artistic position that is forever *en marche*.

These restless patterns of movement are discussed in Part Three, 'Planes', in which we become the *arpenteur* walking around the square and circular topographies that Genet builds into his penitentiary imagination. These grids and circles should feel restrictive: his subjects bound to repetitive revolutions in *Miracle de la rose*; boxed in by iterations of rectangular shapes in *Le Bagne*; Genet himself beset by the vertical and horizontal shapes of Hebrew in *Un captif amoureux*. Yet, their wholeness is only ever partial, and Genet's spatial imagination is more concerned with accentuating what falls out of the frame: the orbit of the conical *tinette à chier*; the *enceinte* of *Le Bagne* that surrounds an empty centre; the *marge frontalière* that encircles the Palestinians in *Un captif amoureux*; the revolving set of an early version of *Le Balcon*; the gauze that filters language in *La Sentence*. Building on Derrida's hermeneutic of the matrix in *Glas* and Sartre's circular interpretation of Genet's writing, this chapter explores what is left behind by Genet's liminal evocation of a subjectivity in which the self is never wholly contained in any part. Through new comparisons with Foucault's analysis of prison geometry in the construction of docile bodies and Samuel Beckett's *Quad*, I consider how Genet sits within a much wider poetics of the void, in which the impossible task of fully containing subjective experience in any representation becomes, quite literally, like squaring the circle.

The Coda, 'Petits dessins géométriques', will offer a visual counterpoint to the book's textual analysis via a study of Genet's geometric sketches. Despite receiving almost no critical attention, these sketches recall the single-line drawings of Cocteau and Picasso: depicting four facial profiles that are abstract and isolated, suspended in mid-air to evoke a fragile sense of detachment that nonetheless calls out for some relation to it. These geometric faces crystallise Genet's desire to outline our individuality as an *arpenteur* would, but what they actually measure is the profound uncertainty that lies within the capacity of any cultural form to make sense of subjective experience. In Genet's mobile geometry, each line gestures to its own undoing, each shape is replaced by another, and all measurement becomes defunct.

Arguably, therein lies Genet's conflation of the competing figures of the surveyor and the geometer. His ontological *arpenteur* promises a cartography of selfhood, but what his geometric figures produce instead is a critical hermeneutic that exposes the violent sedimentation of such essentialising measurement. Geometry restlessly resists entrenchment in Genet's texts, cannibalising the metrics of the surveyor to draw our attention instead to the anti-identitarian possibilities of abstraction where the subject is rescued from comprehension. Where the French engineer Edme-François Jomard, who took part in Napoleon's commission to Egypt, claimed that 'la géométrie, plus qu'aucune autre branche de connoissances offre le moyen de parvenir à la vérité; en effet, les théorèmes de géométrie ne laissent point de prise à de vagues interprétations' [geometry, more than any other branch of knowledge, offers the means of achieving truth. In effect, the theorems of geometry do not allow vague interpretations to hold], Genet's geometric shapes respond by exposing the hawkish standpoint behind that knowledge.[28] Instead, his geometry directs us to the unresolved question scribbled aphoristically in his 1977 essay on the perils of nationalism, 'Cathédrale de Chartres': 'se connaître — où est notre étalon?' Genet returns us to the shifting materiality of the *arpent* and the *borne* as his *étalon*, or ruler, strives to gauge a self-understanding by using the same tools that tie the individual to the politicised spaces of territory, nationality and kinship that erode any such self-governance. This book argues that Genet reappropriates those instruments that have become such contrived vehicles of power, bombastically serving the authors of empire who weaponised mensuration for subjugation, to plot the intangible terrains of a subjectivity whose measure is found in the poetics of space, and in the points, lines, squares and circles, that dance in abstraction alone.

Notes to the Introduction

1. Jean Genet, *Un captif amoureux* (Paris: Gallimard, 1986), pp. 178–79; *Prisoner of Love*, trans. by Barbara Bray, intro. by Ahdaf Soueif (New York: New York Review of Books, 1986), p. 150 (hereafter referenced in main text as *CA*). Thomas Lynch, 'Euclid', in *The Walking Papers* (London: Jonathan Cape, 2010), pp. 3–4 (p. 3).

2. Jean Genet, 'Cathédrale de Chartres — "Vue cavaliere", Notice', in *L'Ennemi déclaré: textes et entretiens*, ed. by Albert Dichy (Paris: Gallimard, 1991), pp. 381–84 (p. 383); 'Chapter 27: Chartres Cathedral, Introductory Note', in *The Declared Enemy*, ed. by Albert Dichy, trans. by Jeff Fort (Stanford, CA: Stanford University Press, 2004), pp. 343–46 (p. 344) (hereafter referenced in main text as *ED*).

3. 'Les Valises de Jean Genet', exhibition, IMEC, Caen, 30 October 2020–24 April 2021; Jean Genet, *Romans et poèmes*, ed. by Emmanuelle Lambert and Gilles Philippe, with Albert Dichy (Paris: Gallimard/ Pléiade, 2021).

4. *Les Valises de Jean Genet: rompre, dispaître, écrire*, ed. by Albert Dichy (Saint-Germain-la-Blanche-Herbe: IMEC, 2020), p. 9.

5. Ibid., p. 166.

6. Ibid., p. 22.

7. Ibid., pp. 173–74.

8. For an expansive genealogy of subjectivity, see Étienne Balibar, *Citoyen sujet et autres essais d'anthropologie philosophique* (Paris: Presses universitaires de France, 2011), or, more recently, Annabel Kim's astute overview of 'subjecthood' in *Unbecoming Language: Anti-identitarian French Feminist Fictions* (Columbus: Ohio State University Press, 2018), p. 5.

9. *Les Valises de Jean Genet,* ed. by Dichy, pp. 41–42.

10. Véronique Lane makes a passing reference to the text as a whole in 'Trois mille ans d'histoire à treize mille mètres d'altitude', in *Jean Genet, toujours en fuite*, ed. by Véronique Lane (= *Spirale*, 240 (Spring 2012)), 45–47, and to its thematic echoes with Genet's previous article on the Vietnam war, 'Un salut aux cent milles étoiles', in *ED*, pp. 321–28, written in September 1968 on his arrival in America.

11. Herodotus, *The Histories*, trans. by Aubrey de Sélincourt (London: Penguin, 1954), p.109 (Book 2).

12. For a compendium on the history of the walker in European thought, see Frédéric Gros, *Marcher, une philosophie* (Paris: Carnets Nord, 2009); Matthew Beaumont, *Nightwalking: A Nocturnal History of London, Chaucer to Dickens* (London: Verso, 2016). See also Walter Benjamin,

Arcades Project, trans. by Howard Eiland and Kevin McLaughlin (Cambridge, MA: Harvard University Press, 1999), pp. 10–18, 423; Charles Baudelaire, *Œuvres complètes II*, ed. by Claude Pichois (Paris: Gallimard/ Pléiade, 1990), p. 695; Michel de Certeau, *L'Invention du quotidien* (Paris: Gallimard, 1980), Chapter 7; Guy Debord, 'La Théorie de la dérive', *Les Lèvres nues*, 9 (December 1956), pp. 6–10 (repr. *Internationale Situationniste*, 2 (December 1958), 19–23); 'Theory of the *dérive*', in *Situationist International Anthology*, revised and expanded edn, ed. and trans. by Ken Knabb (Berkeley, CA: Bureau of Public Secrets, 2006), pp. 135–45.

13. As Carl Lavery has shown, time and space are never static or punctual in Genet's writing, they are always frantic and synchronic: 'To Perform Genet: Transversalité, Blessure, Pouvoir', in *Genet et les arts*, ed. by Agnès Vannouvong (Paris: Presses du réel, 2013), pp. 133–47 (p. 137); while Mairéad Hanrahan's seminal work on Genet's whole corpus, but particularly on his relationship to space and time, has long argued that 'writing — and art in general — is a fixing that inscribes the fluidity it ends; the fluidity and the fixing together': 'Sculpting Time', in *Genet*, ed. by Mairéad Hanrahan (= *Paragraph*, 27.2 (July 2004)), 43–58 (p. 46).

14. Euclid, *The First Six Books of the Elements of Euclid, with a Commentary and Geometrical Exercises*, ed. by D. Lardner, 9th edn (London: Printed for Taylor & Walton, 1846), p. 1.

15. Proclus, *A Commentary on the First Book of Euclid's Elements*, trans. by Glenn R. Morrow (Princeton, NJ: Princeton University Press, 1970), p. 143 (my emphasis).

16. This philosophy of the limit derives from Kant's interpretation in the *Prologomena* of the difference between the limit (*die Schranke*) and the boundary (*die Grenze*), perimeter and periphery, barrier and gate. See Alain Badiou's reading in *L'Être et l'évènement* (Paris: Seuil, 1988) to understand how Hegel takes up these terms ontologically to argue that 'every point of being is between itself and its mark'. Here, Genet is playing with these philosophical terms with great ambiguity, but is certainly using the border as a construct simultaneously to constrain and liberate the individual who seeks their own territory.

17. Most notably, of his critics: Georges Bataille and his claim that Genet's poetics are radically non-communicative (Georges Bataille, *Œuvres complètes*, 12 vols (Paris: Gallimard, 1970–88), IX, 314–15); Leo Bersani's reading of his anti-relational gay ethics, *Homos* (Cambridge, MA: Harvard University Press, 1995), pp. 113–81; Ivan Jablonka and Éric Marty's claims of anti-semitism as a form of anti-socialism (Ivan Jablonka, *Les Vérités inavouables de Jean Genet* (Paris: Seuil, 2004), and Éric Marty, *Bref séjour à Jerusalem* (Paris: Gallimard, 2003); *Genet: Post-scriptum* (Paris: Verdier, 2006)); Kadji Amin's interpretation of his queer kinships as fetishist and atomising in *Disturbing Attachments: Genet, Modern Pederasty, and Queer History* (Durham, NC: Duke University Press, 2017). Carl Lavery's *The Politics of Jean Genet's Late Theatre: Spaces of Revolution* (Manchester: Manchester University Press, 2010) offers a rich counter argument that supports Genet's utopian ethics of equality, resonating with readings by Edward Said, *On Late Style: Music and Literature Against the Grain* (London: Bloomsbury Academic, 2017), Abdelkébir Khatibi, *Figures de l'étranger* (Paris: Denoel, 1987), Clare Finburgh, 'The Anti-monumental Cemetery: Ghosts in Jean Genet's "Quatre heures à Chatila"', *French Studies*, 74.4 (October 2020), 587–604, and Mairéad Hanrahan, 'Genet socialiste ?', *Revue Europe*, 1103 (March 2021), 86–99.

18. Abdelkébir Khatibi, *Jacques Derrida en effet* (Neuilly sur Seine: Al Manar, 2007), p. 14.

19. Reading Genet geometrically lends a new voice to the critical practice of surface reading, which troubles Frederic Jameson's belief that the role of the critic is to reveal a latent meaning behind a manifest one (*The Political Unconscious: Narrative as a Socially Symbolic Act* (London: Methuen, 1981)). Where many partisans of this school of 'symptomatic reading' (Sigmund Freud, Paul Ricoeur, Louis Althusser, Eve Kofosky Sedgwick) plumb the depths of a text to unearth what is repressed by it, to fill its lacunae, and solve the 'issue' at stake, surface reading finds meaning within its formal, aesthetic properties. I propose that interpreting the geometric figures in Genet's texts teaches us not to hanker after any 'ideological demystification' of his art — as Bruno Latour, Elaine Scarry and Susan Sontag have warned against in criticism more generally — but to assemble the diverse portrayals these geometric signifiers bring to a picture of subjectivity. See Stephen Best and Sharon Marcus's article 'Surface Reading: An Introduction', *Representations*, 108.1 (Fall 2009), 1–21; as well as Susan Sontag, 'Against Interpretation', in *Against Interpretation and Other Essays* (New York: Dell, 1966), pp. 6–14; Bruno Latour, 'Why

Has Critique Run Out of Steam? From Matters of Fact to Matters of Concern', *Critical Inquiry*, 30.2 (Winter 2004), 225–48.

20. Bersani, *Homos*; Éric Marty, *Genet: Post-scriptum* (Paris: Verdier, 2006); Jablonka, *Les Vérités inavouables de Jean Genet*; Jean-Paul Sartre, *Saint Genet: comédien et martyr* (Paris: Gallimard, 1952); *Saint Genet: Actor & Martyr*, trans. by Bernard Frechtman (London: Heinemann, 1988) (hereafter referenced in main text as *SG*).

21. Blaise Pascal, *De l'esprit géométrique; entretien avec M. Sacy; Écrits sur la grâce et autres textes*, ed. by André Clair (Paris: Flammarion, 1985); René Descartes, *Discours de la methode; plus La Dioptrique; Les Météores; et La Géometrie* (Paris: Fayard, 1986).

22. Vitruvius, *On Architecture* (London: Penguin, 2009), Book 6.

23. Aimé Césaire, 'Poésie et connaissance', *Tropiques*, 12 (January 1945), pp. 157–70 (p. 157); 'Poetry and Knowledge', in *Lyric and Dramatic Poetry 1942–82*, trans. by Clayton Eshleman and Annette Smith (Charlottesville: University of Virginia Press, 1990), pp. xlii–lvi (p. xlii).

24. Jacques Derrida, *Edmund Husserl's Origin of Geometry: An Introduction*, trans. by John. P. Leavey (Lincoln & London: University of Nebraska Press, 1989), p. 160. See Peg Rawes's excellent exploration of geometry in Kantian, Husserlian and Deleuzian thought in *Space, Geometry and Aesthetics: Through Kant and Towards Deleuze* (Basingstoke: Palgrave Macmillan, 2008).

25. Sontag, *Against Interpretation*, p. 79.

26. Christina Howells, *Sartre's Theory of Literature* (London: MHRA, 1979), p. 84.

27. Sara Ahmed, *Queer Phenomenology: Orientations, Objects, Others* (Durham, NC, & London: Duke University Press, 2006); Lee Edelman, *No Future* (Durham, NC: Duke University Press, 2004); Michel Foucault, 'De l'amitié comme mode de vie', in *Dits et écrits: 1954–1988*, 4 vols (Paris: Gallimard, 1994), II, 163–67; 'Friendship as a Way of Life', in *Ethics: Subjectivity and Truth. The Essential Works of Michael Foucault, 1954–1984*, ed. by Paul Rabinow, trans. by Robert Hurley and others (New York: New Press, 1997), pp. 135–40.

28. Edme-François Jomard, *Mémoire sur le système métrique des anciens égyptiens* (Paris: Imprimerie royale, 1817), p. 205.

❖

CHAPTER 1

Points

In my work, I do not belong to the species, but am a cosmic point. (Paul Klee)[1]

Geometry moves between the point and the circle as between its beginning and its end: and both of these are antithetical to the certainty characteristic of this science, for the point cannot be measured at all, since it cannot be divided, and the circle cannot be measured precisely, since, being curved, it cannot perfectly be squared. (Dante Alighieri)[2]

These lines are from Dante's second book of the *Convivio*, his encyclopaedic banquet of philosophical musings on astronomy, metaphysics and the immortality of the soul, which offers a valuable ingress into the enduring conceptual importance of the geometric point. The point is where geometry begins; it is the smallest figure, a singular atom defined by Euclid as 'that which has no parts'.[3] Despite being itself indivisible, the point is a unit that forms the basis of union and unity; positioned at the centre of a circle or at the extremities of a line, it provides the coordinates for the plane figures that are formed from it. Yet, the point remains independent of the very lines of connection it enables: by definition, it stands alone. The point that underpins geometry as a science of measurement cannot be made quantifiable by its principles, since without height, weight or volume this one-dimensional figure collapses all attempts at calculation. Dante highlights the paradox that not only is the point anathema to the axiomatic certainty characteristic of geometry, but that it is this very symbol of indeterminacy and inaccessibility, this ultimate unknown, that makes measuring the relation of objects in space both possible and necessary.

At the heart of such mathematical abstraction lies a series of ethical and aesthetic questions that are central to Genet's poetic vision. His texts are littered with the figure of the point, which tessellate to make manifest a pattern of singularity that positions the individual forever on the outside, unreachable and unquantifiable, in the shared isolation of communal solitude. This chapter reads how the point is tied to the impenetrability of characters who beckon for a connection that is always perforated by ultimate detachment. Yet I argue that Genet's points offer more than a static image of existential inaccessibility. They also atomise what can be made legible in representation, the point pricking its way into Genet's language to produce a restless discursive style, refusing to be pinned down, ontologised or quantified by fixed conceptual values. Genet's geometric point not only channels the post-structuralist disruption that Derrida has long attributed to the indeterminacy of his prose, but, by its very definition as an incommensurable shape, it defies any fixed metric that tries to essentialise our subjective experience of the world. Just as Paul Klee's geometric paintings turn people into dots, scattered irreducibly and inaccessibly across the canvas, so I see Genet's embodied point gambolling around his writing in sheer defiance of ever trying to quantify the individual.

Lou-du-Point-du-Jour

An example from Genet's 1946 novel, *Miracle de la rose*, dramatises the anthropomorphic nature of the point in Genet's imaginary. Here, we witness the hermetic worlds of Fontevrault prison and Mettray penal colony where Genet was incarcerated for three months. Ever the author of people, rather than places, Genet brings the arid space of the prison to life by inscribing his experience of it into the names and stories of an intimate fraternity of inmates living within its walls: 'Fontevrault, comme Mettray, pourrait s'écrire par une longue liste de ces couples formés par des noms' [Fontevrault, like Mettray, could be rendered by a long list of the couples which were formed by names].[4] The pairs that Genet invents — Botchako and Bulkaen, Sillar and Venture, Lou-du-Point-du-Jour and Jo — all operate metonymically: their names become substitutes for a closed prison world that is otherwise inexplicable. These pseudonyms promise to grant access to what resists direct communication, yet as epithets they can only ever act as replacements for the proper names they conceal. In this complex web of meaning, Genet invites us to understand the worlds he describes not through diegesis, but through patterns of signifiers bound together by repeated codes. Names allow Genet to tell his stories, and never is this more apparent than in the alias 'Lou-du-Point-du-Jour' [Lou Daybreak]. Genet presents Lou as 'le plus isolé de nous par son nom' [Lou Daybreak, the most isolated of us because of his name], explaining that:

> Le nom de Lou était une buée qui enveloppait toute sa personne et cette douceur franchie quand on s'approchait de lui, quand on avait passé à travers son nom, on se déchirait à des épines, à des branches aiguës et sournoises dont il était hérissé.

> [Lou's name was a vapor that enveloped his entire person, and when you pierced the softness and approached him, when you passed through his name, you scraped against the thorns, against the sharp branches with which he bristled.]
> (*MR*, pp. 238; 22)

The signifier of the 'point' in Lou's pseudonym evokes the same properties as a geometric point: constitutively singular; an independent unit that has no parts; atomised and isolated. If Euclid's point is found at the extremities of a straight line, here Genet plays with precisely that spatial limit by positioning Lou at the very margins of the relations forged between the other couples.[5] It is at dawn when the executions are held in Genet's Fontevrault, thus held within the very name, 'Lou-du-Point-du-Jour' offers a double image of rupture. The solitude of the geometric point breaks away from any hope of a relation with others, while the absolute finality of the 'point-du-jour' forecloses our ability to relate to the radical unknowability of the execution. Like a geometric point within a circle, Lou's 'point-du-jour' is located at the very centre of what is most ineffable, inaccessible and poignantly affective within the prison.[6] Such poignancy is built into Genet's description of the sharp, piercing, scraping point in Lou's name, whose spiny thorns prick those who attempt to draw near. The symbolic violence of the point thus warns against any proximity, and Genet's vaporous figuration of Lou's name, which is already emblematic of separate particles or discrete points, is further atomised whenever someone approaches. The point of Lou's name exerts not only an ethical separation, sundering the intimate couples within the text, but also a symbolic one, since when we peel back the layers of his name to draw closer to Genet's textual world, all we are left with is the image of an abstract, unmeasurable point.

While the point imposes itself as a signifier in Genet's language, it seems nonetheless to signify what is scarcely imaginable within it. Lou's point forges a wound in the onlooker, pricking the inmates with the same affective potency as Barthes's *punctum* does in *La Chambre claire*. As the chain of punctuating objects moves from 'épines' to 'branches aiguës', so Genet's verbs ('se déchirait' and 'était hérissé') create a grammar of laceration that pierces both characters and readers alike. Passing through the pointy symbolism of Lou's name symbolises the process of interpreting Genet's texts more widely: as a reader, we seek a solid relation with the subjects that occupy his texts, or simply a way into his hermetic worlds; yet, Genet's poetics prick us with the sharp edges of unknowability, scraping us against the bristles of his text so that we find ourselves marked by his writing and yet unable to pinpoint the source of our wound. The signifier of the point in Lou's name thus draws attention to a singular yet indefinable discomfort in Genet's writing at large. His point is anathema to the teleological finitude of idioms which ask 'what is the point?' in order to assert that 'the point is...'. Instead, it seems to be a vital and disruptive energy within his texts that makes creative play with epistemological assertions about what we know and how we can put that into words. The point is intimately connected with the borders of language itself, and its relation to language is made manifest in Wassily Kandinsky's theorisation of the basic elements of abstract art in his 1926 treatise on abstraction *Point and Line to Plane*. Here, he argues that:

> The geometric point is an invisible thing. Therefore, it must be defined as an incorporeal thing. Considered in terms of substance, it equals zero. Hidden in this zero, however, are various attributes which are 'human' in nature. We think of this zero — the geometric point — in relation to the greatest possible brevity, i.e. to the highest degree of restraint which, nevertheless, speaks. Thus we look upon the geometric point as the ultimate and most singular *union of silence and speech*. The geometric point has, therefore, been given its material form, in the first instance, in writing. It belongs to language and signifies silence.[7]

The geometric point — both graphically as a punctuation mark and figuratively as a signifier — marks the silences within writing. It helps to visualise that silence, to listen to it and to experience what speaks without any signified attached. If language is a network that constructs meaning through the interrelation of words and letters, then the geometric point stands both without and within that linguistic relation: a lone figure that asserts meaning spatially, an ineffability that nonetheless speaks. Kandinsky thus imbues the geometric point with hermeneutic significance: a figure he inserts into language in order to signify, but which in fact conveys a silence that challenges that signification. Despite Kandinsky's reading of it as 'zero', the point is not a sign of emptiness. Rather, as a 'small world cut off more or less equally from both sides and almost torn out of its surroundings', Kandinsky's geometric point makes manifest a sensation of radical isolation, of being uprooted rather than belonging, its singularity imposing itself on the page away from wider neighbourhoods of meaning.[8]

If we consider the geometric point in language as a full stop, then we might regard it, as Derrida does, as a vital silence that enables the text to breathe: 'ponctuer c'est écrire [...] la punctuation [...] est, on ne le dira jamais assez, le cœur et comme le souffle vivant, le poumon de l'écriture' [to punctuate is to write [...] punctuation [is] the heart and the living breath, the very lungs of the writing].[9] As the point is anthropomorphised as an organ of writing, developing Kandinsky's interpretation of it as deeply human, it breaks free of any static conceptualisations of it as a sign of fixity, pinioning, limitation, conclusion, cessation. Its silence is neither the end of language, nor the failure to articulate, but rather an interruption which enables writing to move forth and to continue living. As David Wills suggests in his interpretation of Hélène Cixous's own analysis of points, 'un point par exemple ne représente pas un son parlé, plutôt son absence, disons une espèce de pause' [a full stop does not represent a spoken sound, but rather its absence, or let's say a type of pause].[10] Rather than a figure that stops or stifles language, Wills shows how Cixous reconfigures the point into a figure which suspends in order to make room for contemplation, allowing thought to continue after writing has drawn to a close. Both as grammatical figure and as poetic signifier, the point provides a sign that lightens language from the heaviness of assertion. We could argue it achieves what Barthes is searching for in *Roland Barthes par Roland Barthes*, when he laments the way in which the writer is 'condamné à l'assertion' because 'il manque en français (et peut-être en toute langue) un mode grammatical qui dirait légèrement (notre conditionnel est bien trop lourd), non point le doute intellectuel, mais la valeur qui cherche à se convertir en théorie' [being condemned to assertion: we lack in French (and perhaps in every language) a grammatical mode which would speak lightly (our conditional is much too heavy), not intellectual doubt, but the value which strives to convert itself into theory].[11] Just as Barthes eschews maxims, which promote a way of thinking that suggests we can know how things always are, this chapter reads the point in Genet's own highly mobile texts turn as providing just such a new grammatical mode of lightness, flouting dialectical modes that try to pin meaning, affect and thought down to a definite position.

The *pointe*: Poetic Perforations

The reception of Genet's early novels was marked by a lengthy debate about his writing style, since the beauty of his poetry was perceived to be in tension with the political, ethical and moral challenge of his content.[12] It was Sartre who first tackled those who sought to divorce Genet's language from its meaning in his 1952 *Saint Genet*, by issuing a 'prière pour le bon usage de Genet' [Please use Genet properly] (*SG*, pp. 536; 584). Naturally, the sermonising nature of Sartre's request is highly problematic as it places him as the guardian of meaning in Genet's texts; overwhelmingly, though, it is Sartre's insistence on forging an alliance between Genet's words and a fixed conceptual meaning that best explains why Genet's writing is so resistant to being pinned down. Sartre corrects those who:

> Lisaient sans broncher les récits les plus crus: 'Ces deux messieurs couchent ensemble? puis ils mangent leurs excréments? Après quoi, l'un court dénoncer l'autre? la belle affaire! C'est si bien écrit.' Ils s'arrêtaient au vocabulaire de Genet pour se garder d'entrer dans son délire; ils admiraient la forme pour se défendre de réaliser le contenu. Mais forme et contenu ne font qu'un: c'est ce contenu qui exige cette forme.

> [Can read the coarsest passages without turning a hair: 'Those two gentlemen sleep together? And then they eat their excrement? And after that, one goes off to denounce the other? As if that mattered! It's *so* well written.' They stop at Genet's vocabulary so as not to enter his delirium; they admire the poem so as not to have to *realize* the content. But form and content are one and the same: it is *that* content that requires *that* form.] (*SG*, pp. 537; 585)

Sartre seems to suggest that by reading Genet *à la lettre*, by focusing only on the sophistry of his rhetoric, we are avoiding a stable reality or truth that repels us underneath. Those who abstractly admire Genet's language do so as a means of taking refuge from a content that revolts their sensibilities. However, it is precisely within Genet's vocabulary that we encounter the very source of this repulsion: not a moral revulsion as Sartre implies; but a linguistic rebuke of any reader who seeks to reify his words into stable concepts from which an objective content might be gleaned. Sartre reads the disturbance that is so central to Genet's novels through a thematic prism, concentrating on the social discomfort of 'sa voix [qui] est de celles que nous souhaitions ne jamais entendre; elle n'est pas fait pour analyser le trouble mais pour le communiquer' [his voice is one of those that we wanted never to hear; it is not meant for analysing disturbance but for communicating it] (*SG*, pp. 539; 587), but I want to explore here how perhaps the most troubling aspect of his voice is the unrest generated by the words themselves.

Genet's poetics are punctured by several geometric points that mobilise a verbal choreography that uproots fixed meaning. In addition to his 1948 ballet 'Adame Miroir, his 1957 elegy to his tightrope-walker lover Abdallah in *Le Funambule* and his later fascination with Palestinian dancers in his 1986 text *Un captif amoureux*, Genet ubiquitously extols the expressive virtues of dance over the heaviness of language. In his free-flowing debut novel *Notre-Dame-des-Fleurs* (1943), Genet challenges the suitability of words as viable modes of expression because they are so laden with precision. As he embarks on narrating the story of his protagonist, the young Louis Culafroy who later transforms into the transvestite prostitute Divine, Genet laments his use of a discursive medium over an abstract, figurative one: 'La Divine-Saga devrait être dansée, mimée, avec de subtiles indications. L'impossibilité de la mettre en ballet m'oblige à me servir de mots lourds d'idées précises, mais je tâcherai de les alléger d'expressions banales, vides, creuses, invisibles' [The Divine Saga should be danced, mimed, with subtle directions. Since it is impossible to make a ballet of it, I am forced to use words that are weighed down with precise ideas, but I shall try to lighten them with expressions that are trivial, empty, hollow and invisible].[13] The precision of language is figured as binding and oppressive, words become bloated with heavy ideas that weigh them down to a determinate meaning that Genet absolutely rejects. Instead, he attempts to reconfigure discourse, lighten it, hollow out its substance and put levity in its place. Rather than pinpointing meaning, he privileges a melodious language of movement and flux, producing a fluid hybrid where words seem to mimic their dance equivalents. Indeed, he lingers over the balletic quality of language itself in his description of the Russian ballet dancer and choreographer Nijinsky, relishing the visual mobility of calligraphy by revelling in:

> L'allure du *mot* Nijinsky (la montée de l'N, la descente de la boucle du j, le saut de la boucle du k et la chute de l'y, forme graphique d'un nom qui semble vouloir dessiner l'élan, avec ses retombées et rebondissements sur le plancher, du sauteur qui ne sait sur quel pied se poser) il devina la légèreté de l'artiste, comme il saura un jour que Verlaine ne peut être que le nom d'un poète musicien [...] tous ses actes furent servis par des gestes nécessités non par l'acte mais par une chorégraphie qui transformait sa vie en un ballet perpétuel. Il réussit vite à faires des pointes, il en fit partout.

> [The aspect of the *word* Nijinsky (the rise of the N, the drop of the loop of the j, the leap of the hook on the k and the fall of the y, graphic form of a name that seems to be drawing the artist's élan, with its bounds and rebounds on the boards, of the jumper who doesn't know which leg to come down on), he sensed the dancer's lightness, just as he will one day realize that Verlaine can only be the name of a poet-musician [...] his every act was served by gestures necessitated not by the act itself, but by a choreography that transformed his life into a perpetual ballet. He quickly succeeded in dancing on his toes, and he did it everywhere.] (*NDF*, pp. 94; 130)

Even if the physical mobility of the text fails, Genet designs a language replete with the same undulations and momentum as live ballet. Words are made agile, not cumbersome or immutable, and as the letters leap forth, Genet envisages words as transient images that create meaning through soundscapes, patterns, impressions, rather than concrete definitions. It is the shape of the language that matters, the internal contours of the letters themselves more evocative to Genet than their external referents. Even the reference to Verlaine helps to further disencumber language, prioritising musicality and mood over didactic meaning. Just as Culafroy loses himself in the beauty of poetic gesture, cutting himself off from external referents so that his life is orientated only towards movement itself, so Genet's balletic language vaunts a new way of making meaning: exalting pure expressiveness rather than referential signification.[14]

The *pointe* exemplifies Genet's process of troubling the conceptual stability of language. His desire for a balletic discourse staunchly rejects the connotation of the point as a figure that constrains, pins down, and pinions; and yet the fluidity of Culafroy's movement is comprised of just such points. To return to Kandinsky:

> Already in the classical ballet form existed 'points' — a designated terminology which unquestionably is derived from 'point'. The rapid running on the toes leaves behind on the floor a trace of points. The ballet dancer leaps to a point above, clearly aiming at it with his head and, in landing, again contacts a point on the floor [...] the brief states of rigid immobility can be looked upon as points. Thus, we have active and passive point formations which bear a relationship to the musical form of the point.[15]

Genet's balletic steps (*pas*) are constituted by a sequence of small points which do not simply glide over the surface, they mark it (*en pointe*). As the balletic *pas* becomes *point(e)* (the reader might imagine the grammatical negation of *ne... pas* moving to *ne... point*, as though in the midst of this balletic discourse, nothing can be affirmatively asserted), we see an effortless sylph-like flight comprised, paradoxically, of moments of anchorage: mobility composed of 'rigid immobility'. If Genet seeks to transform his narrative into dance in order to avoid the oppressive fixity of *idées précises*, his fixation on the balletic motif of 'la pointe, comme un fer de lance, fichée au sol' [her toe rooted to the floor, like a spearhead] (*NDF*, pp. 94; 130) seems to simply replace one precision for another. On the one hand, he constructs an opposition between the balletic *pointe* and 'les mots lourds d'idées précises', yet, on the other, his very use of the point as a signifier, with all of the weighty accuracy such a symbol implies, seems to collapse that difference. While he seeks a replacement for the impossible balletic form of his text, choosing to lighten his words instead with 'expressions banales, vides, creuses', he re-evokes that ballet by using the *pointe* as itself a puncture that creates a *creuse*, which, in turn, is analogous with the geometric figure of the point a sort of *vide* as it can contain no substance, no-thing, no inside.

The trace of points created by Culafroy offer a nascent version of the series of points, the *pointillé*, which Genet uses to sign off *Notre-Dame-des-Fleurs*. I will return to this figuration shortly. The signifier of the *pointe* offers a source of textual disruption, it sows illegibility throughout the text by triggering a chain of signifiers that are constantly travelling through conceptual oppositions and thus defying anything that can be definitively asserted. These points imprint Genet's novel to produce writing that echoes the spirit of Deleuze and Guattari's 'lines of flight', which disrupt conceptual fixity in an epistemology that 'nous emportait, à travers nos segments, mais aussi à travers nos seuils, vers une destination inconnue, pas prévisible, pas préexistante [...] cette ligne [...] n'est rien d'autre que le cheminement de l'âme du danseur' [carried us away, across our segments, but also across our thresholds, towards a destination which is unknown, not foreseeable, not pre-existent [...] this line [...] is nothing other than the progression of the soul of the dancer].[16] Genet's *pointe* achieves this movement across the segments or thresholds of language itself, moving the reader through the inner shapes of words and the sensations they evoke rather than through their the hard segmentation of their meaning. Genet's signifier thus echoes Deleuze and Guattari's conceptual resistance to the immutable structural positions that govern meaning in *Mille plateaux*. Yet, figuratively speaking, his point stands in stark contrast to their rally cry: 'faites la ligne et jamais le point!' [run lines, never plot a point].[17] In his 1987 book of interviews with Claire Parnet, *Dialogues*, Deleuze argues that the point belongs to structuralism, which he explains as

> Un système de points et de positions, qui opère par grandes coupures dites signifiantes, au lieu de procéder par poussées et craquements, et qui colmate les lignes de fuite, au lieu de les suivre, de les tracer, de les prolonger.

> [A system of points and positions, which operates by cuts which are supposedly significant instead of proceeding by thrusts and crackings. It warps the lines of flight instead of following them and tracing them.][18]

For Deleuze, the point binds us to systems that organise life in a manner which excludes, stops or halts the organic movement promised by a fluid 'ligne de fuite' which he considers a much more realistic model of the subject's creative, contradictory and disordered engagement with the world. The point enforces strict boundaries: its extreme position at either end of a line offers a definite trajectory which Deleuze sees as structurally restrictive; where the point blockades, the line runs freely. When conceptualising the 'ligne de fuite' in *Dialogues*, he explains that 'il y a des lignes, qui ne se ramènent pas au trajet d'un point, et qui s'échappent de la structure, lignes de fuite, devenirs' [there are lines which do not amount to the path of a point, which break free from structure — lines of flight, becomings].[19] For Deleuze, these legato 'lignes de fuites' help collapse fixed positions, offering a mode of writing that 'nous y engage' [engage us]. These lines of flight propose an agitation of static structures to engage actively with writing as a creative rather than descriptive endeavour. To write is not to inscribe these patterns, but to follow them; to pursue poetic impulses as a means of accessing reality rather than attempting to recount it — thus fix it — in language. However, the point does not pull Genet's writing back as it does for Deleuze. Rather, it invades and kindles his expression to produce a rhetoric that is unfettered by stable oppositions. This contradicts the finitude of Deleuze and Guattari's point which always being a point of origin symbolises a discrete position that prevents a 'logique du ET' that would 'annuler fin et commencement' [a logic of the AND [that would....] nullify endings and beginnings].[20] Yet, Genet's point does trouble the teleological linearity of a beginning and end that Deleuze and Guattari so vehemently resist: its perpetual mobility does cripple any such stable position by simultaneously inhabiting both mobility and fixity, both fluidity and puncture.

Just as Deleuze and Guattari's linearity drives their fluid mode of existence, somewhat paradoxically so does Genet's point rally his writing. In *Notre-Dame-des-Fleurs*, Genet writes of Mignon and Notre Dame that:

> Ils vécurent à ne rien faire [...]. Ils devisaient sur les jambes des femmes; comme ils n'avaient pas d'esprit, leurs remarques étaient sans finesse. Leur émotion n'étant déchirée par aucune pointe, tout naturellement ils glissaient sur un fond stagnant de poésie.

[They spent their time doing nothing [...]. They made comments about the women's legs, but as they were not witty, their remarks had no finesse. Since their emotion was not torn by any point, they quite naturally skidded along on a stagnant ground of poetry.] (*NDF*, pp. 66; 102)

The *pointe* is positioned here as a central feature of Genet's poetics, located at the junction between affective torpor and crude expression, and poised to break through and rupture both. More than simply an existential commentary on the empty lethargy of daily life, Genet constructs the point as a figure that will unsettle the smooth surface of a language that seeks simply to statically depict the world as it is perceived. The absent-minded remarks of Mignon and Notre Dame simply translate the outside world into a flat discourse, their conversation rendering them merely passive recipients of the space around them rather curators of any engaged meaning. Their discursive approach would fit, albeit inelegantly, into Barthes's depiction of classical language in *Le Degré zéro de l'écriture*,[21] in which:

Les mots [...] ne reproduisent pas comme plus tard, par une sorte de hauteur violente et inattendue, la profondeur et la singularité d'une expérience; ils sont aménagés en surface [...] une pensée toute formée accouche d'une parole qui l''exprime', la 'traduit'.

[Words [...] do not, as they later do, thanks to a kind of violent and unexpected abruptness, reproduce the depth and singularity of an individual experience; they are spread out to form a surface [...] a ready-made thought generates an utterance which 'expresses' or 'translates' it.][22]

Where Barthes presents classical discourse as the process of making thought accessible in language, of bearing across a meaning that is able to be communicated by words, he suggests that modern poetics seeks rather to condense all of the violent ineffability of the world into speech. Here, Genet's *pointe* houses all of the poignant energy that Barthes attributes to modern poetics, pricking what is easily communicable in the dormant poetics of the pair's repartee in order to awaken a mode of thought that transcends the act of purely bearing witness or actualising ready-made thoughts into language. The point that affectively breaks through these utterances testifies to a need to express precisely what cannot be perceived or explained in discourse. Where Mignon and Notre Dame 'devisaient' — the verb suggesting a division or splitting up of speech into parts — Genet advocates for the serrated poetics of a singular, indivisible *pointe* that eschews any such digestible communication. Slipping mindlessly through life creates an inert form of discourse that immobilises and desensitises the individual, whereas it is the sharp tip of an affective, engaged ineffability that Genet's *pointe* tries to harness. The *pointe* is poised to impale language, tearing through emotion to prompt a response that is articulated with a balletic finesse that is 'dansée, mimée, avec de subtiles indications' rather than encumbered by concrete communication.

Genet thus constructs the point as a form of thought as much as of action; the *pointe* inspiring not only the gymnastics of the body but also of the mind. In order to disrupt their existential somnambulism, Mignon and Notre Dame must be pricked by the affectively inexpressible and the linguistically inaccessible. Genet develops this idea only a few sentences later when revelling in the idea of penetrating the disengaged stupor of his fellow men:

> On s'y déplace comme des ombres. Est-ce à dire que mon âme de cambrioleur extatique n'épargne aucune occasion d'entrer en transe? Sentir que l'on vole sur la pointe des pieds, quand la semelle des humains pose à plat! Ici même et à Fresnes, ces longs couloirs parfumés qui se mordent la queue, me redonnent, malgré la dureté précise, mathématique, de la paroi, cette âme du rat d'hôtel que je veux être.
>
> [People move about like shadows. Does this mean that my ecstatic crook's soul lets slip no opportunity for falling into a trance? Oh to feel yourself flying on tiptoe while the soles of humans move flat on the ground! Even here, and at the Fresnes Prison, the long fragrant corridors that bite their tails restore to me, despite the precise, mathematical hardness of the wall, the soul of the hotel thief I long to be.] (*NDF*, pp. 66; 102)

Here, the metaphor of the *pointe des pieds* breaks through the symbolic lassitude Genet sees in the community around him. Habitual walking patterns are metamorphosed into positions of engagement where one sides either with action or apathy, whether one mimics the trance-like state of existence or whether one creeps through it eyes-open. This image of the *pointe des pieds* is picked up by Slavoj Žižek in *The Puppet and the Dwarf: The Perverse Core of Christianity* as a means of describing the marginality of those 'living constantly at a tiptoe stance, never knowing what to expect next, and plagued with outer fears and inner resentments'.[23] Yet, it is precisely this liminal instability that Genet valorises as he embraces the *pointe des pieds* over 'la semelle [...] à plat' [the flat sole] in a metonymic gesture where gait is symbolic of conformity or resistance: one cannot slide through language, one must tiptoe through it, penetrating at each interval. Genet's metaphor not only privileges a vertical disruption of a horizontal mass trance, but it demonstrates a desire to break through a natural flow or order and actively engage. The *pointe des pieds* becomes symbolic of a solitary mode of revolt that troubles the mass order: stealing from it; hiding from its laws; profiting from its myopia. Where the masses glide through life as spectres, the point penetrates to produce a thrill, a moment of sensation. Curiously, then, the *pointe* is both implacable and hard to pin down: it ruptures, and yet clandestinely avoids being trapped. Both rigid and invisible, Genet's *pointe* operates as a guerrilla figure of affect which rouses his poetics and troubles the oppositions which would allow us to fix them to signification.

Perhaps Genet's furtive *pointe des pieds* symbolises a contrapuntal way to generate meaning. Gesturally, tiptoeing first touches solid ground, then immediately unsettles it in a dynamic mobility that will never commit to any one dwelling place. In an article on the poetics of the step, Carl Lavery explains the paradox that:

> The motion that attaches us to being by establishing a ground (an *ethos*) is undone by a step (un *pas*) [...] this is to affirm an impossible doubleness: to fix an abode and to engage a line of flight at the same time.[24]

Poetically, then, the *pointe des pieds* both posits one idea and its counterpoint, repelling any conceptual fixity, or as Lavery suggests, any fundamental or underlying ethos, within a language that will never stay put. In 'Comment jouer *Les Bonnes*', Genet is directive about how:

> Le jeu [théâtral] sera furtif afin qu'une phraséologie trop pesante s'allège et passe la rampe [...]. Il serait bien qu'à certains moments elles marchent sur la pointe des pieds [...] non pour ne pas être entendues des voisins d'en dessous, mais parce que ce geste est dans le ton.

> [The performance will be furtive so that the heavily overblown language feels lighter and gets across more easily to the audience [...]. It would be good if, at certain moments, they walked on tiptoe [...] not so as not to be heard by the neighbours below, but because this kind of movement is in keeping with the tone.][25]

In their Pléiade edition of Genet's *Théâtre complet*, Michel Corvin and Albert Dichy note that the etymology of the term *furtif* derives from *voleur* [thief], and here we can see how the *pointe des pieds* exerts such theft by physically enacting Genet's poetic ambition to steal something away from the stable grounds of assertion. Genet inscribes the non-committal movement of tiptoeing into the very tone of the maids' discourse, such that their *pointe* generates a refusal to seize hold of the elusive nature of meaning through a language that is too 'pesante'. Instead, their *pointe* is characterised by a disruptive process of uprooting and unsettling, flouting what Judith Butler has called 'the violence of [a] language' that tries to 'capture the ineffable, and hence to destroy it'.[26]

Hélène Cixous's *Stigmata: Escaping Texts* also wrestles with the point's conceptual dimensions of fixity, while situating it as a principal catalyst for the fluidity of writing. *Stigmata* is an anthology of non-fiction texts from the 1980s and 1990s, described by Derrida as a 'poetic treatise on the scar at the origin of literary writing'. The twelve texts are subtended by a common struggle:

> All these texts aim to flee the fatal nail, the sword, the knife, the axe which threatens to fix, to nail, to immobilize them in, by, death. Their first and best ally in the evasion is the poetic use of the languages of language. If only we listen, a language always speaks several languages at once, and runs with a single word in opposite directions.[27]

For Cixous, contradictory impulses are a constitutive part of language which works tirelessly against itself in order to avoid the immobilisation of stable meanings. This deconstructive tug of war produces signification through the multiplicity of a single word and the frictions of its connotations. This is certainly redolent of Genet's texts which, as we have seen, constantly unsettle dialectical readings. Cixous, like Genet, galvanises language not simply by revealing its internal vibrations, but by engaging them. The point that is eschewed conceptually as the 'fatal nail' that pinions the text is simultaneously embraced as the affective instrument which brings writing into being. As Derrida points out in his foreword, Cixous's point is configured as a spike from the Greek *stigmē* which 'points poignantly', and thus becomes the catalyst of writing.[28] Cixous explains that:

> Stigmata are traces of a sting. *Piquer* in French, to prick, to sting, to pinch, pricks in order to take, in order to prick *piquer* steals, strikes and removes,

sows, speckles signs its blows, leaves behind and takes way, annoys and excites at the same time, gives back what it takes, serves the interests of the thief and the police. *Piquer* has the resources of Figaro in French: it has innumerable aptitudes and identities. One can be stung by the bug of (se piquer de) literature or philosophy as others can shoot (se piquer de) drugs. With *piquer* and stigmata we have what we need to explore the scene of writing.[29]

I will return to the wounding effect of stigmata in the second section of this chapter, focusing here on how writing is not restrained by the point, but reliant upon it. Rather than an instrument of restriction or a trap which halts movement, Cixous's point provokes, incites and, just like Genet's furtive *pointe des pieds*, here the point purloins as it imprints by 'strik[ing] and remov[ing] [...] giv[ing] back what it takes'. Cixous's point 'pierces, makes holes, separates with pinched marks and in the same movement distinguishes — re marks — inscribes, writes', enacting a figural violence which advances writing, while also physically limiting the words imprinted on the page.[30] The point — both as fatal nail and the mark produced by this pinion — is reminiscent of a Derridean *pharmakon* whose hallmark is, ironically, 'impossible d'y *faire le point*' [impossible to *point* it out].[31] Not only does the point wound writing by provoking an affect that seeks expression, but like the *pharmakon*, it also constitutes 'le milieu dans lequel s'opposent les opposés' [the medium in which opposites are opposed].[32] Like Deleuze's linear logic of 'et... et... et' [and... and... and], Genet's point marks out a point in writing which denies any oppositional discourse, and instead places itself as an indeterminate and ineffable interstice which any attempt to explain motivates the very recourse to writing in the first place.

I want to explore how the affective impulse of the point drives writing in more detail. In *L'Atelier d'Alberto Giacometti* Genet exposes the point in Giacometti's artworks as emotive and dynamic:

> Je reviens encore à ces femmes, maintenant en bronze (généralement doré et patiné): autour d'elles l'espace vibre. Rien n'est plus en repos. C'est peut-être que chaque angle [...] ou courbe, ou bosse, ou crête, ou pointe déchirée du métal ne sont eux-mêmes en repos. Chacun d'eux continue à émettre la sensibilité qui les créa. Aucune pointe, arête qui découpe, déchire l'espace, n'est morte.

> [I keep coming back to those women, now in bronze (for the most part gilded and patina'd): around them space vibrates. It may be because each angle [...] or curve, or bump, or ridge, or shattered tip of metal is itself not at rest. Each of them continues to emit the sensibility that created them. No point, or edge that cuts, tears apart space, is dead].[33]

Once again, the *pointe* evinces a mutability that we would not expect from a figure that is often associated with immobilisation. Genet invests the angular tips of Giacometti's sculptures with emotive energy, the point lacerating and bursting through the still space of its static form. Genet seems less interested in the fixed sculpture than the discomfort, the precariousness, 'la sensibilité' that created it. I am drawn to a comparison Deleuze makes in his *Cinéma 1: L'Image-mouvement*:

> C'est une violence en acte, avant d'entrer en action; c'est une violence non seulement intérieure ou innée, mais statique, dont on ne trouve d'équivalent

que chez Bacon en peinture, lorsqu'il évoque une 'émanation' qui se dégage d'un personnage immobile, ou chez Jean Genet en littérature, quand il décrit l'extraordinaire violence qui peut habiter une main immobile au repos.

[It is a violence which is not merely internal or innate, but static, whose only equivalent is that of Bacon in painting, when he summons up an 'emanation' which arises from an immobile character, or that of Jean Genet in literature, when he describes the extraordinary violence which can be contained in a motionless hand at rest.][34]

As Geir Uvsløkk has noted, this is the only time Deleuze makes reference to Genet.[35] His citation comes from Genet's opening pages of *Journal de voleur* where he describes the figural violence of a 'dessin de la main unique de Stilitano, immobile, simplement posée sur la table, et qui rendait inquiétant et dangereux le repos' [design of Stilitano's only hand, simply lying on the table, still, rendering the repose disturbing and dangerous].[36] The drawing becomes poignant to Deleuze not because of the (in)action of Genet's artwork, but because of the affective violence of his *reaction* when encountering it. For Tom Conley:

A detail — generally a part of the body — can capture and cause to vibrate or to tremble everything that surrounds it [...] the reader's eye [...] wanders upward to wonder if the hand at rest owes any of its latent violence to the very words that convey or embody the description [...]. Put otherwise, would Genet's words, when they are taken as images themselves be of a nascent violence that the philosopher of cinema attributes to their descriptive effects?[37]

Deleuze as the spectator to Genet's imagined artwork would thus be affected not by the image of 'une main immobile au repos' but by the terms in which it is conveyed; the violence of that figural detail governed more by anxiety created by Genet's suspense: 'immobile; inquiétant; dangereux'. It is precisely this dormancy that Genet depicts as a spectator to Giacometti's artworks, the figural violence of the artwork generated from Genet's own description of its *pointe* which he experiences as penetrating the space of the spectator. The *pointe* becomes poignant because it never reaches a comfortable conclusion, its lingering precariously in mid-air provokes a profound discomfort which is contained by the literal *pointe* that pricks Genet as witness, and which, in turn, symbolically pricks us as reader. Indeed, the *pointe* is a signifier of Genet's choosing; it, like the hand which for Deleuze 'tremble sous sa propre violence contenue', contains a latent violence in its own symbolism. As a tip, the point pokes, prods, and thrusts its way into our affective vocabulary as a touching experience. Indeed, if 'aucune pointe n'est morte' then the point ruptures the immobility and the suspense that renders the artwork so troubling; instead, the term mobilises the artwork by generating a poignancy that *moves* the spectator. Both Deleuze's analysis of Genet, and Genet's of Giacometti, latently attributes the violence of the image to a figural violence embedded in the terms which move the artwork from object to text. The *pointe* as a signifier in *L'Atelier d'Alberto Giacometti,* and as a concept in Deleuze's analysis of 'l'extraordinaire violence qui peut habiter une main immobile au repos', communicates this shift from image to affect. Notably, in both the drawing of Stilitano's hand, and Genet's description of Giacometti's *pointe*, we are in the realm of pure singularity: the 'main unique' and 'aucune pointe', both singular images whose simple presence, or what Deleuze calls 'haecceity', animates sensation.[38] It is that singularity which inculcates an affect that gestures to a referent beyond codification.

On the one hand, Genet's point may inspire his language, but on the other, its singularity and puncture generate an affective vitality that challenges the fidelity of any attempts to express it. Consider the affective vitality of Genet's signature at the end of *Notre-Dame-des-Fleurs*, his paean to the point in the form of an ellipsis. In Mignon's last letter to Divine, he writes:

> *Tâche de reconnaitre le pointillé. Et embrasse-le. Reçois, ma chérie, mille bons baisers de ton Mignon.*
>
> Ce pointillé dont parle Mignon, c'est la silhouette de sa queue. J'ai vu un mac bandant en écrivant à sa môme, sur son papier sur la table poser sa bite lourde et en tracer les contours. Je veux que ce trait serve à dessiner Mignon.
> — Prison de Fresnes, 1942
>
> [*Try to recognise the dotted lines. And kiss it. A thousand big kisses, sweetheart, from Your Darling.*
>
> The dotted line that Darling refers to is the outline of his prick. I once saw a pimp who had a hard-on while writing to his girl place his heavy cock on the paper and trace its contours. I would like that line to portray Darling.]
> (*NDF*, pp. 207; 237)

The *pointillé*, an ellipsis marked by a discontinuous series of points, has been read by several scholars as a phallic, phantasmatic signature. For example, Uvsløkk considers it to be 'la silhouette de sa queue en pointillé [...] fonctionne comme une sorte de signature [...] il est bien naturel que ce livre termine sous le signe du phallus' [The silhouette of his phallus as an ellipsis [...] functions like a sort of signifier [...] it is entirely natural that this text is signed by a phallus];[39] François Bizet argues that 'une fin en "pointillé" exhibant une dernière fois la nature discontinue, poreuse et interminable du fantasme, ainsi que celle de tout tracé signifiant' [an ellipsis at the conclusion reveals the discontinuous, porous and interminable nature of the fantasy, as well as that of any signifying trace].[40] For Pierre Laforgue, the ellipsis is the privileged figure of Genet's primary endeavour in *Notre-Dame-des-Fleurs*:

> Reste l'essentiel: la bite dessinée selon un pointillé. Nul trait continu ne peut la reproduire, seul un pointillé en donne l'image. Peut-être cette image en pointillé est-elle l'image d'une image, un fantasme; elle est, plus encore un signifiant sans signifié, quelque chose en quoi le sens se rassemble, mais qui lui-même n'est pas le sens, seulement sa trace, un signe, et pour l'occasion une signature [...] le pointillé donne à voir tout en retirant la vision; le pointillé impose la présence d'un référent, mais en donne à lire l'absence. En cela il est parfaitement accordé à l'idée même que l'on se fait du désir.[41]

> [Only the essential remains: the phallus drawn by a dotted line. No continuous line can reproduce it, only a dotted line can provide the image. Perhaps this dotted image is the image of an image, a fantasy; moreover, it is a meaningless signifier, something in which the meaning is gathered, but which itself is not the meaning, only its trace, a sign, and for the occasion a signature [...] the dotted line enables us to see at the same time as it removes our vision; the

dotted line imposes the presence of a referent, yet only absence can actually be
read. In this he is perfectly attuned to the very idea of desire].

In all three interpretations what is emphasised is the virtual nature of the *pointillé*,
these dotted marks invested with futurity, sexuality, longing, but which can never
come to fruition. For all three, the *pointillé* is embedded into a discourse of desire,
representing a *broken* linear continuity which configures the points as incomplete,
and which kindle desire by gesturing to a possible wholeness. In such a reading,
what seems to be upheld is the lack contained by the points, the *pointillé* framed as
a Lacanian *objet a* which offers substitution for the object that is missing, a signifier
of privation and wanting described by Parveen Adams as:

> Not part of the signifying chain; it is a hole in that chain. It is a hole in the
> field of representation, but it does not simply ruin representation. It mends as
> it ruins. It both produces a hole and is what comes to the place of lack to cover
> it over.[42]

Wrought *as* and *out of* a discourse of desire, the *objet a* is both located in language
and points to an extra-discursivity, as a pointer to what spills over the edges of
language.[43]

Despite Genet's quotation being laden with visceral and sexual overtones, I
would argue that to read the *pointillé* as purely a cipher for desire and a screen for
lack, is to misunderstand the profoundly disruptive nature of the points themselves.
Rather than reading the *pointillé* as a broken linearity, a failed attempt at continuity,
perhaps we should recognise the value of the points as discrete markers which
gesture to a relation while ultimately remaining single entities. The points of
Genet's inscription form a synecdoche: they use their parts to posit a whole, but this
whole is always partial. In perforating the outline of the whole phallus, Genet offers
us both a puzzle and a solution explaining that 'ce pointillé dont parle Mignon,
c'est la silhouette de sa queue'. He therefore renders the points *additional* to the
phallus, different to it, not merely figures which reveal its lack. In fact, the only
figure that is whole is the 'queue' itself; it is its traced image which reveals the series
of perforations. The effect is one where the marks that are made in the drawing
actively show the evacuation of their referent: they demonstrate not the failure of
reproducing the 'whole' phallus, but rather actively assert a vigorous absence within
that whole.

The *pointillé* marks a series of gaps which actively disrupt legibility: they gesture
to the negative space which lies between them and it is this interstice which is
fetishised, not the phallus itself. Loaded with phallic overtones, the *pointillé* can
be read as a virile driving force which impregnates the text with absence, making
room for that which is yet to be coded. Indeed, for Derrida in his 'Être juste avec
Freud', he too remarks that 'les pointillés d'une écriture suspendue *situent* avec une
redoutable précision' [The dotted lines of a suspended writing *situate* with a terrible
precision].[44] The points in this formation are remarkably unsettling because they
are complete but they point to incompletion; they promise wholeness, but in fact
actively assert the gaps around them. Such unease is certainly palpable at the end of
Notre-Dame-des-Fleurs not because an ordinary ellipsis or aposiopesis marks the end

of the text where we might be able to rely on an external meaning, but because Genet phallically injects these troubling absences into the heart of all the writing that has gone before. This final autograph does not sign a lack, an omission, but asserts instead the positive presentation of a negative, a revelation of an a priori void which Genet is constantly trying to represent, and which in fact gives life to a future scene or stage of writing.

Read as a signature, this series of discontinuous points offers the trademark of Genet's authorial persona: its serial singularity proposing a form of relation deeply motivated by questioning how the singular point fits in to a wider series. For Derrida, such plural singularities are an inherent feature of the signature, an idea he conceives in relation to Genet in *Glas* when he argues that 'la signature est un cliché. Sans droits de reproduction' [the signature is a cliché. Without rights of reproduction], and again in 'Countersignature' when he describes the betrayal of the signature which relies upon its own singularity in reproduction.[45] In order to function, we must trust the inimitability of the signature, which is then replicated *ad infinitum*. We rely on the individual nature of each imprint, but also require the sequence of repetition for it to have any meaning. Genet's elliptical autograph therefore becomes the form that contains this paradox: it undermines the prospect of uniqueness while radically refusing assimilation into a wider community. The points in the *pointillé* are relational without being continuous, and so is Genet's writing: it makes its solitary marks, while abstracting itself from connections that enable us the reader to fathom the bigger picture. The points of Genet's inscription are not ones which pinpoint specific, precise meanings; they encourage a re-reading of language like the ellipsis of Derrida's *Points de suspension* where a new chapter begins on a promising new page. As Genet's *pointillé* signs off one novel, its indeterminacy prompts the production of new chapters to decipher its blanks. Just as Euclid defines the geometric point as the determining coordinate for a line or a circle which, in joining up its dots, relinquishes the singularity that constitutes it as a point, so Genet lines up his points to gesture to a connection he never creates. The *pointillé* offers a privileged form of discontinuity that safeguards the singularity of points which refuse to cohere; this atomicity is a metaphor of Genet's authorial signature which signs his text with a radical singularity that perforates any relation to definitive meaning or wholeness itself.

Sore Points: The *punctum*

One etymological definition of the point is the *punctum*: 'the past participle of the Latin verb *pungere* meaning to prick or pierce and a noun meaning a small hole, dot, or lesion' (*OED*). In this section, I will extend the ways in which the figure of the point elicits an affective ineffability by reading it as a *punctum*, or wound, that both prompts and scars Genet's writing. Through a theoretical engagement with two texts that explore how this *punctum* catalyses the need for artistic expression — Barthes's *La Chambre claire* and Cixous's *Portrait de Jacques Derrida en jeune saint juif* — I consider how the *punctum* galvanises the emergence of a radically solitary subjectivity in Genet's writing. I respond directly to Leo Bersani's interpretation of

Genet's anti-relational ethics to propose that, instead, Genet establishes a perforated relation in which individuals reach out as lone points in a shared separation.

Most canonically, it is Roland Barthes's 1980 text on photography, *La Chambre claire*, which theorises the relationship between the *punctum*, language and subjectivity. Seeking a new critical form in which to talk about the uniqueness of individual experience, Barthes opens his essay by expressing discomfort with his reliance on the language of semiology, psychoanalysis and sociology, which all systematise ways of thinking about the self through a hardened language of order and classification. His 'résistance éperdue à tout système réducteur' [desperate resistance to any reductive system], inspires a critical shift in his *œuvre* that will turn to photography as the artform he believes could be able to produce 'la science impossible de l'être unique' [the impossible science of the unique being].[46] Barthes's urge to theorise what drives our idiosyncratic, affective responses without imposing a rationalised system of standards or principles that suggest a generalisable truth, leads him to launch what he perceives as the curious quest for a '*Mathesis singularis* (et non plus *universalis*)' [a *mathesis singularis* (and no longer *universalis*)].[47] In an article on his endeavour, Øyvind Vågnes explains that a '*mathesis universalis* implies a systemic approach to the object to be analyzed, the establishment of a theoretical apparatus'.[48] Barthes rejects any such hermeneutic that reifies the subject into a static object of analysis, subjecting the individual to patterns and systems that are anathema to the distinctiveness of ontological difference. Instead, a *mathesis singularis* aims to explore the singular in the universal, that impossible science of identifying the specificity of our personal impulses, while trying to understand what is broadly true for all people. Barthes elusively identifies this as 'une science du sujet dont peu m'importe le nom [...] pourvu qu'elle parvienne à une généralite qui ne me réduise ni ne m'écrase' [a science of the subject, a science whose name is of little importance to me, provided it attains to a generality which neither reduces nor crushes me].[49] Linguistic codifications and theoretical fields of study break down in this pursuit of the science of the individual, as though lending it a discipline or conceptual domain ossifies it into an essentialised and abstracted truth too far removed from the singularity of affect. Perhaps, then, a *mathesis singularis* could take its inspiration from the geometric point itself: an a priori singularity, which, when serialised, forms the image of a continuous line. This implies a connectivity between each individual point, as though a broader general association joins the units together, while never sacrificing the uniqueness of each point that cannot, by its very definition, actually cohere.

To understand this tension between the particular and the general, Barthes chooses a handful of photographs he believes to be directly addressed to him. He explains his pull towards certain images, rather than others that remain inert, because of a wound wrought in him as an onlooker: 'Comme *Spectator*, je ne m'intéressais à la Photographie que par "sentiment"; je voulais l'approfondir, non comme une question (un thème) mais comme une blessure: je vois, je sens, donc je remarque, je regarde et je pense' [as *Spectator* I was interested in Photography only for 'sentimental' reasons; I wanted to explore it not as a question (a theme) but as a wound: I see, I feel, hence I notice, I observe and I think].[50] The sensation of being pulled toward the image, which then demands rationalisation is encapsulated by an inexplicable affliction caused by the photograph. He breaks this sensation down into two affective impulses. The initial, voluntary '*studium*', which he explains as our nonchalant desire for the image, enticing the onlooker without troubling us: 'elles me plaisent ou me déplaisent sans me poindre' [they please or displease me without pricking me].[51] Our emotional response hinges on this involuntary pinprick that wounds us when we look, a spontaneous reflex that Barthes calls the *punctum*:

> C'est lui qui part de la scène, comme une flèche, et vient me percer. Un mot existe en latin pour designer cette blessure, cette piqure, cette marque faite par un instrument pointu; ce mot m'irait d'autant mieux qu'il renvoie aussi à l'idée de ponctuation et que les photos dont je parle sont en effet comme ponctuées, parfois même mouchetées, de ces points sensibles; précisément, ces marques, ces blessures sont des points [...] piqure, petit trou, petite tache, petite coupure — et aussi coup de dés. Le *punctum* d'une photo, c'est ce hasard qui, en elle me point (mais aussi me meurtrit, me poigne).

> [It is this element which rises from the scene, shoots out of it like an arrow, and pierces me. A Latin word exists to designate this wound, this prick, this mark made by a pointed instrument: the word suits me all the better in that it also refers to the notion of punctuation, and because the photographs I am speaking of are in effect punctuated, sometimes even speckled with these sensitive points; precisely, these marks, these wounds are so may points [...] *punctum* is also: sting, speck, cut, little hole — and also cast of the dice. A photographs' *punctum* is that accident that pricks me (but also bruises me, is poignant to me).][52]

Barthes identifies a dual directionality of the point as both an agent, darting out of the static image like an arrow to arrest the spectator, and the object that the spectator pursues, a chance encounter with an unknown aspect that re-opens old wounds. The metatextual reference to Mallarmé's 'Un coup de dés', and to his celebration of chance and the unknown, invites us to consider the poignancy of these points as tapping into what is most unpredictable, and thus unclassifiable, about who we are and how we feel. The *punctum* resonates because the spectator projects meaning onto the image, as much as being struck by an entirely unexpected connection, in a mutual flow of energy that Derrida has described as a point 'me vise à l'instant et au lieu où je le vise; et c'est ainsi que la photographie ponctuée me point' [aims at *me* at the instant and place where I aim at it; it is thus that the punctuated photograph pricks me].[53] The *punctum* is not solicited; rather, it wounds by touching on an aspect of the self that is innately singular, that breaks through codification and yet that nonetheless is elicited by the very encounter with an external other. Derrida picks up on how Barthes's point reveals an ethical quandary:

> Le *punctum* traduit d'ailleurs, dans *La Chambre claire*, une valeur du mot 'détail': un point de singularité troue la surface de la reproduction — et même de la production — des analogies, des ressemblances, des codes. Il perce, il vient m'atteindre d'un coup, me blesser ou me meurtrir et d'abord, semble-t-il, ne regarde que moi. [...] S'adresse à moi la singularité absolue de l'autre.

> [The word *punctum*, translates, in *Camera Lucida*, one meaning of the word 'detail': a point of singularity that punctures the surface of the reproduction

— and even the production — of analogies, likenesses, and codes. It pierces, strikes me, wounds me, bruises me, and first of all, seems to concern only me. Its very definition is that it addresses itself to me. [...] The absolute singularity of the other addresses itself to me.][54]

The *punctum* enters where the subject experiences the re-emergence of affect from seemingly neutral codes, images or analogies which bear no ostensible relation to them. Such wounding arises from this unexpected encounter in which the absolute singularity of the other becomes singularly poignant to the onlooker. As a form of relation, the point qua *punctum* forges a link between image and spectator, subject and other, witness and referent, because of a recognition of an insurmountable difference that nonetheless resonates: I relate in my intransigent solitude.

The incipit of *Notre-Dame-des-Fleurs* is galvanised by a *punctum* that Genet locates in twenty photographs of guillotined murderers that his first-person narrator sticks to his prison cell wall. Seized by an ineffable point of contact with these images, Genet's subject becomes a passive recipient of these 'assassins maintenant morts [qui] sont pourtant arrivés jusqu'à moi' [these murderers, now dead, have nevertheless reached me], those who elusively touch him like 'astres de deuil [qui] tombe[nt] dans ma cellule' [these luminaries of affliction fall into my cell] (*NDF*, pp. 12; 47–48). The spatial invasion of criminals that reach out and fall into Genet's affective consciousness carries an ethical weight, as here Genet's 'moi' succumbs to the absolute singularity of those who rupture normative codes of relation. They become poignant to him in their double unreachability: spatially remote, these stars of death are scattered like points in a constellation of inaccessibility outside the prison; and temporally disconnected, both in their literal death and in their immortality as partial images immobilised in a newspaper that makes its way in tatters to the cell. Genet's ethical posture is based on such fragmentation, since what connects him to these individuals is no communitarian ideal, but rather, like Barthes's *mathesis singularis*, a form of relation that allows him to extrapolate from their singularity a quality that responds to his own subjectivity. Only by co-opting the poignant inaccessibility of these photographic scraps can Genet externalise a fraction of his own selfhood, 'une parcelle de me vie intérieure' [a small fragment of my inner life] (pp. 13; 50). The narration of selfhood is imbricated with the affective penetration of the other, such that the *punctum* that pricks from without then re-emerges on the page as a point or particle of subjectivity.

This figurative connection between self and image is mimed physically when Genet enshrines the photographs as pin-ups, a gesture that pierces back the very *punctum* that pricks him:

Quelques-unes sont épinglées avec des petits bouts de fil de laiton [...] j'ai fabriqué pour les plus purement criminels des cadres en forme d'étoile [...] sourires et moues, les uns et les autres inexorables, m'entrent par tous mes trous offerts, leur vigueur pénètre en moi et m'érige. Je vis parmi ces gouffres.

[Some are pinned up with bits of brass wire [...] I have made star-shaped frames for the most purely criminal [...] smiles and sneers, alike inexorable, enter me by all the holes I offer, their vigour penetrates me and erects me. I live among these pits.] (*NDF*, pp. 13; 49)

Genet responds erotically to the *punctum* that drives home the unreachable singularity of the most criminal, as though imagining their transgression of social values is then experienced as a phantasmic, phallic penetration. The images are pinned up in part because they dramatise a radical break away from any communitarian ethics, those who stand alone titillating Genet as he conjures up the phantasmagoria of vigorous puncture: 'ta verge traversait ma bouche avec l'âpreté soudain mauvaise d'un clocher crevant un nuage d'encre, une épingle à chapeau un sein' [your rod, unsheathed and unbrandished, went through my mouth with the suddenly cruel sharpness of a steeple puncturing a cloud of ink, a hatpin a breast] (*NDF*, pp. 13; 49). The *punctum* of the photographs catalyses a series of symbolic penetrations, all of which atomise the possibility of wholeness or unity: the cloud, breast, mouth are split open by skewers that prioritise the singular part over the group. If read in terms of relation, we might argue that Genet eroticises the feeling of atomising cohesion itself, the *punctum* of these images resonating in him as a poignant sensation of disbanding, his own solitude paradoxically finding solace in theirs.

Genet's imagination is full of such pinpricks. The poignant sensation of the *punctum* not only forges holes in the onlooker, but also operates inside the 'trous offerts' of those orifices poised to be entered. The *punctum* that wounds does so precisely at those sites that Genet describes as voluntarily open and eager to be penetrated, his holes not purely laden with sexual overtones but constructed also as symbolic fissures which resist closure or remediation. Both aspects are related: Genet is enthralled by hollowness, rationalising his selection of images as not 'par hasard que j'ai découpé dans des magazines ces belles têtes aux yeux vides' [by chance that I cut those handsome, vacant-eyed heads out of the magazines] since, 'si je l'ai cloué à mon mur, c'est qu'il avait selon moi, au coin de la bouche ou à l'angle des paupières, le signe sacré des monstres' [if I have nailed him to my wall, it was because, as I see it, he had the sacred sign of the monster at the corner of his mouth or the angle of the eyelids] (*NDF*, pp. 12; 48). These pin-ups pierce Genet by channelling a vacuity that evacuates any symbolic or moral standing: the monstrosity to which Genet refers is as ethically ambiguous as it is lacking a tangible referent, as though the singularity that bears into him cannot be ontologised by any set position. The *punctum*, too, multiplies and moves as it emanates from the mouth, eye, facial flaw and gesture of the criminal who becomes poignant to Genet as an 'illumination qui montre le vide' [illumination that shows the void] (pp. 13; 107) that later becomes the guiding principle on which his theatre is based. The *punctum* that strikes from these empty eyes is compared to a litany of inert, defunct spaces that once active or filled with life, have now been evacuated: 'ils sont, ces yeux, comme certaines villes closes [...] ils m'hypnotisent autant que les théâtres vides, les prisons désertes, les machineries au repos, les déserts, car les déserts sont clos et ne communiquent pas avec l'infini' [these eyes [...] are like certain closed cities [...] and they hypnotise me as much as empty theatres, deserted prisons, machinery at rest, deserts, for deserts are closed and do not communicate with the infinite] (pp. 10; 49). The anaphora of 'desert' which slips from adjective to noun, from the description of isolation to the status of solitude, insists on an image of abandonment that Genet fetishises in all of his writing. With their function rendered obsolete and their marginal presence even further neglected, these empty spaces are funnelled by Genet's sentence into the symbolic repository of the *desertum*, the solitary retreat, which in turn becomes the *punctum* itself. Bearing witness to that solitude is a serrated, jarring experience in Genet's writing, the inaccessibility of the other rendered all the more poignant as he is unable to delve into the very image he creates: the emptiness that pierces him only re-emerges as another iteration of a new void. He explains that:

> Les hommes de tels visages m'épouvantent, quand je dois les parcourir à tâtons, mais quelle éblouissante surprise quand, dans leur paysage, au détour d'une venelle abandonnée, je m'approche, le cœur éperdu, et ne découvre rien, rien que le vide dressé, sensible et fier comme une haute digitale!

> [Men with such faces terrify me, whenever I have to cross their paths warily, but what a dazzling surprise when, in their landscape, at the turning of a deserted lane, I approach, my heart racing wildly, and discover nothing, nothing but looming emptiness, sensitive and proud like a tall foxglove.] (*NDF*, pp. 10; 48)

Genet maps out a spatial cartography of this nothingness in which every image forms a synecdoche whose parts stand in for the void they seek to enter. The deserted lanes only lead onto a new image of puncture: the foxglove, a naturally phallic flower that stands erect ready to pierce its onlooker. The 'rien' is thus animate: both the *punctum* that penetrates and the empty hole that imitates the result of such puncture.

Sartre moralises on the nature of such isolation in Genet's society of criminals, arguing that there can be no 'solitude en commun' [solitude in common] but only 'une juxtaposition de solitudes individuelles' [a juxtaposition of individual solitudes]. He plots this contrapuntal alienation along the horizontal and vertical lines of a sort of ethical geometry:

> Le rapport vertical, qui sert d'épine dorsale à cette pseudo-communauté [...] le dur, droit comme une verge, crève le ciel, émerge dans le vide. Et le mou, maniaque crispé, se rue dans l'esclavage et l'abjection pour y retrouver la solitude; jusque dans l'accouplement ils sont seuls.

> [The vertical relationship, which serves as a backbone to this pseudo-community [...] the tough, upright as a penis, pierces the sky and drifts into the void. And the soft, that fidgety zealot, rushes into slavery and abjection to find solitude. Even in copulation they are alone.] (*SG*, pp. 116; 119)

Sartre imitates Genet's own spiked rhetoric when considering how any community in his writing is necessarily the site of a rupture. He suggests that individuals come together in order to break off coldly into untouchable separateness. Yet, his metaphor positions the couple along a perpendicular axis that necessarily produces a point of convergence, the individuals brought together to experience the other's solitude and thus *realise* their own. What is unique about the point as a *punctum* is that its piercing establishes just such a connection between individuals, a collision that Genet experiences affectively, compassionately even, in the recognition of the ultimate singularity of being. Rather than an existential failure, the point formalises a self-awareness in Genet's writing. Any encounter with the other — whether acrimonious, erotic or even inadvertent (as Genet's quasi-religious revelation on a train in 'Ce qui est resté d'un Rembrandt' suggests) — is experienced as a wound in the self, not a disconnected desertion of the other as Sartre implies.

The *punctum* caused by the encounter with the other also bears into Genet's subjects as a stigmata. *Notre-Dame-des-Fleurs* is born partly out of the invasive memory of fellow thief Roger, later transformed into Mignon, the lover of Notre Dame, whom Genet describes bursting through his narrative as a character who 'va surgir, s'ériger et m'introduire au point que j'en garderais les stigmates' [will rise up, become erect and penetrate me so deeply that I will be marked with stigmata] (*NDF*, pp. 29; 66). Similarly, *Pompes funèbres* is a text pitted by stigmata that Genet eulogises through the points of the wounds created 'par une rafale de mitraillette'. He fantasises that:

> Le personnage le plus important qu'exalte le récit de ma douleur et de mon amour pour lui sera ce monstre lumineux, exposé à la plus splendide solitude, celui devant qui je connais une sorte d'extase *parce qu'*il lui déchargea dans le corp [*sic*] une rafale de mitraillette.
>
> [The most important character glorified by the account of my grief and of my love for him will be that luminous monster who is exposed to the most splendid solitude, the one in whose presence I experience a kind of ecstasy *because* he discharged a burst of machine-gun fire into his body.][55]

As Genet stands before the perpetrator who, he fantasises, caused the wounds in his lover's body, Riton's luminous monstrosity becomes a literal embodiment of the driving force of the *punctum*. His lone presence penetrates both physically, causing the open wounds in Jean's body, and symbolically, through Genet's own experience of a palpable poignancy, an affective disruption from which he writes the text. Such poignancy is galvanised by this contingent *parce que*: Genet afflicted *par* (through, via, by) *ce* (that which) fired through Jean's body to pierce him with multiple stigmata. Genet is aroused physically by the abrasion caused by Riton's disavowal of relation itself, as though, paradoxically, it is only by falling outside of the system of social norms that Riton can reach the apotheosis of human individuality. Solitude is both painful and enticing as Genet's response echoes what Georges Bataille calls an 'ecstatic anguish' in which 'l'inconnu nous donne de l'angoisse, mais il est la condition de l'extase. L'angoisse est peur de perdre, expression du désir de posséder' [the unknown gives us great anguish, but often this is the condition for ecstasy. Anguish is the fear of losing, the desire for possession].[56] Riton represents precisely this 'inconnu' insofar as his solitude renders him inscrutably singular, his position as a traitor alienating him further from any relation, so that his solitude strikes in such a way that anguish turns to ecstasy. There is a complex mimetic web of the *punctum* at play: just as Riton's creation of multiple wounds in Jean's body in turn wounds (Jean) Genet, so Genet iteratively re-wounds the body of his lover Jean by writing to keep open his wounds, while also forging open a wound at the heart of the perpetrator such that 'un vide effrayant troua le ventre de Riton qui rentra à la caserne, seul avec sa solitude au milieu de lui' [a terrifying void pierced Riton who returned to the barracks, alone with his loneliness within him] (*NDF*, pp. 143; 190). The void which hollows out Riton's body is commensurate with the holes made in Erik's body from the 'rafale de mitraillette'; these holes striking Genet as though through a *punctum* that mimetically reinforces its points, its wounds, each time it pierces.

Bersani reads Genet's exaltation of solitude not as a failure to relate personally as Sartre implies, but as a negation of all symbolic systems that create a community of shared understanding. Solitude wounds language since it:

> Replaces the rich social discursiveness of good-and-evil, with what might be called the empty value of solitude, a value that literature, always circulating within a symbolic network, can only name. Solitude is evil because it is a betrayal, but not a betrayal defined by any opposition to loyalty. It is betrayal of that opposition, a betrayal opposed to nothing because it consists merely in a movement out of everything.[57]

By opting out of a dialectical relationship between transgression and allegiance, Bersani argues that Genet destroys the very codes and dynamics of the social relation itself. However, perhaps the revolutionary power of Genet's wounding points is that by emptying out the communitarian norms of social interaction, they create a new symbolic language that speaks to the shared experience of the individual. His *punctum* is fissiparous: it may divide subjects into their innermost singularity, but it also multiplies the points of connection between selves who are all wounded by falling outside of the boundaries of social recognition. Before delving further into this ontological wound and its 'radical democratic potential' as Carl Lavery contends, it is worth briefly exploring how Genet's trope of stigmata is figured as anything but an empty sign; rather, its points are etched into his text as the wounding origin from which to write about subjectivity itself.[58]

Stigmata then become the site of writing in both *Notre-Dame-des-Fleurs* and *Pompes funèbres* as both texts speak *out* of the holes forged in the skin of their prose, and *in* to them as part of a cultivation of those wounds. Writing is directly linked to the wound also in *Un captif amoureux* when Genet describes his discomfort in encountering Hebraic writing which is etched from a discontinuous series of points:

> La plupart des caractères étaient carrés, à angles droits, se lisant de droite à gauche et présentant tous une ligne horizontale mais discontinue. Un ou deux caractères étaient coiffés de l'aigrette, celle des grues; trois minces pistils soutenant trois stigmates antés sur les trois pistils attendant les abeilles qui poudraient le monde d'un pollen plusieurs fois millénaire, ou mieux, original.
>
> [Most of the letters were squat and rectangular; they read from right to left in a broken horizontal line. One or two had a crane-like plume on top: three slim pistils bearing three stigmata and waiting for the bees who'd scatter their age-old, nay primeval, pollen all over.] (*CA*, pp. 364; 310)

Hebraic writing is a wound in Genet's metaphor, a stigmatic puncture that perforates its own linearity as a continuous string of letters. Just like the machine gun in *Pompes funèbres*, the points in this scripture successively disrupt any continuity to produce writing as a line of solitary wounds which are as productive as they are disruptive. These linguistic stigmata pollinate the text, these three points waiting to be scattered over Hebraic language only to breed and inculcate their ideas beyond the confines of the page. Language thus transforms from a succession of solitary points into a breeding ground: the singular made multiple in a contagion that causes great unease for Genet. Such discomfort recalls the *punctum* insofar as the poignancy of these points for Genet is in their disjointed singularity, their multiple solitude(s). For Cixous, it is precisely through these multiple stigmata that writing creates meaning:

> Stigma stings, pierces, makes holes, separates with pinched marks and in the same movement distinguishes — re-marks — inscribes, writes. Stigma wounds *and* spurs, stimulates [...] I want stigmata. I do not want the stigmata to disappear. I am attached to my engravings, to the stings in my flesh and my mental parchment. I do not fear that trauma and stigma will form an alliance: the literature in me wants to maintain and reanimate traces.[59]

Differentiating between trauma and stigma, Cixous's remark that 'I do not fear that trauma and stigma will form an alliance' attests to a subtle recalibration of the wound. Where trauma, etymologically derived from the Greek for wound, might demand a static rendering of a traumatic event post-facto or even the iterative re-enactment of a one-off event; stigma produces a new scripture which renders productive the wounds it makes. If 'traumatism as an opening to the future of the wound is the promise of the text', then Cixous elevates the wound as more than simply a product of injury to be healed, transforming it instead into a master metaphor for the text itself.[60] In her mediation on Genet, *L'Entretien de la blessure*, she argues that the wound is a catalyst for writing since 'on entre en littérature par lésion. Par la suite chaque œuvre vit de sa plaie originaire' [we enter into literature through a lesion. Subsequently each text lives on through its original wound].[61] If Genet's writing is produced by a wound, then perhaps we might read his celebration of 'l'univers de l'irrémédiable' [the universe of the irremediable] (*NDF*, pp. 159; 165) and his 'goût de l'irréparable' [the love of the irreparable] (*PF*, pp. 117; 123) as a resistance to healing that wound and to ensuring that this *punctum* is perpetually re-imprinted into his text. Just as we opened this chapter referring to Derrida's concept that punctuation in Cixous's writing represented as 'le poumon de l'écriture', so here do I read Genet's *punctum* and his opposition to its healing as a desire to keep his text alive and breathing. By writing from and through the *punctum,* he stages a return to the origins of his text and continually strives to find new permutations, new rationales, that articulate that original sore.

Sartre has equated Genet's non-remedial thrust with his desire for stasis, and a perennial (re)living in the moment, arguing that:

> Genet porte en lui le vertige de l'irrémédiable, il veut mourir encore. Il s'abandonne à l'instant à des crises cathartiques qui reproduisent et portent au sublime le premier enchantement: le crime, l'exécution capitale, la poésie, l'orgasme, l'homosexualité, en chaque cas nous retrouverons le paradoxe de l'avant et de l'après, l'épanouissement et la retombée, une vie misée sur une seule carte, le jeu de l'éternel et de la fugacité.

> [Genet carries [...] within him the dizziness of the irremediable, he wants to die again. He abandons himself to the instant, to the cathartic crises that reproduce the first enchantment and carry it to the sublime: crime, crime, capital punishment, poetry, orgasm, homosexuality. In each case we shall find the paradox of the before and after, a rise and fall, a life staked on a single card, the play of the eternal and the fleeting.] (*SG*, pp. 12; 4)

However, such longing for the unhealed wound speaks not to a hermetic stuck record, but rather to a positive harnessing of the *irrecuperable*: writing from a radical position of an open wound whose continual dehiscence resists recuperation into structural norms. Genet's literature is not only engendered by a wound, an original openness, but it strives throughout to maintain its gaping-ness and to establish a non-progressive, anti-teleological thrust which is nonetheless productive. For Mairéad Hanrahan, 'cette blessure, omniprésente de n'être jamais présente' adumbrates 'la possibilité de toute création. C'est parce que la plaie demeure ouverte qu'elle permet de s'ouvrir sur autre chose qu'elle-même' [this wound, omnipresent without ever being present [...] the possibility of all creation. It is because the wound stays open that it can open onto something else].[62] She cites his remark in *Miracle de la rose* that 'ces blessures que subit notre enfance et qu'elle-même provoque' [those wounds which our childhood suffers and which it itself causes] (*MR*, pp. 368; 174), to which I add his comment in 'Entretien avec R. Wischenbart et L. S. Barrada' that 'créer c'est toujours parler de l'enfance' [creating always means speaking of childhood] (*ED*, pp. 277; 239), such that the wound at the heart of his writing always returns to a severed relation wrought in an orphaned childhood.[63]

To return to the *punctum* as the points of a stigma, and its neighbouring resonances as a fertile source of writing, how might we read Cixous's analysis of Derrida's stigmata in *Portrait de Jacques Derrida en jeune saint juif*, in which she asserts, 'A quel point avec le *point* il a maille à partir, tout le corpus de son œuvre en porte les stigmates' [The point to which the *point* is a thorn in his side, the whole corpus of his work bears the stigmata]?[64] Recognising the lexical connection of the point as a stitch, Cixous unpicks the fabric of Derrida's text to highlight the ubiquitous points. There is no doubt that Derrida's writing is marked by the traces of an inherent wounding, such that in his 'Circonfession' he compares the instrument of writing to a catheter where he explains that 'toujours je rêve d'une plume qui soit une seringue, une pointe aspirante plutôt que cette arme très dure avec laquelle il faut inscrire, inciser, choisir, calculer' [I always dream of a pen that would be a syringe, a suction point rather than that hard weapon with which one must inscribe, incise, choose, calculate].[65] The upward movement of the injection which withdraws, which removes an abject part that is both me and no longer me mirrors Cixous's own description of stigmata when she states that 'the mark of the pointed object [...] This hole enters into my skin. The scar adds, the stigma digs, excavates'.[66] This impulse of localised evacuation and extraction central to the stigma is certainly at play in Derrida's *Circonfession*, a whole text which, like in *Pompes funèbres*, elegises the wound at its core. He realises that his entire philosophical project is shaped by:

> Circoncision, je n'ai jamais parlé que de ça, considérez le discours sur la limite, les marges, marques, marches, etc. la clôture, l'anneau (alliance et don) le sacrifice, l'écriture du corps, le *pharmakos* exclu ou retranché, la coupure/ couture de *Glas*, le coup et le recoudre.

> [Circumcision, that's all I've ever talked about, consider the discourse on the limit, margins, marks, marches, etc., the closure and the ring (alliance and gift), the writing of the body, the *pharmakos* excluded or cut off, the cutting/ sewing of *Glas*, the blow and the sewing back up.][67]

While Derrida may use the wound of circumcision as an inscriptive, mark-making trope, he denies the possibility of pinning down and reading its marks (as a stigmatic reading would demand). Indeed, Derrida seems to assert their presence rather than their legibility, investing the language of these wounds with the power of self-cancellation: 'tout le lexique qui obsède mes textes, CIR-CON-SI, s'imprime dans l'hypothèse de la cire, non ça c'est faux et mauvais, pourquoi, qu'est-ce qui ne marche pas, mais scie, oui, et tous les points sur les *i*' [the whole lexicon that obsesses my writings, CIR-CON-SI, imprints itself in the hypothesis of wax, no that's false and bad, why, what doesn't work, but saws, yes and all the dots on the i's].[68] Derrida's glorious homophony of 'scie', 'oui' and 'i' lets the reader slide between adjacent signifiers which attest both to the division and dissection inherent in even the most emphatic of affirmations: *si* becomes *scie*, and the positive 'yes' is torn up, cut through and its fixed assertions put into question. Genet's own analysis of *ici* in *Pompes funèbres* homophonically echoes the disintegration of Derrida's 'scie', as he riffs on the serrated sounds of his syllables:

> 'Ici' et les mots qui devaient suivre: 'qu'on l'a tué' prononcés, fût ce men-talement, apportaient à ma douleur une précision physique qui l'exaspérait. Les mots étaient trop cruels. Puis je me dis que les mots sont des mots et qu'ils ne changeaient rien aux faits. Je me forçais à dire, à me redire avec l'agaçante répétition des scies I-ci, I-ci, I-ci, I-ci, I-ci. Mon esprit s'aiguisait sur l'endroit que désignait 'Ici' [...] 'I-ci, I-ci, I-ci, I-ci, I-ci. Qu'on l'a tué, qu'on l'a tué, qu'on l'a tué, con l'a tué, con l'a tué...' et je fis mentalement cette épitaphe: 'Ici con l'a tué'.

> [The uttering of 'here' and, even if only mentally, of the words meant to follow, 'that he was killed,' gave to my pain a physical precision that aggravated it. The words were too cruel. Then I said to myself that the words were words and did not in any way change the facts. I forced myself to say over and over, inwardly, with the irritating repetitiveness of a saw, He-re, He-re, He-re, He-re, He-re. My mind was being sharpened at the spot designated by 'Here' [...] 'that he was killed, that he was killed, that he was killed, that heels killed, that heels killed...' and I mentally composed the following epitaph: 'Here that heels killed'.] (*PF*, pp. 39; 130)

Genet's anaphora *ici* repeatedly lacerates him, metamorphosing the spatial *ici* into an affective *punctum* that poignantly evokes his lover's death. He responds by wounding language itself and by disintegrating its signifiers into their phonetic parts. By rupturing the syllables that fix facts as immutable, Genet wields language as an aggressor against itself, atomising whole words into their constituent, etymological parts in order to break apart any determinacy. Even when keeping words whole, he equips his terms with a sharpness that recalls the perforation of the *punctum*: his 'esprit s'aiguisait', his mind sharpened like the *punctum* which wounded it in the first place, Genet wounded by the very word, *ici*, that gestures to the locus of wounding itself. The *scie* that is so equivocal for Derrida arguably finds its blueprint here as Genet renders *ici* a malleable signifier that draws on its own experience of being wounded to re-wound language in turn. Genet atomises language like the machine gun that created the wounds in Jean's body, his 'agaçante répétition' firing through the fixity of terms to refigure their reality.

Derrida's reference to the idiomatic 'mettre tous les points sur les i' signals, albeit less violently, how the point destabilises language. He shows how language always has the possibility of being read another way, an equivocation which *can resist* the completion of dotting the 'i's and crossing the 't's. Derrida in fact prolongs this indeterminacy by reducing the number of 'points' or full stops within each section of the text, so that each section remains both meandering and incomplete, and is then jerkily drawn to a close by the machine of its inscription:

> 'Entre l'aléatoire et le calculable [...] la chance et la nécessité': la loi provisoire de *Circonfession*, une machine — avec laquelle il fallut calculer son souffle, ponctuer chaque période, arrêter le contour de la périphrase, circoncire en un mot pour que l'événement défie ou surprenne l'autre machination.

> ['Between the aleatory and the calculable... chance and necessity': the provisional law of *Circumfession*, a machine — with which breath had to be calculated, each period punctuated, the contour of the periphrasis arrested, in a word, circumcision performed so that the event might challenge or surprise the *other* machination.][69]

Circonfession's artificial conditions of restraint undeniably put the process of writing, and more specifically the process of 'pointing' or concluding, under the microscope. Analagous to Genet's *pointillé*, Derrida offers us a series of fifty-nine singular, individual *périodes*: one to mark each year of his life at the time he wrote the text, each concluded by only one full stop pre-organised by the matrix of the text to avoid the software's warning 'cette commande va créer un paragraphe trop long' [this command will create a paragraph that is too long].[70] Derrida speaks of how this 'matrice pourtant s'ouvre, laissant place à l'inanticipable singularité de l'événement, elle reste par essence, par force, non saturable, non suturable, invulnérable, donc seulement extensible et transformable, toujours inachevée' [this matrix nevertheless opens, leaving room for the unanticipable singularity of the event, it remains by essence, by force, nonsaturable, nonsuturable, invulnerable, therefore only extensible and transformable, always unfinished].[71] He thus emphasises how the only driving force for all of these characteristics is the point which draws each *période* to a close. All of the qualities Derrida cites — singularity, un-suturable, always incomplete — are deeply reminiscent of the *punctum* in Genet's writing, such that once again we are encouraged to forge a connection between the point and the wound as intertwined sites that both deeply problematise and motivate writing. As much as Derrida's text foregrounds the wound as its main theme, so does it assert the significance of the 'point' as more than simply its cipher, but as a trope which forces the reader to think about singularity, fixity, stability and the point as an aggressor, a wound-er of writing in general.

The point never sounds the death knell of finality in Derrida's writing, because it refuses the totalising catharsis of *un point c'est tout*. Instead, it becomes the symbolic site on which his deconstructive project is acted out: a geometric figure of indivisibility that Derrida endlessly strives to dismantle. Cixous forensically magnifies his relation the point by claiming that:

> Le point c'est l'unité absolue, sans dimensions, dit le discours mathématique [...].
> Or, l'axiome fondamental de tout ce qu'il dit partout, tout ce qu'il écrit, tout

ce qu'il pense est une protestation contre le point comme indivisible. Il écrit, divise, pour le diviser, le point. Il pense, il vit, la divisibilité, il divit [...] cette protestation, c'est son point d'honneur. Jamais il ne met de point, le mot, le signe, qui n'entraine des tremblements. Celui qu'il est, quel qu'il soit, ne reste jamais au point mort. Dès qu'il y a point en vue le voilà partant, le voilà partir, le voilà parti. En sens contraire. En tous les sens contraires.

[The point is the absolute unit, without dimension, says mathematical discourse [...]. Everything he writes, everything he thinks is a protest against the point as indivisible. He writes, divided, in order to divide it, the point. He thinks, he lives, divisibility, he divives [...] this refusal is his point of honor. Never does he put a point, a dot, a period, the word, the sign without a shudder. The minute he sights a point he is on the mark, he is off, he is gone.][72]

The 'point(s)', or as Cixous sees them, the stigmata, are not just central to Derrida's work in *Circonfession*, rather they act as the catalyst and motivation for his whole project of deconstruction which seeks to disrupt, shake-up, dissect and destabilise. Where the *punctum* for Barthes produced an enforcement of expression, 'donc je remarque', so here does the point in Cixous' estimation produce Derrida's reason for writing: 'il écrit [...] pour le diviser, le point'. The agitation Derrida produces around the figure of the point in some ways only serves to re-instate a new point, a counterpoint, ad infinitum; a divisive movement Derrida sees not as aggressively and unnecessarily disruptive in *Points de suspension*, but rather as the inevitable, protective structure of living itself:

La signification de la division elle-même se divise. D'une part, c'est la fatalité, sous une certaine face douloureuse, l'incapacité à rassembler dans l'un. C'est la nécessité, c'est l'inévitable. En ce sens, c'est ce qui expose à la dissociation, ce qui expose à la déhiscence; et, en même temps, autre signification, la division peut être aussi une ligne de stratégie, un mouvement profond de la garde elle-même. Dès lors qu'on se divise, on garde toujours en réserve, on ne s'expose pas totalement d'un seul coup à la menace.

[The meaning of division itself divides. On the one hand, it is fate, seen in its painful aspect: the inability to bring together in the one. It is necessity, inevitable. In this sense it is what exposes to dissociation, to dehiscence; and at the same time, on the other hand, in another meaning, division can also be a line of strategy, a profound movement of keeping itself. From the moment one divides oneself, one keeps something always in reserve, one doesn't expose oneself all at once to the threat.][73]

Form becomes content here as Derrida cleaves the very term 'division' in two. His argument that there can be no access to an indivisible singularity in language can also be mapped onto the conditions of subjectivity itself: no self can be contained by one indivisible form. This is where Genet's divisive *punctum* becomes such a productive sign of subjectivity, since it channels both such thrusts of division. Firstly, dehiscence as Genet's desire to constantly write through the open wound he locates in the self, re-inscribing it through the process of writing which creates its own metaphorical wounds. Secondly, division as self-preservation: Genet's *punctum* creates a subject-forming wound that cannot be located in any one site, but which proliferates itself throughout his writing in an act of resisting identitarian fixity.

This *punctum* becomes as abstract and unmeasurable as the point in geometry: not a space that can be pinpointed, but a stigma that defines the self and yet whose affect is uncontainable in any form. This solitary point is buried inside the divisive *punctum* and becomes what Genet explores in *L'Atelier d'Alberto Giacometti*, as the secret source of individuality itself.

Like Samuel Beckett's austere aesthetic that strives to tear apart the veils of his language 'in order to get at the things (or the Nothingness) behind it', so Genet seems drawn to Giacometti's trenchant sculptures because they pull apart the artistic ornamentation that cloaks 'ce lieu secret, en nous-mêmes' [this secret place, within ourselves] (*AAG*, pp. 41; 42).[74] Beckett's desire to express an existential void that is not contained by words, grammar or style finds echoes in Genet's attraction to Giacometti's artwork precisely because it seems able to 's'aventurer ailleurs que dans le mensurable' [venture forth beyond the merely measurable] (*AAG*, pp. 41; 42). In order to understand the conditions of our subjectivity, Genet is moved by forms that resonate beyond the realm of the empirical or the visible, beckoning him instead to access the solitary point from which these figures must be seen. These lone sculptures demand that the spectator recognise and relate to what is most solitary, and yet most shared, about our human experience. Genet attributes this incommensurable point to an ontological wound within the subject: 'Il n'est pas à la beauté d'autre origine que la blessure, singulière, différente pour chacun, caché ou visible, que tout homme garde en soi, qu'il préserve et où il se retire quand il veut quitter le monde' [Beauty has no other origin than a wound, unique, different for each person, hidden or visible, that everyone keeps in himself, that he preserves and to which he withdraws when he wants to leave the world] (pp. 41; 42). Genet's wound is a Derridean site of reserve: less the product of a fatal fragmentation; it is rather a subject-forming wound which is essential to consolidation of the self. It is precisely within that which is divided that Genet locates a radical singularity which is 'différente pour chacun', perhaps a realisation of the generalised singularity to which Barthes refers in his *mathesis singularis*. Genet's division is not purely dehiscent; rather it seems to subtend both parts of Derrida's division as both disassociative and self-protective. The wound separates subjects from one another in a singularity that is inherently solitary:

> Chaque être m'est révélé dans ce qu'il a de plus neuf, de plus irremplaçable — et c'est toujours une blessure — grâce à la solitude où les place cette blessure dont ils ont à peine connaissance, et où pourtant tout leur être afflue [...] la solitude, comme je l'entends, ne signifie pas condition misérable mais plutôt royauté secrète, incommunicabilité profonde mais connaissance plus ou moins obscure d'une inattaquable singularité.

> [Each being is revealed to me in its newest, most irreplaceable quality — and it's still a wound — thanks to the solitude where this wound places them, about which they know almost nothing, and yet in which their entire being flows [...] solitude, as I understand it, does not mean a miserable condition, but rather a secret royalty, a profound incommunicability, but a more or less obscure knowledge of an unassailable singularity.] (*AAG*, pp. 53; 51)

The wound becomes a site in which the self can seek solitude, a rare and robust space which offers protection. And yet, the idea of a contained site is deeply problematic in Genet's writing. An image in *Pompes funèbres* helps unpack such a paradox, as Genet configures a similar fortification but in a form which rejects containment: the form of a diamond whose facets radiate, unrestrictedly: 'le goût de la *singularité* [...] d'une forme aux lignes sévères et nettes, d'une manière inattaquable, une sorte de diamant, justement appelé solitaire' [a taste for singularity [...] a shape formed by sharp, severe lines, of an unattackable matter, a kind of diamond rightly called solitaire] (*PF*, pp. 66; 80). Another definition of the point as a singular entity is the 'solitaire', a precious stone set apart or by itself, and the diamond is considered to be the gem or 'solitaire' par excellence.[75] Thus, Genet's astute matching of a singular, solitary item with one whose morphology is multifaceted, seems to reconfigure our notion of singularity as something not inherently singular itself. Indeed, read via the multivalence of the diamond, Genet's pointing to an 'inattaquable singularité' does not yield an image where a single container houses and protects the self; but rather, it is one which protects itself precisely because it cannot be encapsulated. Genet configures the solitaire as sublime: 'le plus éclatant diamant; la solitude, ou sainteté, c'est-à-dire encore le jeu incontrôlable, étincelant, insupportable de sa liberté' [the most sparkling diamond; solitude, or sanctity, that is to say the uncontrollable game, dazzling, unbearable in its freedom] (pp. 66; 80), an unbreachable, multifaceted singularity whose hostility protects it from infiltration. Indeed, Genet asserts his own inaccessible solitude through the same metaphor, situating himself at the very heart of this diamond in *Journal du voleur*: 'je m'établissais dans ma richesse participant du diamant, dans cette ville des diamantaires, et dans cette nuit de la solitude égoïste dont les facettes miroitent' [I was establishing myself in my diamond-like wealth, in the city of diamond cutters, and in that night of self-centred solitude whose facets sparkled] (*JV*, pp. 300; 289). Ensconced in the 'solitaire', Genet inscribes his solitude into a metaphor whose many facets not only challenge the singularity of solitude, but whose glistening brilliance deflects any deeper access into the nature of his singularity. Allying himself to the diamond motif, Genet asserts an authorial identity as dazzling as it is impenetrable; terms that recall Bataille's later criticism of the 'étincelante parade des mots' [sparkling parade of words] of Genet's prose, whose beauty he considers to be 'celle des bijoux' [that of jewels].[76] For Bataille, the jewel evokes the cold hardness of Genet's texts ('rien de plus froid, de moins touchant' [nothing more cold, nothing less touching]) which, asserting the solitude of its characters, render his writing 'incommunicable'.[77] As much as Genet labels his solitude 'égoïste', thus self-centred and singular, he also serialises that solitude by establishing himself as one diamond in a whole town of diamonds: his writing addressing a generalised solitude that is independently experienced and which communicates a unique irreducibility we all share in common.

To return to Bersani, Genet's 'solitaire' does not isolate itself from relatability by moving out of everything and away from everyone. Rather, it atomises the very language of relation: as a *punctum* it provides a form of relation which operates affectively and beyond codification. It is inherently inaccessible, just like Derrida's second rendering of division in *Points de suspension*, which protects the subject because 'il y a toujours un autre lieu, il n'y a pas une seule face, un seul lieu, il y a toujours plusieurs lieux, et cette différenciation est une protection' [there is always another place, there is not just one side, just one place; there are always several places, and this differentiation is a protection].[78] Genet offers a radical configuration of relation as *multiple* singularities, the point as *multiple* counterpoints: less total anti-communitarianism, but a community of hostile, solitudes whose 'incommunicabilité profonde' rejects any form of cohesion. Such a perforated relation reflects Derrida's analysis of Barthes's *punctum*, in which he perceives as a:

> Théorie contrapuntique ou défilé des stigmates: une blessure vient sans doute au lieu du point signé de singularité, au lieu de son instant même (stigmê), en sa pointe. Mais au lieu de cet événement, la place est laissée, pour la même blessure, à la substitution qui s'y répète ne gardant de l'irremplaçable qu'un désir passé.

> [Contrapuntal theory or a procession of stigmata: a wound no doubt comes in (the) place of the point signed by singularity, in (the) place of its very instant (stigme), at its point. But *in (the) place of* this event, place is given over, for the same wound, to substitution, which repeats itself there, retaining of the irreplaceable only a past desire.][79]

Derrida's counterpoint, his procession of stigmata attests to the serial, relational quality of the point and the wound. By suggesting that the wound operates contrapuntally, by which we can understand any different voices all speaking at once, he evokes its plural singularity: it endlessly repeats the singularity it provokes. Derrida refers here to Barthes's *punctum* whose poignancy is directed toward a specific singularity in the onlooker, but whose affective penetration of the onlooker causes a wound which in turn becomes a substitute marker of the place we can never access, contain, read or get hold of, that which is considered by both Genet and Derrida as '(de plus/ l') irremplaçable'. The *punctum* is thus singularly poignant and iteratively played out; a feature of the subject's irreplaceable singularity, which has been replaced. Bersani argues that Genet turns away from relation because of a 'pure destruction [which] does not choose its objects; to the extent that all objects are available for relations, there can be no loyalty, no connection, to any object. In Genet there is an antirelational thrust'.[80] I see instead a form of subjective relation based on this procession of wounds which serialise subjects, a form which is relational without being continuous. The fact of these poignant wounds that are so crucial to Genet's writing means that there is a relational energy at play in the texts, but it is one which he renders profoundly indecipherable.

What is described in *L'Atelier d'Alberto Giacometti* as truly poignant, and as such destabilising, is precisely this serialised solitude *constituted of points*: 'ce point précieux où l'être humain serait ramené à ce qu'il a de plus irréductible: sa solitude d'être exactement équivalent à tout autre' [that precious point at which the human being is brought back the most irreducible part of him: his solitude of being exactly the same as any other] (*AAG*, pp. 51; 49). It is to this precious point that Genet directs his concept of subjectivity, a point which holds a generalised, irreducible wound at the heart of all selves; a wound which is constructed as a fleeting, dehiscent and self-protective point rather than a corporeal injury. Perhaps the heuristic value of the point as *punctum* is that it enables the reader to conceptualise the process of delivering affect as something both violent and ephemeral, whose traces provide the prospect of something legible, but which, in reality, are always foreign to the moment itself. The *punctum* is both inherently relational and yet atomises the very language of connection, unity, cohesion; as a wound, it generates Genet's writing, a dynamic affect which offers a form of relation that breaks with everything to which we can relate. Arguably, the greatest poignancy of Genet's geometric point is not that it promotes a 'diabolical individualism', as Edmund White has claimed of his early novels, but that it painfully reveals the common isolation of subjectivity itself.[81] The sore point behind Genet's *punctum* then is that it imagines a selfhood that is only possible when it holds itself apart, in parts, like a Kandinskian point forever turned inwards.

Compass Points: Navigating the Self

As Kandinsky reminds us in *Point and Line to Plane*, the geometric point is an organic form found throughout nature. Whether the seeds of a poppy, a cosmic constellation or a desert full of sand, he perceives such phenomena to 'have been originated from points, to which point — in its original geometric essence — everything returns [...]. The smallest, self-contained, wholly centrifugal shapes actually appear to the naked eye as points seemingly loosely related to each other'. In this stippled perception of the world and its objects, Kandinsky seems to usher in a return to a 'primordial state of geometric being' in which the singular and self-contained origin of all things is made manifest.[82] Whole compounds and identities break down in this starkly elemental perception of the outside world, and it is amidst this fragmentation that I understand Genet's own vital and anthropomorphic geometry. Where the point exemplifies the innermost concise form for Kandinsky, it also formalises the inward-facing nature of subjectivity in Genet's writing. In this concluding section, I explore how Genet abstracts the self in his early novels, plotting characters like the points on a compass as he strives to navigate what he calls the 'internal astronomy' of each individual.

In *Pompes funèbres*, we encounter the bodies of Riton and Erik interlaced in erotic bliss. Filtered through Riton's inner consciousness, we witness the experience of being together as way to draw the self inwards as the other's presence catalyses the subject's withdrawal, not its relation. Genet imagines Riton's personal retreat via an affective geometry:

> Le sentiment de certitude de sa présence rassemblait son corps des quatre coins de l'horizon, battait le rappel vers un point idéal, au centre de lui-même, en y portant sur une houle bienheureuse, depuis la fin bout des doigts et des orteils, ce message de paix et le bon ordre des membres, des extrémités, de la tête elle-même jusqu'à ce point vague du corps (ce n'est pas le cœur) où les lignes de force convergeaient.

> [The feeling of certainty of his presence assembled his body from all parts of the horizon, sent out a call to arms toward an ideal point in the middle of himself by carrying to it, on a blissful surge, from the outermost tips of his fingers and

toes to that imprecise point of the body (it is not the heart) where the lines of force converged, a message of peace and orderliness of the limbs, of the extremities, of the head itself.] (*PF*, pp. 110; 143–44)

Paradoxically, the desire for the other exerts a centripetal influence on the self. It is because of Erik's comforting presence next to him that Riton finds himself finally at one. His previously disjointed person — whose fragmentation is rendered literally through the spatial depiction of a subject dispersed across far-flung points in the distance — is at last united in a centre of existential security. Genet transforms Riton into a linear perspective drawing, geometrically imagining his split sense of self like convergence lines that only ever meet at a vanishing point on the horizon. When alone, Riton is externally displaced and cast outwards; when next to Erik, Genet describes the sensation of a magnetic pull inwards, the self coming back together to find unity within 'ce point vague du corps'. Genet is careful to codify this point as an affective, not a corporeal, site; a centre of individual harmony, rather than a centre of love (given the otherness that is associated with the heart). Indeed, to reach this ideal, unknown point of internal unity, Genet implies that Riton must relate to the other only to experience a discrete separation from him. To be as one, the self must not lose themselves in the other, but rather use the other's presence to catalyse a retreat into this singular, yet unifying point. It may be misleading to equate the ethics of such a relation with a Levinasian reading, in which self-formation is achieved by recognising the alterity of the other.[83] I see a subtly different dynamic at play. Genet's ideal point of selfhood is reached when in contact with the other, but only because such a relation facilitates the euphoric realisation of introverted solitude. Riton is no solipsist, he is a character who enjoys the emotional succour of feeling unified in this imprecise point that can never be breached by the other, precisely because it is only made accessible when Genet's characters are together. The relation is thus a perverse one, connecting selves to themselves rather than to one another.

Sartre has argued that the overriding quality of Genet's writing is its ethical disconnection, metaphorically describing his texts like going to a brothel 'en souhaitant n'y rencontrer personne; et quand on y est, on y est tout seul' [hoping not to meet anyone; and when one is there, one are alone] (*SG*, pp. 651; 589). Yet, focusing on the geometric aspects of Genet's poetics renders this isolation far less sordid or transgressive. Genet's *point idéal* curates a relation in which units are held together and apart from one another in such a way that this separation becomes a mathematical certainty. Consider the metaphor of an invisible compass in *Pompes funèbres*, which Genet evokes in admiration of the discontinuity of his subjects:

Ma main était dans la sienne, mais de la main de l'image la mienne restait à dix centimètres. [...] Et chaque fois que j'étais auprès d'un objet qu'il avait touché, ma main ne s'en approchait qu'à dix centimètres, si bien que, dessinées par mes gestes, les choses paraissaient gonflées extraordinairement, hérissées de rayons invisibles ou augmentées de leur double métaphysique à mes doigts enfin sensible. Quelle démonstration de la force géométrique que l'angle de lumière, les branches mobiles et rigoureusement immobiles du compas qu'étaient ses deux jambes quand il marchait!

[My hand was in his, but mine was four inches away from the hand of the image [...]. And each time I was near an object he had touched, my hand would stop three inches from it, with the result that things, outlined by my gestures, seemed to be extraordinarily inflated, bristling with invisible rays, or enlarged by their metaphysical double, which I could at last feel with my fingers. What a demonstration of geometrical force there was in the angle of light, the mobile yet rigorously immobile legs of the compass which his legs were when he walked!] (PF, pp. 63; 83)

Genet fractures reality and perception by portraying Erik and himself with their hands enlaced, while the image of this image plays out in slow motion, revealing the 'rayons invisibles', the puppet strings, which facilitate the scene. The meta-image is hyper-sensitive, its ephemeral light-rays producing a fine membrane that separates the bodies in the scene. The gap is incontrovertible, the bodies vulnerable to the point that Genet describes how any transgression of their borders — any real connection between the two — would result in their mutual dissolution. The geometric force used to describe the movement of Riton's legs re-instates this separation, as the central point of the compass marks out a threshold that Genet seems both anxious to respect, and eager to behold. Like the solitaire diamond whose facets radiate outwardly, here Genet's compass uses its single point to push away and keep at a distance any potential breach. Such is the axiomatic principle of the compass in geometry, as Kant has argued:

> The science of geometry seems to comprise some of its dignity if it confesses that on its elementary level it needs instruments to construct its concept, even if only two: compass and ruler [...]. Yet even when we call compass (zirkel) and ruler (lineal) circinus et regular, instruments, we mean not the actual instruments, which could never produce those figures (circle) and (straight line) with mathematical precision, but only the simplest ways [these figures can] be exhibited by our a priori imagination, [a power] that no instrument can equal.[84]

Kant establishes a dynamic relationship between implement and concept: the abstraction of geometry can only be conceived of in a tangible execution which brings to life figures already in our imagination. In other words, Genet's compass seeks to sublimate and materialise that gap that is experienced affectively between characters who doggedly strive to quantify their separation. His geometric metaphor provides a way of measuring that imagined distance, the compass and its fixed point visualising an implacable distance between individuals always held apart by the 'rayons invisibles' that emanate from each untouchable being in Genet's universe. His compass is stripped of the symbiosis we find in John Donne's metaphysical conceit, in which two souls:

> [...] are two so
> As stiff twin compasses are two;
> Thy soul, the fixed foot, makes no show
> To move, but doth, if the other do.[85]

Genet only imagines a pair of individuals' legs, rigidly split from one another, and which demarcate the ephemeral boundary that cordons Erik off from Genet's desiring touch. His compass resonates more with the image Beckett depicts in his novel *Watt* (1944), in which he describes a picture hanging in Mr Erskine's room of a 'circle, obviously described by a compass, and broken at its lowest point [...] Watt wondered how long it would be before the point and the circle entered together upon the same plane'.[86] Watt's sense of torment upon witnessing a point that does not come together with the outer circumference it helps to produce becomes a source of admiration for Genet. He revels in the fact that the compass is geometrically defined by the breach it forms between point and line, between single unit and continuous plane, and seems to delight in the almost axiomatic legitimacy it offers to his celebration of a metaphysical gap between all selves.

The only relation possible in Bersani's analysis of *Pompes funèbres* is one of 'fundamental sameness [...] as if [Erik and Riton] were relay points in a single burst of erotic energy toward the world. Relationality here takes place only within sameness'.[87] This homogenising impulse, which Bersani nonetheless admonishes in Genet's work, is perhaps worth readdressing if we recognise these invisible gaps between subjects as safeguards Genet puts in place against any mutual cohesion. Rather than being subsumed by sameness that then dissolves relation, Genet endlessly problematises the connectivity between his subjects to build subject relations based on introversion and renunciation. Isolated by their own unassailable singularity, their recognition of sameness only prompts a turning inward that he describes in *L'Atelier d'Alberto Giacometti* as reaching 'ce point qui le fait identique à tous et plus précieux que le reste du monde: ce qui subsiste quand il s'est reculé en lui-même, aussi loin que possible' [the point that makes him identical to everyone and more precious than the rest of the world] (*AAG*, pp. 68–69; 63). It is the *recul* that Genet valorises, this active distance from a subjective parity that he recognises to be true, and yet profoundly isolating. Giacometti's statues as invested with an impulse which both equates, and separates: a perverse connection of a radical solitude that cannot connect 'à ce point [...] ce qui pourrait les unir serait une reconnaissance de la solitude de tout être et de tout objet' [at this point [...] what could unite them is the recognition of the solitude of every being and of every object] (*AAG*, pp. 73; 68). The 'point' at which such aporias coincide is not only ineffable, but, by definition, *unclear*.

What is the nature of this point that abstractly loiters around Genet's subjective vocabulary? Is it always the same point? Genet's acknowledgement that this solitary point is an 'endroit secret que je ne puis ni décrire ni préciser' [a secret place, which I can neither describe nor clarify] (*AAG*, pp. 69; 64) testifies to his difficulty in discerning the moment at which the self relates to the world and then renounces it. Perhaps 'ce point précieux' is a metaphorical blind spot, a *punctum caecum*. Both a function of the visual and yet hidden from sight, the blind spot turns vision in on itself in a process of self-cancellation that Derrida sees in the example of self-portraiture in *Mémoires d'aveugle*. He defines the

> '*Punctum caecum*' comme une simple image à son tour, un index analogique de la vision elle-même, de la vision en général, celle qui se voyant voir, ne se réfléchit pourtant pas ne se 'pense' pas sur le mode spéculaire ou spéculatif —

et donc s'aveugle par le même, en ce point du 'narcissisme' en cela même où elle se voit regarder.

['Punctum caecum', as itself a mere image, an analogical index of vision itself, of vision in general, of that which, seeing itself see, is nevertheless not reflected, cannot be 'thought' in the specular or speculative mode — and thus is blinded because of this, blinded at this point of 'narcissism' at this very point where it sees itself looking.][88]

Derrida here explores the blind spot as an inherent feature of artistic production, the act of inscription generating a momentary blindness for the artist. Aware of his mark-making, the artist turns inwards and the object of perception collapses into a narcissism where one is trapped in the process rather than the destination of sight. While Genet is not lost in his own artistic endeavour when looking upon Giacometti's sculptures, the principle is nonetheless the same: it is in encountering the familiar solitude of the sculptures that prompts Genet-as-onlooker to retreat into himself. To look upon them is to get lost in his own inward self-reflection. The object of perception does not cause outward empathy, but self-facing interiority in which 'c'est donc la solitude de la personne ou de l'objet représentés qui nous est restituée, et nous qui regardons, pour la percevoir et être touchés par elle devons avoir une expérience de l'espace non de sa continuité, mais discontinuité' [it is thus the solitude of the person or the object represented that is restored to us, and we, who look, in order to perceive it and be touched by it must have an experience of space — not of its continuity but its discontinuity].[89] The spectator looking upon the artwork does not experience a connection, but rather a disconnection, lost not in the object of perception but in one's own sense of looking. In this self-reflexive moment of discontinuity, the blind spot offers a protective enclave which Genet seems to suggest is the moment the subject comes into his own, shielded from any outside connection. The blind spot is the moment at which Genet comes across commonality, but for him the condition of such recognition is to reject any continuity and instead retreat further into one's own solitude. What is extraordinary about Genet's retreat to the *punctum caecum* is that he illuminates this myopia: he uses distance and the absence of relation to speak a truth about the essentially solitary, self-facing nature of subjectivity. The blind point is therefore a useful metaphor that not only expands on the sanctuary proposed in the point as *punctum*, but that exposes the aporetic nature of the point as a constitutive site which exists beyond, between or beneath modes of access.

How might this subjective interiority provide a model for Genet's world outlook? Derrida reads an externality into the blind spot, suggesting that the condition of seeing oneself seeing, of narcissism where one is trapped in one's own process of vision, is to momentarily be outside of oneself.[90] I am interested in how this outside might function in Genet's writing, not traditionally as a phenomenological exteriority, but as a construction of what Genet refers to as his internal astronomy: a cosmic outside which collapses inwards and retreats into a point which is inaccessible not because it is beyond the world, but because it defies its organising principles. In *Notre-Dame-des-Fleurs*, Genet muses that:

Le monde des vivants n'est jamais trop loin de moi. Je l'éloigne le plus que je peux par tous les moyens dont je dispose. Le monde recule jusqu'à n'être qu'un point d'or dans un ciel si ténébreux que l'abime entre notre monde et l'autre est tel qu'il ne reste plus, de réel, que notre tombe. Alors j'y commence une existence de vrai mort [...] le vrai monde est étalé à vingt mètres d'ici, tout aux pieds des murailles.

[The world of the living is never too remote from me. I remove it as far as I can with all the means at my disposal. The world withdraws until it is only a golden point in so sombre a sky that the abyss between our world and the other is such that the only real thing that remains is our grave. So I am beginning here a really dead man's existence [...] the real world is spread out twenty yards away, right at the foot of the walls.] (*NDF*, pp. 114; 64)

As Genet reflects on his writing process, he becomes aware of the gap between his original intention of the text to exalt his criminal existence, and the reality of its spatial detachment, his rejection of a world in which such exaltation might take place. Although he is describing the liminal space of the prison, his withdrawal reaches far beyond the physical boundaries that alienate him as he actively seeks to disengage from all the trappings of a 'real' existence. The shrinking retreat of the world into the figure of a 'point d'or' is a deeply astral image, this golden fleck reminiscent of a burgeoning and withering star whose proportions are always distorted from our earthly viewpoint. As reality bends according to these deformed perspectives, Genet capitalises on the abyssal nature of the interstice between the empirical world and the spectral world of an incarcerated existence. As a signifier, the 'point d'or' which encapsulates this existence stages a homophonous return to Cixous's own linguistic play in *Portrait de Jacques Derrida* in which the title 'Point donneur' becomes read as 'point d'honneur'.[91] As a point of capital importance, the 'point d'honneur' asserts an idiomatic homophony with 'point d'or', such that on the one hand Genet creates a visual image of deterioration where the world shrinks into a mere point, but on the other he creates a linguistic image where the significance of the point is magnified by its semantic slippage from 'd'or' to 'd'honneur'. An abbreviation of 'mettre un point d'honneur', Genet's idiom 'mettre un point d'or' puts the visual and the linguistic at odds with one another once again, so that the images with the greatest significance in Genet's writing seem to be those that most trouble their spatial representation.

In parallel to the distance Genet sublimates between Erik and his hands, here Genet stages an abyss between him and the world, eager to keep the two not simply apart, but as worlds apart, universally un-connectable. Genet's originality in his defiance toward the world is not predicated on his actions within it, but his extrication from it. By sublating the world into a 'point d'or', he idealises it, and in so doing, renders it an inaccessible constellation in his literary universe. Such withdrawal is total: the abyss he forges between his existence 'de vrai mort' and 'le monde des vivants' is merely a manifestation of an already-existent internal alterity. He explains that 'je crois que cette vie je la portais en moi jusqu'alors secrète et qu'il me suffit d'être mis à son contact pour qu'elle me soit, de l'extérieur, révélée dans sa réalité' [I think that hitherto I bore that life within me secretly and that all I needed was to be put into contact with it for it to be revealed to me, from without, in its reality] (*NDF*, pp. 115; 64). The space of the prison therefore enables him to validate his subjective detachment, a perverse retreat which enables him to eschew a worldly existence for an indomitable equivalent: 'j'accepte d'y vivre comme j'accepterais, mort, de vivre dans un cimetière' [I accept living there as I would accept, were I dead, living in a cemetery] (pp. 114; 64). Genet's seriality returns once more, eager to be a single part amidst a group of incommunicable solitudes.

Genet's representation of the world in *Notre-Dame-des-Fleurs* is often subject to spatial disruptions that atomise the whole into its parts, championing the process of decomposing the whole into its original particles just as Kandinsky describes. Like a black hole, which consumes a greater mass than itself and thus entirely changes the constellations of its system, so Genet imagines a process of rejecting the world by assimilating and digesting the world into its individual molecules. He claims to want to 'm'avaler moi-même en retournant ma bouche démesurément ouverte par-dessus ma tête, y faire passer tout mon corps, puis l'Univers, et n'être plus qu'une boule de chose mangé qui peu à peu s'anéantirait' [I wanted to swallow myself by opening my mouth inordinately and turning it around over my head so that it would take in my whole body, and then the Universe, until all that would remain of me would be a ball of eaten thing which little by little would be annihilated] (*NDF*, pp. 27; 154). The metaphor is not necessarily nihilistic. Perhaps it suggests Genet's desire to return to a primal, inchoate space in which nothing can be encapsulated by a whole identity or fixed system. He spatialises his revolutionary spirit here, encouraging us to regard his geometric vision as abstraction of a political process of breaking down the social and relational structures to which we are bound.

The image is extended in *Miracle de la rose* when Genet envisages Harcamone's inner universe as a geometric labyrinth that leads towards a rose:

> Au cœur de la rose: c'était une sorte de puits ténébreux. Tout au bord de ce trou noir et profond come un œil, ils se penchèrent et l'on ne sait quel vertige les prit firent tous les quatre les gestes de gens qui perdent l'équilibre, et ils tombèrent dans ce regard profond.

> [The heart of the rose. It was a kind of dark well. At the very edge of this pit, which was as murky and deep as an eye, they leaned forward and were seized by a kind of dizziness. All four made the gestures of people losing their balance, and they toppled into that deep gaze.] (*MR*, pp. 464; 388)

Rather than the world falling into Divine's body, here it is the inmates that fall into Harcamone's: the black points symbolised by the well, the black hole and the pupil all become sites of vertigo that entice the outside in. The black hole that consumes and invites such interiority is nonetheless outwardly perceived as a mere dot, an obscure point in a wider universe. By empowering this small particle as a site which can contain the whole universe, Genet invests the point with what Guattari reads in *L'Inconscient machinique* as 'not [an] emptiness but rather [a] hyper-concentration of energy and matter [...] what black holes and lack share, it would seem, is a common origin in the emergence of language and a collapse into the signifier'.[92] For Guattari, the point as a black hole differs from Lacan's lack precisely because it is generative:

it is here that new universes of reference are produced, new signs radiate outwards and creation can begin.[93] As a black hole, Genet's internal cosmos both annihilates the outside world and radically re-configures it: generating an ontological outlook in which all subjects are returned to their disassociated and irreducible singularity. This disruptive energy boils over in all of Genet's writing, and any totalising form of containment, whether political, social, ethical or identitarian, explodes into a new constellation of abstract particles. As he describes in *Pompes funèbres*:

> Au fond de nous, ces années déposèrent une vase où éclosent des bulles. Chaque bulle, habitée d'une individuelle volonté d'être, se développe, se déforme, transforme, seule et selon les autres bulles, pour former un ensemble irisé, violent, manifestant une volonté sortir de cette vase.

> [Within us, these years have deposited a mud in which bubbles appear. In each bubble lives a single will to be, which develops, becomes deformed, transformed, alone and according to the other bubbles, and forms an irridescent, violent ensemble, manifesting a will which has emerged from this mud.] (*PF*, pp. 144; 226)

These transparent bubbles, empty particles of energy which surge up against the heavy silt that fetters them, create an extraordinary metaphor of subjective revolt. Mired in the thick sediment of experience, Genet energises, pressurises and inflates these effervescent molecules of willpower, such that the subject is forged in the same explosive way as the universe: a corporeal big bang which creates space for a revolutionary spirit.

Amidst all of these astronomical metaphors, whether directed inwards or bursting outwards, Genet is building a dynamic, spatial constellation that maps how his selves relate to the world and how those relations are being endlessly displaced. Atomising the world and its structures becomes greatly politicised in Genet's later writing; however, as we have discovered in his early texts, such a process adopts a far more philosophical and erotic posture that weds itself to understanding the individual and their affective experience, rather than revolutionising any societal system. The points scattered among the pages of *Notre-Dame-des-Fleurs* plot a cartography from Divine's and Mignon's sperm, which 'giclant haut, tracé sur le ciel une voie lactée ou s'inscrivent d'autres constellations que je sais lire' [spurts high and maps out on the sky a milky way where other constellations that I can read take shape] (*NDF*, pp. 39; 19). In this erotic solar system, Genet writes over any fixed, universal patterns that might transcend the individual in order to create a new cartography in which each body finds itself inscribed. Cocooned in Divine's attic, Genet has his characters star-gaze at the way in which their own bodily fluids are able to artistically re-invent the universe. He empowers his characters to reconfigure the symbolic codes of the outside world and launch themselves into a new space of their own creation. The gesture is remarkably democratic, and as Genet navigates his subjects through their fleshy interaction, he abstracts them from any concrete social standing to cast them upwards like a speckled constellation of single units. These celestial points lend the individual the autonomy to reproduce their own way of being in the world, a way that only becomes legible to those prepared to renounce the symbolic norms and systemic patterns that circulate in the realm of the living. Genet inscribes these constellations onto the bodies of the inmates themselves in *Notre-Dame-des-Fleurs*, fashioning a language that is constituted by individual pinpricks:

> Mille et mille petits coups d'une fine aiguille frappent jusqu'au sang la peau et les figures les plus extravagantes pour vous s'étalent aux endroits les plus inattendus [...] des étoiles, des croissants de lune, des traits, des flèches, des hirondelles, des serpents de bateaux, des poignards triangulaires et des inscriptions, des devises, des avertissements, toute une littérature prophétique et terrible.

> [Thousands and thousands of little jabs with a fine needle prick the skin and draw blood, and figures that you would regard as most extravagant are flaunted in the most unexpected places [...] pansies, bows and arrows, hearts pierced and dripping blood, overlapping faces, stars, quarter-moons, lines, swallows, snakes, boats, triangular daggers and inscriptions, mottoes, warnings, a whole fearful and prophetic literature.] (*NDF*, pp. 113; 271)

Reifying the point as the dot produced by a tattoo needle, Genet etches a new sign language into the skin of his subjects. This visual discourse is not only full of geometric shapes — lines, triangles, circles, points, stars — but it can only be deciphered by those who either break free from, or are marginalised by, the accepted codes of normative, social practices. Only by reading the discrete singularity heralded by Genet's body-writing can we understand how his subjects communicate with one another: their tacit understanding of these extravagant figures and unexpected emblems crafts a new form of relation in which each inmate can be both connected and discontinuous. The subject is quite literally marked by a physical point towards which they will always affectively retreat: whether a unique wound, an individual cipher, an inaccessible 'solitaire', a poignant *punctum* or the elliptical insignia of the *pointillé*, it is from this singular, indeterminate site that we are able to apprehend the perforated relations of Genet's texts. The geometric point makes no attempt to forge a continuum, but nor does it demand a wholly anti-social isolation; rather, it affords Genet the aesthetic potential to imagine subjectivity as a form of standing together, while being apart.

Notes to Chapter 1

1. Paul Klee, *The Diaries of Paul Klee, 1898–1918* (Berkeley & Los Angeles: University of California Press, 1964), p. 345.
2. Dante Alighieri, *Convivio*, II.xiii. 25–27; *The Banquet*, trans. by Christopher Ryan, Stanford French and Italian Studies, 61 (Saratoga, CA: Anma Libri, 1989), p. 70.
3. Euclid, *The First Six Books of the Elements of Euclid*, p. 6.
4. Jean Genet, *Miracle de la rose*, in *Œuvres complètes*, 6 vols (Paris: Gallimard, 1952–79), II, 261–469 (p. 231); *Miracle of the Rose*, trans. by Bernard Frechtman (New York: Grove Press, 1966), p. 14 (hereafter referenced in main text as *MR*).
5. Euclid, *The First Six Books of the Elements of Euclid*, ed. by Lardner, p. 1.
6. Ibid., p. 99 (Proposition IX: Theorem 338).
7. Wassily Kandinsky, *Point and Line to Plane* (New York: Dover Publications, 1979), p. 25.
8. Ibid., p. 32.
9. Jacques Derrida, *H.C. pour la vie, c'est-à-dire...* (Paris: Galilée, 2002), pp. 58 & 63; *H.C. For Life, That's to Say...*, trans. by Lauren Milesi (Stanford, CA: Stanford University Press, 2006), p. 62.

10. David Wills, 'La Techno-poétique de l'autre... en pointillé', in *Rêver, croire, penser autour d'Hélène Cixous*, ed. by Bruno Clément and Marta Segarra (Paris: Campagne première, 2010), pp. 115–27 (p. 115).

11. Roland Barthes, *Roland Barthes par Roland Barthes* (Paris: Seuil, 1975), p. 59; *Roland Barthes by Roland Barthes*, trans. by Richard Howard (London: University of California Press, 1994), p. 55.

12. See Philip Thody, *Jean Genet* (London: Hamish Hamilton, 1968), pp. 36–37, for a thorough discussion.

13. Jean Genet, *Notre-Dame-des-Fleurs*, in *OC*, II, 7–207 (p. 24); *Our Lady of the Flowers*, trans. by Bernard Frechtman, intro. by Jean-Paul Sartre (London: Faber & Faber, 1973), p. 61 (hereafter referenced in main text as *NDF*).

14. It is worth noting the gendered implications of Genet's use of the *pointe*. Traditionally, men do not dance *en pointe*, but in ballets such as *A Midsummer Night's Dream*, men used *pointe* technique to symbolise the hooves of Bottom the donkey. It seems the balletic metaphor allows Genet to transform meaning from the literal to the allegorical, as his *pointe* not only disrupts gendered conventions, but does so to insist on an animalistic, instinctive mobile construction of impressions (riffing on the trot, the footstep), not concretised ideas.

15. Kandinsky, *Point and Line to Plane*, p. 42.

16. Gilles Deleuze and Claire Parnet, *Dialogues* (Paris: Flammarion, 1997), p. 152; *Dialogues II*, trans. by Hugh Tomlinson and Barbara Habberjam (London: Continuum, 2002), p. 125.

17. Gilles Deleuze and Félix Guattari, *Mille plateaux* (Paris: Minuit, 1980), pp. 36–37; *A Thousand Plateaus: Capitalism and Schizophrenia*, trans. by Brian Massumi (London: Continuum, 1987), p. 27.

18. Deleuze and Parnet, *Dialogues*, pp. 48; 37.

19. Ibid., pp. 34; 26.

20. Deleuze and Guattari, *Mille plateaux*, pp. 37; 25.

21. Barthes defines this mode of writing as discourse that existed before 'la poésie moderne, celle qui part, non de Baudelaire, mais de Rimbaud' [modern poetry, which springs not from Baudelaire, but from Rimbaud]: *Le Degré zéro de l'écriture* (Paris: Seuil, 1953), p. 36; *Writing Degree Zero*, trans. by Annette Lavers & Colin Smith (London: Cape, 1984), p. 42.

22. Ibid., pp. 36–37; 43–44.

23. Slavoj Žižek, *The Puppet and the Dwarf: The Perverse Core of Christianity* (Cambridge, MA, & London: MIT Press, 2003), p. 18.

24. Carl Lavery, 'Preamble: A Panegyric for the Foot', *Performance Research*, 17.2 (January 2012), 3–10 (p. 8).

25. Jean Genet, 'Comment jouer *Les Bonnes*', in *Théâtre complet*, ed. by Michel Corvin and Albert Dichy (Paris: Gallimard, 2002), pp. 125–27 (p. 125) (hereafter referenced as *TC*); 'How to Play *The Maids*', trans. by Julie Rose, in programme to *The Maids*, Sydney Theatre Company, 2013, pp. 8–10 (p. 8).

26. Judith Butler, *Excitable Speech: A Politics of the Performative* (New York: Routledge, 1997), p. 9.

27. Hélène Cixous, 'Preface: On Stigmatexts', in *Stigmata: Escaping Texts*, trans. by Eric Prenowitz (London & New York: Routledge, 1998), pp. x–xiv (p. xi). Although a longer text, 'Stigmates', was first published in *Lectora*, 7 (2001), 195–202 (English version in *Philosophy Today* (Spring 1997), 12–17), this preface does not appear there.

28. Jacques Derrida, 'Foreword', in Cixous, *Stigmata*, p. ix.

29. Cixous, Stigmata, p. xi.

30. Ibid.

31. Jacques Derrida, *Positions: entretiens avec Henri Ronse, Julia Kristeva, Jean-Louis Houdebine, Guy Scarpetta* (Paris: Minuit, 1972), p. 58; *Positions*, trans. by Alan Bass (Chicago: University of Chicago Press, 1981), p. 42.

32. Jacques Derrida, *La Dissémination* (Paris: Seuil, 1972), pp. 145–46; *Dissemination*, trans. by Barbara Johnson (Chicago: University of Chicago Press, 1981), p. 130.

33. Jean Genet, *L'Atelier d'Alberto Giacometti*, in *OC*, V, 41–73 (p. 65); *The Studio of Alberto Giacometti*, in *Fragments of the Artwork*, trans. by Charlotte Mendell (Stanford, CA: Stanford University Press, 2003), pp. 41–68 (p. 60) (hereafter referenced in main text as *AAG*).

34. Gilles Deleuze, *Cinéma 1: l'image-mouvement* (Paris: Minuit, 1983), p. 191; *Cinema 1: The Movement Image*, trans. by Hugh Tomlinson and Barbara Habberjam (London: Continuum, 1986), p. 136.

35. Geir Uvsløkk, *Jean Genet: une écriture des perversions* (Amsterdam & New York: Rodopi, 2011), p. 210.

36. Jean Genet, *Journal du voleur* (Paris: Gallimard, 1949), p. 14; *The Thief's Journal*, trans. by Bernard Frechtman, preface by Jean-Paul Sartre (New York: Grove Press, 1964), p. 11 (hereafter referenced in main text as *JV*).

37. Tom Conley, 'A Restive Word', in *Genet*, ed. by Mairéad Hanrahan (= *Paragraph*, 27.2 (2004), 77–84 (pp. 77–78).

38. See Deleuze and Guattari, *Mille plateaux*, p. 291, in which 'haecceity' refers to individual singularity.

39. Uvsløkk, *Jean Genet*, p. 128.

40. François Bizet, *Une communication sans échange: Georges Bataille critique de Jean Genet* (Geneva: Droz, 2007), p. 296.

41. Pierre Laforgue, *Notre-Dame-des-Fleurs, ou La Symphonie carcérale* (Toulouse: Presses universitaires du Mirail, 2002), pp. 16–17.

42. Parveen Adams, *The Emptiness of the Image: Psychoanalysis and Sexual Differences* (London & New York: Routledge, 1996), p. 151.

43. Tim Dean, 'Lacan and Queer Theory', in *The Cambridge Companion to Lacan*, ed. by Jean-Michel Rabaté (Cambridge: Cambridge University Press, 2003), pp. 238–52 (p. 244).

44. Jacques Derrida, '"Être juste avec Freud": l'histoire de la folie à l'âge de la psychanalyse', in *Penser la folie: essais sur Michel Foucault* (Paris: Galilée, 1992), pp. 141–95 (p. 180); "To Do Justice to Freud": The History of Madness in the Age of Psychoanalysis', trans. by Pascale-Anne Brault and Michael Naas, *Critical* Inquiry, 20.2 (Winter 1994), 227–66 (p. 255).

45. Jacques Derrida, *Glas* (Paris: Galilée, 1974), p. 257b; *Glas*, trans. by John P. Leavy Jr. and Richard Rand (Lincoln & London: University of Nebraska Press, 1986), p. 208b (hereafter referenced as *G*); and 'Countersignature', in *Genet*, ed. and trans. by Hanrahan, pp. 7–42

46. Roland Barthes, *La Chambre claire*, in *Œuvres complètes: 1962–1967*, ed. by Eric Marty, 5 vols (Paris: Seuil, 2002), v, 785–892 (pp. 795, 847); *Camera Lucida*, trans. by Richard Howard (New York: Hill & Wang, 1982), pp. 8, 71.

47. Ibid., pp. 847; 71.

48. Øyvind Vågnes, 'Working Through Contradiction Interminably? Towards a *Mathesis singularis*', *Nordic Journal of English Studies*, 2.2 (2003), 325–44 (p. 326).

49. Barthes, *La Chambre claire*, pp. 801; 18.

50. Ibid., pp. 805; 21.

51. Ibid., pp. 809; 26.

52. Ibid., pp. 809; 26–27.

53. Jacques Derrida, *Psyché: inventions de l'autre*, 2 vols (Paris: Galilée, 1998–2003), I, 278; *Psyche: Inventions of the Other*, ed. by Peggy Kamuf and Elizabeth Rottenberg, 2 vols (Stanford, CA: Stanford University Press, 2007–08), I, 269.

54. Ibid., pp. 277–78; 269.

55. Jean Genet, *Pompes funèbres*, in *OC*, III, 7–162 (p.103, my emphasis); *Funeral Rites*, trans. by Bernard Frechtman (London: Grove Press, 1994), p. 161 (hereafter referenced in main text as *PF*).

56. Georges Bataille, *L'Expérience intérieure* (Paris: Gallimard, 1943), p. 169; *Inner Experience*, trans. by Stuart Kendall (Albany: State University of New York Press, 2014), p. 147.

57. Bersani, *Homos*, p. 168.

58. Lavery, *The Politics of Jean Genet's Late Theatre*, p. 75.

59. Cixous, *Stigmata*, p. xiii.

60. Ibid.

61. Hélène Cixous, *L'Entretien de la blessure* (Paris: Galilée, 2011), additional loose leaf entitled 'Prière d'insérer'.

62. Mairéad Hanrahan, 'L'Exhibition du vide: la blessure indicible à l'origine de l'art', in *Jean Genet: rituels de l'exhibition*, ed. by Bernard Alazet and Marc Dambre (Dijon: Éditions universitaires de Djion, 2009), pp. 13–24 (p. 18).

63. The point as an originary wound evokes Hélène Cixous's leitmotif of the *point de départ* in *Philippines* where the texts is motivated by a psychoanalytic return to an origin that is figuratively elusive: 'revenons au point de départ, allons viens avec moi. Et c'est cela que je veux par-dessus tout: qu'un livre fasse rêve et me ramène aux enfances' [let's return to the starting point, come on, come with me. And that's what I want above all: I want a book to make itself dream and bring me back to childhoods': *Philippines: prédelles* (Paris: Galilée, 2009), p. 50; *Philippines*, trans. by Laurent Milesi (London: Polity, 2011), p. 31. Analogous to the point in geometry as the form to which everything departs and returns, so Genet's writing prompts a return to a *point de départ* which, as a wound, is forever rendered inaccessible.

64. Hélène Cixous, *Portrait de Jacques Derrida en jeune saint juif* (Paris: Galilée, 1991), p. 59; *Portrait of Jacques Derrida as a Young Jewish Saint*, trans. by Beverley Bie Brahic (New York: Columbia University Press, 2004), p. 62.

65. Jacques Derrida, 'Circonfession', in Geoffrey Bennington and Jacques Derrida, *Jacques Derrida* (Paris: Seuil, 1991), pp. 7–291 (p. 13); 'Circumfession', in Geoffrey Bennington and Jacques Derrida, *Jacques Derrida*, trans. by Geoffrey Bennington (Chicago: University of Chicago Press, 1993), pp. 3–315 (p. 10).

66. Cixous, *Stigmata*, p. xiv.

67. Derrida, 'Circonfession', pp. 70; 70.

68. Ibid.

69. Ibid., pp. 37; 35.

70. Ibid.

71. Ibid., pp. 36; 34.

72. Cixous, *Portrait de Jacques Derrida en jeune saint juif*, pp. 59; 63–64.

73. Jacques Derrida, 'Dialangues', in *Points de suspension: entretiens*, ed. by Elisabeth Weber (Paris: Galilée, 1992), pp. 141–65 (p. 156); 'Dialangues', in *Points: Interviews 1974–1994*, trans. by Peggy Kamuf and others (Stanford, CA: Stanford University Press, 1995), pp. 132–55 (p. 146).

74. Samuel Beckett, *Disjecta* (New York: Grove Press, 1984), pp. 171–72.

75. Solitaire, a single gem whose jewel-like qualities Genet himself reconnects to mathematics in his aphorism in *Notre-Dame-des-Fleurs* of being 'brillant comme un bijou ou comme un théorème' [gleaming as a jewel or a theorem] (*NDF*, pp. 49; 25).

76. Georges Bataille, *La Littérature et le mal* (Paris: Flammarion/ Folio, 1957), p. 143.

77. Ibid., pp. 143, 153.

78. Derrida, 'Dialangues', pp. 156; 146.

79. Derrida, *Psyché*, I, 304; 297.

80. Bersani, *Homos*, p. 169.

81. Edmund White, *Genet* (London: Chatto & Windus, 1993), p. 437.

82. Kandinsky, *Point and Line to Plane*, p. 65.

83. Emmanuel Levinas, *Time and the Other*, trans. by Richard A. Cohen (Pittsburgh, PA: Duquesne University Press, 1987).

84. Immanuel Kant, *Critique of Judgement*, trans. by Werner S. Pluhar (Indianapolis, IN: Hackett, 1987), p. 388 (n. 6).

85. John Donne, 'A Valediction: Forbidding Mourning', in *The Complete English Poems*, ed. by A. J. Smith (London: Penguin, 1971), p. 84 (ll. 25–28).

86. Samuel Beckett, *Watt* (London: Faber & Faber, 2009), p. 109. See further analysis of the relation between Kandinsky, the point and Beckett in C. J. Ackerley, *Obscure Locks, Simple Keys: The Annotated 'Watt'* (Edinburgh: Edinburgh University Press, 2010), p. 129, n. 4; Tim Lawrence, *Samuel Beckett's Critical Aesthetics* (Basingstoke: Palgrave Macmillan, 2018), p. 147.

87. Bersani, *Homos*, p. 170.

88. Jacques Derrida, *Mémoires d'aveugle: l'autoportrait et autres ruines* (Paris: Réunion des musées nationaux, 1990), p. 57; *Memoirs of the Blind*, trans. by Pascale-Anne Brault and Michael Naas (Chicago & London: University of Chicago Press, 1993), p. 53.

89. Ibid., pp. 49; 47.

90. See John D. Caputo, *The Prayers and Tears of Jacques Derrida: Religion Without Religion* (Bloomington: Indiana University Press, 1997), p. 320.

91. Cixous, *Portrait de Jacques Derrida en jeune saint juif*, p. 59.

92. Cited in Janell Watson, 'Guattari's Black Holes and the Post-Media Era', in *Holes, Burrows, Lines of Flight: Media and Spatiality in Deleuze and Guattari*, ed. by Janelle Blankenship (= *Polygraph*, 14 (2001)), 23–54 (p. 24).

93. Ibid.

CHAPTER 2

❖

Vectors I — Lines

L'horreur était surtout en ce que je n'étais qu'une ligne. Dans la vie normale, on est une sphère, une sphère qui découvre des panoramas [...]. Ici seulement une ligne. Une ligne qui se brise en mille aberrations [...]. Tout moi devait passer par cette ligne.

[The horror of it was that I was no more than a line. In normal life one is a sphere, a sphere that surveys panoramas [...]. Now only a line. A line that breaks up into a thousand aberrations [...]. All of my self had to pass through that line.]
— Henri Michaux[1]

Admirez le pouvoir insigne
et la noblesse de la ligne.

[Admire the remarkable power
And the nobility of the line.]
— Guillaume Apollinaire[2]

Across the anarchic pages of *Mille plateaux*, Deleuze and Guattari's experimental philosophy of how to map new pathways through the machines of capitalism, politics and power that regulate our day to day lives, we discover a boldly geometric way of thinking about being in the world. In seeking to liberate the individual from any epistemological or familial structures that bind us to static or inherited postures rooted in the past, Deleuze and Guattari imagine life to flow along lines that accelerate and proliferate uninterruptedly. These lines are the product of encounters that do not mark us, but extend us, producing a subjectivity forged out of relation and difference, infinite multiplicity and contradiction. In Deleuze and Guattari's spatial imaginary, subjects are composed of these linear paths in a legato kind of ontology that is more attuned to becoming than being. True to Euclid's definition of the line in geometry as being 'that which lies evenly between extremities', so Deleuze and Guattari look to a figure that brings together two fixed poles that might not otherwise meet to create connections that bring an unanticipated coherence to their relation.[3] Along these invisible, interweaving lines of deviance and alliance, Deleuze and Guattari picture a continuous form of self-creation that is born out of the evenness of our relations: the symmetry of the line never privileging one voice over another, but allowing a social practice of collaboration within and across groups of people. This is an ontology of growing along a trellis, not moving up a ladder; both philosophers reinventing the possibilities of how we think about identity as being forged from organic relations that, like the trellis, promote growth by scaling unknown territory in several directions at once. As Todd May explains, while 'ontology has been thought to be an ontology of identity since Plato', it can also be considered 'an ontology of difference [...] that does not reduce being to the knowable, but instead seeks to widen thought to palpate the unknowable'.[4] To live, in a Deleuzo-Guattarian sense, means to lift off from some putative notion of belonging, identity or individuality, and inhabit the line as the ultimate figure of a collective, provisional and multiple subjectivity.

Mary Bryden notes that it is literature that helps Deleuze to think through the possibilities of this linear mode of being. Deleuze slights the French canon for being wedded to 'epochal awareness, continuity, hierarchy' and lauds Anglo-American authors who channel a 'geographical rather than historicist outreach'.[5] Where Hardy, Woolf, Melville, Fitzgerald all bound forth in pursuit of new territory, their fluid, escapist engagement with the outside world attesting to a desire to understand themselves in relation to it, Deleuze and Guattari criticise his French literary ancestry for using art to retreat from the unknown. He laments that:

> Le roman français est profondément pessimiste, idéaliste, 'critique de la vie plutôt que créateur de vie' [...]. Il ne conçoit que des voyages organisés, et de salut que par l'art [...]. Il passe son temps à faire le point, au lieu de tracer des lignes, lignes de fuite active ou de déterritorialisation positive. Tout autre est le roman anglo-américain. 'Partir, partir, s'évader... traverser l'horizon...'. De Thomas Hardy à Lawrence, de Melville à Miller, la même question retentit, traverser, sortir, percer, faire la ligne et pas le point.

> [The French novel is profoundly pessimistic and idealistic, 'critical of life rather than creative of life' [...]. It can only conceive of organized voyages, and of salvation only through art [...]. It spends its time plotting points instead of drawing lines, active lines of flight or of positive deterritorialization. The Anglo-American novel is totally different. 'To get away. To get away, out!'... To cross a horizon...'. From Hardy to Lawrence, from Melville to Miller, the same cry rings out: Go across, get out, break through, make a beeline, don't get stuck on a point.][6]

For Deleuze, French texts tend to turn inwards. They look away from the world, either towards the nostalgic postures of Frenchness enshrined in the canonical works of 'Racine, Molière, Boileau, les bons auteurs du Louis XIV' [Racine, Molière, Boileau, the great authors of Louis XIV], or to the Mallarmean dream of hermeticism where life only serves art.[7] Such solipsism has no place in Deleuze's desire for writing to help produce new relations that encourage us to move beyond the predetermined, the 'voyage organisé', and traverse national frontiers in the pursuit of a fluid, unfixed and potential mode of existence.

Naturally, Genet bucks the trend of any such French literary nationalism and, unbeknownst to Deleuze and Guatarri at the time of writing *Mille plateaux*, his own 'roman français' creates a philosophy of the line that intersects importantly with theirs. Uprooting himself to Palestine in *Un captif amoureux*, the place without nation, he laments the impossibility of art to capture the reality of experience. From the very first lines of his text, we learn that the homage to the Palestinian revolution that follows can only betray the events it tries to describe; his words immobilising their truth into abstract black signs that obscure or blot out the experiences that first inspired them. As Genet tells us to doubt what we will read over the next 504 pages, he plays with the textual cliché of reading between the lines, telling us that 'lire entre les lignes est un art étale, entre les mots aussi, un art à pic' [reading between the lines is a level art; reading between the words a precipitous one] (*CA*, pp. 11; 3). He exploits the metaphor literally, such that understanding what escapes direct representation becomes itself a linear practice: a way of reading that is both 'étale', horizontal, and 'à pic', vertical. To read between the lines of Genet's text is to become sensitive to the geometry of travel, to be deterritorialised by his writing in a way that prevents the authoritarianism of exegesis or social critique that Deleuze denounces in the French novel. Although Genet tells us that the interstice between the words is 'plus rempli de réel que ne le sera le temps nécessaire pour les lire' [contains more reality than does the time it takes to read them] (pp. 11; 3), he also codifies that space as a geometric vector that carries an ineffable reality. There is a meaning that Genet invites us to develop along the horizontal and vertical axes of his text; a meaning he embeds into the cartography of lines, threads, cords, contours, horizons, his tightrope walker's *fil*, the lineaments of Léonor Fini, Giacometti or Rembrandt's faces, which help us to read between the lines of what can be directly communicated by his words.

The linear imagination we find in *Un captif amoureux* is not incidental; Genet is building a way of looking at his relation to the Palestinians as one not based on hackneyed, orientalist hierarchies that subordinate their reality to the dominance of his French pen. Rather, his geometric focus on the line makes us think harder about the spatial process of mapping that ethical distance between self and other, demanding we measure our appropriation of any foreign ground in order to weave a more Euclidian, more even alliance with it. When Genet answers his own rhetorical question as to whether he had failed to understand the Palestinian revolution in the affirmative ('la révolution palestinienne m'aurait donc échappé? [...] tout à fait', p. 12), he redirects his reader towards a form of understanding not located in imperial knowledge, but in lines of flight that build relations beyond inherited power structures of legacy. Genet's critical methodology of reading 'entre les lignes' actually directs us towards nomadic affiliations that, like Deleuze and Guattari's lines of becoming, are unforeseen and unessentialising.

In this chapter, I analyse the line as a Genet's means of engaging with reality beyond language, his insistent linear figurations providing a *fil conducteur* which pieces together new relations that contribute to a Deleuzo-Guattarian form of becoming. Although the line etymologically implies lineage, blood lines, a family tree, this chapter will argue that Genet's writing does not construct an arborescent genealogy that is repressed by the weight of history or yoked to roots. Rather, his linear figurations echo Deleuze and Guattari's own shift from the point to the line when they advocate for a rhizomatic form of relation: 'il n'y a pas de points ou de positions dans un rhizome, comme on en trouve dans une structure, un arbre, une racine. Il n'y a que des lignes [...] l'arbre est filiation, le rhizome n'est qu'alliance' [there are no points or positions in a rhizome, such as those found in a structure, tree, or root. There are only lines].[8] Deleuze and Guattari's rhizome agitates the bondage of ancestry to free up the possibilities of relations that are constructed, not born. For Genet, the orphan whose 'père reste inconnu' [father remains unknown] (*JV*, pp. 22; 26), filiation will always be a poetic fabrication. His linear language of threads, or *fils*, or their cognate, *fils* or son, becomes an incantation for an endlessly coveted bond that he finally discovers with his adopted kin in Palestine. The solitude of the point is reborn in *Un captif amoureux* through the linear weft of relations that Genet conceives of as material, an 'invisible écharpe [qui] se serait tissée, sans que nous n'y prissions garde, nous liant les uns aux autres' [invisible scarf [which without our realizing it] had been woven between us, binding us all together] (*CA*, pp. 83; 68). Plaiting together linear forms, Genet uses the *fil* to invoke relations that are bonding, not binding. From his exaltation of Giacometti as an artist of the line in the 1950s, to his encomium to the *fil* in *Le Funambule*, Genet's insistent linear poetics insist on the fragility of human relations that strive for connection without coercion.

Lifelines: The Giacometti Moment

After Genet's prolific creativity in the 1940s, which culminated in five novels and two plays by 1947, a more sober period of artistic reflection ensues over the next decade. The baroque prose of his literary works gives way to a more conceptual sensitivity towards abstraction and the possibilities of art to explore human life. Genet's gaze on the external world seems to turn inwards as he muses on the hermetic role art plays in figuring lived experience, breaking away from representation towards a need for containment. It is perhaps unsurprising, then, that Genet's sensibility towards geometric figurations abounds in his art criticism, and in his 'Lettre à Léonor Fini' in 1950, when teasing out how truth is constructed by the fable of painting, Genet privileges the line as the form along which to read the subject:

> Je suis un poète qui sait que l'œuvre d'art doit résoudre le drame, non l'exposer. Ces haillons, ces houx qui les déchirent, ces bêtes, ces fleurs, ces maladies somptueuses, ces passions personnifiées, je veux qu'elles ne soient lisibles que dans la brisure ou la courbe des lignes du plus clair des visages.

> [I am a poet who knows that the work of art must resolve the drama, not display it. These rags, these holly trees that destroy them, these animals, these flowers, these these sumptuous diseases, these personified passions — I want them to be legible only in the break or the curve of lines of the clearest face].[9]

The flat lineaments that Fini uses to create her artwork, and to generate any form of likeness or recognisability in her images, are galvanised by Genet as the inscrutable site of the drama that plays out on the canvas. The contour offers a way to harbour that legibility, as though meaning is being re-routed by Genet away from the mimesis of representation to the interiority of absolute abstraction. As a poet, Genet looks to intensify these lines as vectors of affect: only through their breakage or distortion does he seek to generate the sensibility that might lead the viewer to reflect beyond the empirical. The line should channel us towards something more intuitive, more transcendental than the figurative richness offered by the image of rags, holly branches, beasts, flowers, diseases, passions, which are all copies of the outside world. Rather, in seeking dramatic resolution rather than exposure, Genet seems to use the clean-cut geometry of these lines to call on the detachment of art from reality, to sever the viewer from the secret that it claims to hold, holding us at arm's length as he entices us to move away from the material and towards the conceptual. Sartre attributes this shift to a radical pursuit of freedom in Genet's work, who, he argues, uses his artistic imagination to catapult himself away from the experiential and explore the possibilities afforded by an Idea or Absolute never subordinated to the everyday. Sartre even uses the following geometric analogy to figure the idea:

> Réfléchissant sur ses larcins, il les transforme par un perpétuel 'passage à la limite' en larcins exemplaires, comme le mathématicien transforme les vagues contours des choses naturelles en fermes traces géométriques. La source de tous ces vols parfaits sera pour le lecteur un Genet exemplaire aussi différent du petit voleur de chair et d'os qu'un cercle peut l'être d'un rond tracé dans la poussière.

> [Reflecting upon his acts of larceny, he transforms them, by a constant 'carrying to the limit' into exemplary thefts, as the mathematician transforms the vague outlines of natural things into firm geometric lines. The source of all these perfect thefts will be for the reader an exemplary Genet who is as different from a flesh-and-blood-thief as a circle is from a round figure drawn in the dust.] (SG, pp. 608; 550)

Like the mathematician who seeks the idealisation of form through geometric shapes, so Sartre compares Genet's transformation from an actual thief to an archetypal one through the process of writing as a pursuit of abstraction. These 'fermes traces géométriques' protect the subject, allowing Genet to step away from being totalised by social narratives seeking to reduce him to a known entity, to settle instead within the intangible perfection of contours that are so paradigmatic that they become unreal, so general that they cannot be subjected to the classifying processes of individualisation. Sartre's 'passage à la limite' recalls the idiom *fixer la limite*, to draw the line, as though Genet is pushing himself to the borderlines of the real world to withdraw himself from it. Perhaps we could think of him recast as one of those lineaments in Fini's portrait: the 'courbe des lignes' along which Genet locates the meaning of her artwork resonating with the circular outline of Sartre's analogy, which sublimates Genet as an ephemeral trace, a 'rond tracé dans la poussière' whose impermanence refuses to be pinned down.

The subject is safeguarded by being embedded into this linear contour, and Genet is drawn to the lineament in Fini's portraits because the knowing look it seems to offer refuses any such knowledge to be submitted to our external gaze. The line strips the image of its signification while being asserted at the crux of it, as Genet lauds Fini's 'visages [qui] seront riches, nourris secrètement de tous ces drames qui doivent rester invisibles, happés, mangés par vos héros' [faces [which] will be rich, secretly fed by all those dramas that must remain invisible, swallowed up, eaten by your heroes], precisely because they ravage rather than reveal the drama, swallowing it up in an abstraction which renders the facial contour a site which feeds off experience but which refuses any communication of it.[10] Genet's term 'résoudre' presents an artwork that has shut itself off from outside examination, the lineaments of its characters as impenetrable as those Genet casts for his prisoners in *Le Bagne* where 'personne ne devra avoir un visage en relief, c'est à dire un visage aigu, qui se dirige vers l'extérieur, mais un visage aux traits ramassés, repliés, qui s'enfoncent vers l'intérieur' [nobody should have a face whose contours stand out, that is to say a sharp-featured face, which looks outwards, but a face with the collected, folded lines, which sink inwards].[11] The prisoners' lineaments should be flattened, folding in on themselves to prevent any idiosyncrasy that might individualise them. These flattened lines devour the legibility they seem to promise, their smooth surface eschewing the cartography that Deleuze and Guattari read on the face as a map in *Mille plateaux*, whose 'traits, lignes, rides du visage, visage long, carré, triangulaire' [facial traits, lines, wrinkles, long face, square face, triangular face], promise a form of subjectivation that Genet resolutely denies offering to the external viewer.[12] His prisoners may be incarcerated by the physical space of the prison, but are not bound to the subordination of our gaze.

In his bleak outlook in the early 1950s, after the publication of Sartre's *Saint Genet*, Genet defines himself as a poet of this hermetic linearity, the only clue to gleaning meaning located at the 'brisure' or the 'courbe' of the line. The drama only becomes legible if the continuity of these lines is broken and representational mastery is overcome. We might turn to Bill Martin's reading of Derrida's *brisure* in his text *Matrix and Line*:

> Derrida would say that there are 'ruptures' that lead both to mutations and to retrievals of 'the most hidden and forgotten archives'. Every 'line' of rupture is for Derrida [...] also a 'hinge', a turning point or pivot onto something new.[13]

In this Derridean interpretation, any destruction implied by the *brisure* transforms into a possibility that opens out onto something otherwise inaccessible. The contained drama of Genet's distorted lineaments thus takes on added significance when we consider the *brisure* as a figure both of rupture and of relation, a conjunction that allows meaning to be found both in what is articulated, and what remains open. In an epigraph to his chapter on the *brisure* in *De la grammatologie*, Derrida cites his contemporary critic Roger Laporte, who defines the figure as follows:

> Vous avez, je suppose, rêvé de trouver un seul mot pour designer la différence et l'articulation. Au hasard du 'Robert' je l'ai peut-être trouvé, à la condition de jouer sur le mot, ou plutôt d'en indiquer le double sens. Ce mot est brisure: 'partie brisée, cassée. Cf brèche, cassure, fracture, faille, fente, fragment'.

> [You have, I suppose, dreamt of finding a single word for designating difference and articulation. I have perhaps located it by chance in Robert ['s Dictionary] if I play [jouer] on the word, or rather indicate its double meaning. The word is *brisure* [joint, break] ' — broken, cracked part. Cf. breach, crack, fracture, fault, split, fragment'.][14]

The double meaning of the hinge allows for Derrida to challenge the linear systems of thought he finds problematic in linguistics, whose 'précieux préjugé *continuiste*' [precious *continuist* prejudice] determines meaning through a successive logic where B derives from A and so forth.[15] By contrast, the *brisure* allows for a moment of disarticulation, marking out both a join and a break, and thus transforming signification into something discontinuous and impossible to pin down.[16] Derrida celebrates the hinge precisely because it marks 'l'impossibilité pour un signe, pour l'unité d'un signifiant et d'un signifié, de se produire dans la plénitude d'un présent et d'une présence absolue' [the impossibility that a sign, the unity of a signified and signifier, be produced within the plenitude of a present and absolute presence].[17]

The *brisure* is thus imbricated in a discourse in which resolution is in fact rendered impossible: no stable meaning can be resolved when a hinge promises a rupture that is nonetheless necessary for any meaning to come to the fore. This is writing without resolution, a term that Timothy Mathews asserts in relation to Giacometti's artworks whose lines prompt us to 'think without resolution'.[18] Genet is one such writer who is touched by Giacometti's linear artworks, that touch manifesting itself literally as Genet puts his writing in Giacometti's hands stating, 'mes doigts refont donc ce qu'on fait ceux de Giacometti, mais alors que les siens cherchaient un appui dans le plâtre humide ou la terre, les miens remettent avec sûreté leurs pas dans ses pas' [my fingers do, then, what those of Giacometti have done, but while his sought a support in the wet plaster of the earth, mine put with sureness their steps in his steps] (*AAG*, pp. 53; 48). Walking in his steps, Genet replaces the support Giacometti finds in the materiality of clay for the abstraction of the broken lines in his artworks, drawn to their *brisure*, as he describes:

> Les lignes brisées sont aigues et donnent à son dessin — grâce encore à la matière granitique et paradoxalement assourdie, du crayon — une apparence scintillante. Diamants. Diamant encore plus à cause de la façon d'utiliser les blancs. Dans les paysages par exemple: c'est toute la page qui serait un diamant dont un côté serait visible grâce à des lignes brisées et subtiles, tandis que le côté où tomberait la lumière — d'où serait renvoyée la lumière, plus exactement — ne permettrait pas qu'on voie autre chose que du blanc.
>
> [The broken lines are sharp and give his drawings — a result, too, of the pencil's granitic and paradoxically muted substance — a sparkling aspect. Diamonds. Diamonds all the more because of his way of using the white spaces. In the landscapes, for instance: the whole page could be a diamond of which one side is visible, thanks to broken and subtle lines, while the side on which the light falls — or, more precisely, from which the light would be reflected — will not let us see anything else but white.] (*AAG*, pp. 60; 57)

Sensitive to the contours of the line whose rough edges imbue Giacometti's sketches with scintillation, Genet re-discovers the diamond motif that pervades his writing. Here, the 'lignes brisées' behave like a Derridean hinge: on the one hand, they lend a visibility to the sketch, unlocking a subtle radiance which animates the flat lines on the page; on the other, they reveal the diamond, which we have already explored as a motif of inaccessibility in Genet's writing. In other words, these broken lines construct an image that insists on its own disarticulation. Their *brisure* draws attention to the blank space that bewitches Genet throughout Giacometti's drawings, this gap escaping from codification to make room for pure affect: 'la sensation d'espace est obtenue avec une force qui rend cet espace *presque arpentable*' [the sensation of space is obtained with a strength that makes this space *almost measurable*] (*AAG*, pp. 60; 57). The language of geometry seems to drive home how Giacometti's artworks only give the illusion of quantification: the 'lignes brisées' construct spaces that disavow any navigation; they are only ever *almost* walk-able, *almost* mappable, since their *brisure* ensures that they escape from the containment of form. By disrupting the continuous outline of what they depict, Genet imbues Giacometti's drawings with the full affective charge of experiencing discontinuous space. His landscapes become vast plains where territory gapes without defined borderlines; the page carved up by lines that trick the viewer into thinking that space might be determinable, that the viewer could be an *arpenteur* able to calculate what they see. Yet, in the failure of all measurement, Genet recognises that it is the shared sense of *discontinuity* that lurks at the heart of Giacometti's sculptures: 'c'est [...] la solitude de la personne ou de l'objet représentés qui nous est restituée, et nous, qui regardons, pour la percevoir et être touchés par elle devons avoir une expérience de l'espace non de sa continuité, mais discontinuité' [it's [...] the solitude of each person and each thing which is given back to us, and we, who observe in order to perceive it and be touched by it must have an experience of space — not of its continuity, but its discontinuity] (pp. 49; 47). The broken line awakens the experience of a ruptured relation for Genet, the space it reveals affectively demonstrating the disconnectedness of the subject, each existing in their own atomised world. The space between Giacometti's lines iterates the gap in which Genet locates signification in his own texts, this discontinuous space viscerally experienced as an objectified solitude in which the broken line figuratively ruptures a physical connection with Giacometti's artefacts. Yet, an affective connection is still made; a relational continuum is instated between the viewer and the artefact only for it to be cut off when the solitude it represents is fully experienced in the act of looking.

In *Un captif amoureux* Genet launches what Hadrien Laroche calls 'une attaque poétique contre "le terrifiant discontinue"'' [poetic aggression against the 'terrifying discontinuity'].[19] Here, he encounters a different kind of artwork: the Hebrew alphabet, whose geometric forms Genet finds deeply unsettling when he catches sight of them on a signpost in Beirut. Genet describes the script as three-dimensional: 'dessiné plutôt qu'écrit, sculpté plutôt que dessiné' [sculpted rather than drawn] (*CA*, pp. 365; 309). His chiasmus serves to emphasise the visual nature of Hebrew, a language he describes as etched, sculpted, carved; all man-made constructs that eschew its credibility as a vector of putative truth. Indeed, these oblong characters evoke his childhood memory of seeing the Tablets of the Covenant onto which the Ten Commandments were inscribed, and rather than kowtow to the verbal dictatorship of letters that have long been the bearers of a law by which Western society must live, Genet focuses on the symbolism of their angular surface. Juxtaposed with the curved arabesque of Arabic, Genet recoils at Hebrew's rectangular, right-angled letters, which were organised in a horizontal broken line. Discontinuity elicits an affective response in Genet, who explains his disgust at:

> Ce terrifiant discontinu, chaque lettre épaississant entre elles un espace non mesurable et un temps si tassé que cet espace résultait d'un empilement de plusieurs épaisseurs de temps [...] dans cet espace, plus que le fracas des balles et des obus, le silence nous brisait.
>
> [This terrifying discontinuity: the letters were filled with immeasurable spaces filled with several layers of time [...] in the space between each Hebrew letter [...the] silence shattered us worse than bullets and bombs.] (*CA*, pp. 365; 310)

The passage has been much discussed, with Laroche and Hanrahan brilliantly arguing that Genet's aversion to Hebrew's spread-out writing hangs on its failure to contain or measure time since in the gap between each letter Genet imagines the Jewish race continuing endlessly, generation after generation ushered forth by dominant words that are taken as law.[20] Not only is such authoritative, and self-perpetuating, discourse anathema to Genet's mercurial use of language, but he treats that language as a physical object, this 'écriture [qui] appartenait à l'ennemi' [writing [which] belonged to the enemy] erected as a monument that quite literally makes room for the futurity of its people, while standing in the way of those it seeks to oppress. It is not just time that Genet fears, then, but the profound rupture in communication posed by this discontinuity. Genet experiences space as sound: the gaps produce a silence that breaks down the possibility of a conversation, generating a *brisure* that prevents Genet from being able to relate to the space of meaning itself. In Genet's description, the horizontal broken lines and geometric monoliths of Hebrew create only negative space whose disarticulation violently bursts through the reader looking for a connection. If the discontinuity of Hebraic script is terrifying to Genet, it is perhaps because it ruptures relation itself: a relation to the people who produce, write and speak it; to the referent it seeks to designate (as Hanrahan argues), and to the possibility of understanding (other) times and (foreign) spaces that seem cut off by the very language that tries to articulate them.[21]

It seems that it is not words, but the presence of physical forms that make such detachment bearable for Genet. Giacometti's sculptures may withdraw from a sociable notion of art, but they nevertheless exert a powerful kind of connectivity by asserting our experience of being alone together. Perhaps that is why Giacometti's sculptures are so firmly tied to the figure of the line because they create a form of relation out of discontinuous space. Genet even suggests that Giacometti lends to the abstraction of the line corporeal form when he argues that 'pour lui une ligne est un homme: il la traite d'égal à égal' [a line for him is a man: he treats it as an equal] (*AAG*, pp. 60; 57). Genet conflates the representation with the represented, signifier with signified, the human subject becoming the artistic object as Genet implies that his experience of seeing merges into the object of perception: 'l'image sur la toile se rattache à mon experience de l'espace, à ma solitude de la connaissance de la solitude des objets' [the image on the canvas becomes linked to my experience of space, to my knowledge of the solitude of objects] (pp. 49, 48). The line that Genet perceives as sentient is in fact an extension of his own subjectivity, the geometry before him imbued with a recognition of his own solitude that reaches out but is ultimately unable to connect. Mathews supports this shift from object to subject as he argues that Giacometti 'sees the science of geometry and colour as an attempt not only to see objects as they are, not only to make painting objective, but to become an object and to *be* an object'.[22] What strikes Genet in *L'Atelier d'Alberto Giacometti* is how the artist's geometric shapes always reach outside art to touch on life, how they enable him to grasp the reality of human experience all the more powerfully through the aesthetic.

If 'une ligne est un homme', then Giacometti's embodied lines offer a way for Genet to re-enter the world he sought to renounce in *Fragments* and his 'Lettre à Leonor Fini'. They offer him that metaphorical lifeline back to the notion of human relationality that he had lost, and which, for Albert Dichy, catalyses Genet's move towards a more overtly political subject matter. In an essay written for the 2016 exhibition on Genet, *L'Échappée belle*, he writes:

> Giacometti réaffirme face à Genet l'importance du 'sujet' qui ne s'abime jamais en 'objet', le primat du 'prétexte' et de la 'réalité' qui doit rester extérieure à l'artiste. Il fait ainsi lentement émerger Genet du rêve mallarméen qui le hante — et le hantera toujours — où le monde ne serait fait que pour aboutir à un beau livre [...] tout ce que Genet va écrire par la suite, que ce soit sur les Noirs, sur l'Algérie, sur les Black Panthères ou sur les Palestiniens est tributaire de ce déplacement qui l'arrache à la tentation très littéraire de réaliser une œuvre sur 'rien' détachée comme un ciel d'étoiles de tout ancrage.

> [Giacometti reaffirms the importance of the 'subject' who is never effaced as 'object', the primacy of 'pretext' and 'reality' that must remain outside of the artist. He thus makes Genet emerge from the Mallarmean dream that haunts him — and will always haunt him — in which the world only serves to create a beautiful text [...]. We might consider everything that Genet wrote afterwards, whether on Black people, on Algeria, on the Black Panthers or the Palestinians, as a tribute to this displacement that tears him away from the very literary temptation to produce a work about 'nothing' detached from any anchorage like a ceiling of stars.][23]

If a line is a man to Genet, then this linearity is invested with a renewed ethical purpose that seeks a connection that transcends the gulf of discontinuity that divides individuals. Giacometti's sinewy sculptures reach out to Genet far beyond the space of the studio; as Dichy suggests here, they drive Genet's recognition of the political utility of art to forge links with the human, and with the dispossessed in particular, as his writing turns more explicitly to reach out to those who have fallen into the gap of invisibility. Rather than abstracting himself from the world by exalting its nothingness in art, Genet's essay on Giacometti marks a turning point where geometric abstraction becomes a pathway to Genet's ethical consciousness. The more labyrinthine Giacometti's geometry, the more paradoxically palpable the humanity of his drawings. Genet is struck by the affective potential with which his lines vibrate:

> Le portrait m'apparaît d'abord comme un enchevêtrement de lignes courbes, virgules, cercles fermés traversés d'une sécante [...] un réseau linéaire qui ne

serait que dessins à l'intérieur du dessin [...] à mesure que je m'éloigne [...] le visage, avec tout son modelé, m'apparaît, s'impose [...] vient à ma rencontre, fond sur moi et se reprécipite dans la toile d'où il partait, devient d'une présence, d'une réalité et d'un relief terribles [...] 'relief' convient mal. Il s'agit plutôt d'une dureté infracassable qu'a obtenue la figure. Elle aurait un poids moléculaire extrêmement grand.

[A portrait seems to me first like a tangle of curved lines, commas, closed circles crossed by a secant [...] a linear system that would only be drawings inside this drawing [...]. As I move away [...] the face, with all its contours, appears to me, imposes itself [...] comes to meet me, swoops down on me, and hurries back into the canvas from which it came, becomes a terrible presence, reality, and form [...] 'contours' isn't right. It is rather a question of an unbreakable hardness the figure has acquired. It seems to have an extremely great molecular form.]
(*AAG*, pp. 57; 54)

The language of witness ('m'apparaît', 's'impose') is transformed into a language of relation ('rencontre', 'fond sur moi'), as Genet experiences the techniques of pictorial convention as physical forms that invade the spectator's space. He ossifies those contours, depicting each brushstroke with its own molecular weight such that the portrait becomes an actor in the drama of Genet's encounter. This network of lines that draws us ever deeper into the artifice of the drawing, also becomes an agent that turns that aesthetic into the ethical: it stages a very real confrontation between two humans — the artist behind the artefact and the subject behind the onlooker — in such a way that to look away, to resist that meeting, or deny the experiential shock of the portrait's imposition, becomes a political act of dehumanisation and non-recognition.

Genet uses an uncannily similar vocabulary to Deleuze and Guattari to figure that form of interaction here, presaging their own linear politics thirty years prior to its conception. In *Mille plateaux*, they imagine our political engagements to run along 'trois lignes qui nous traversent et composent "une vie" (titre à la Maupassant). *Ligne de coupure, ligne de fêlure, ligne de rupture*' [three lines traversing us and composing 'a life' (after Maupassant). *Break line, crack line, rupture line*].[24] The '*ligne de fêlure*' is conceived of as a molecular line that helps to create imperceptible fractures through the rigid segments that structure our identities. These cracks help to rend asunder the binary notions of identity — the two sexes for example — in order to allow for identities to separate while being able to cross over endlessly. Genet may be able to break away from the figure that 'fond sur [lui]', but what is troubling is that he still identifies with that mesh of lines. His recognition of the 'poids moléculaire' that lends Giacometti's figures their humanity foreshadows Deleuzo-Guattarian molecular politics of the crack, since what makes these forms so human is precisely that they resist any neat segmentation to respond instead to our imbricated modes of being human. There is no single lived experience that is conjured by the sculptures, these lines not life-like, but bursting with the molecular conditions of life itself: 'une petite masse de vie, dure comme un galet, bourrée comme un oeuf' (p.43) [little mass of life, hard as a pebble, full as an egg] (*AAG*, pp. 43; 42). Giacometti's linear forms exert their humanity precisely because they vibrate with disruptive, molecular potential: like an egg they are full, pregnant, primed to burst forth with the life they contain; yet like the stone they are themselves inanimate, mineral shells that preserve and petrify life.

Giacometti's *lignes de fuite*

The subtlety of the Deleuzo-Guattarian molecular cracks starts to seem insufficient when we recognise that the lines of Giacometti's figures assert a presence which is almost bellicose, the stark force of their 'dureté infracassable' as aggressive as the 'lignes brisées [qui] sont aigues'. When Giacometti's lines do break, their forms are brittle, jagged, sharp, they seem to rupture and tear through the paper on the surface of which they are cast. Perhaps it is more appropriate to consider the inclination of these 'lines as man' in their deep abstraction, the assault of their unassailability mustered in Genet's own terms as, precisely, 'lines of flight':

> Des lignes *qui semblent fuir* en partant de la ligne médiane du visage [...] un visage offre toute la force de sa signification lorsqu'il est de face, et que tout doit partir de ce centre pour aller nourrir, fortifier ce qui est derrière, caché.

> [Lines *that seem to flee* out from the median line of the face [...] a face offers all the force of its significance when it is frontal, and everything must go from this center to nourish and fortify what is behind, hidden.] (*AAG*, pp. 65–66; 61; my emphasis).

This is Genet describing Giacometti's portrait of him in 1957, and the linearity he describes shows the extraordinary prescience of his terms. Prior to any Deleuzo-Guattarian theorisation, Genet makes reference to 'lignes qui semblent fuir', a term which has been so instrumental in Deleuze and Guattari's ontological politics.[25] For Deleuze and Guattari, lines of flight signify a nomadic deterritorialisation: not yoked to singular categories, they flow away from rigid segmentations and catalyse the mobility of all other pathways around them. While inherently abstract, May summarises how these lines of flight 'are not constituted — or imprisoned — in specific identities. But they provide the material that will be actualised into those identities'.[26] The line yields the potential of a life it helps produce, and Genet's 'lignes qui semblent fuir' also seem to reach beyond the lived subject by 'tir[ant] en arrière (derrière la toile) la signification du visage' [that the painter pulls back (behind the canvas) the meaning of the face] (*AAG*, pp. 66; 61). Only in dispersion does the artwork come together in its full force, as though the lines' apparent bifurcation were necessary to create space or make way for a meaning otherwise obscured. Giacometti's lines of flight are said to displace any meaning produced frontally and gesture instead to an inaccessible seat of meaning created behind the image.

But this now begins to clash with Deleuze's lines of flight, which deny the possibility of any antecedence. These lines operate 'comme si quelque chose nous emportait, à travers nos segments, mais aussi à travers nos seuils, vers une destination inconnue, pas prévisible, pas préexistante' [as if something carried us away, across our segments, but also across our thresholds, toward a destination which is unknown, not foreseeable, not pre-existent'.[27] As it flows, the Deleuzo–Guattarian line of flight liberates us from any foreseeable locus of sense, identity or meaning, its constitutive indeterminacy is what pushes the subject beyond its own borders, beyond its perceived sense of self into a nascent, unknown state. This is a process of alienation, and one which Genet corroborates, for his part, since the hidden meaning to which he refers is in fact the signification behind his own portrait. These lines of flight do not represent a generality but rather the particularised contours of his own face. Genet is artistically carried off, severed, from his own sense of self: 'quand on a su que Giacometti faisait mon portrait (j'aurais le visage plutôt rond et épais) on m'a dit: "il va vous faire une tête en lame de couteau"' [When it got around that Giacometti was doing my portrait (supposedly my face is rather round) they told me: 'He's going to make your head into a knife blade] (*AAG*, pp. 65; 61). His own rounded physique is elongated and etiolated, as Genet follows Giacometti's lines of flight to discover a meaning he now perceives in his own face, an affect only achieved through this estranged equivocation through which he can arrive at any sense of the centre, *his* centre. Mobilised by the dynamism of these lines, Genet is sensitive to how lines of flight have the potential to tap into a valve of meaning not even he can access — even as the subject of the portrait — and to reveal him in a different light otherwise imperceptible.

Giacometti's portrait of Genet is abstracted by these lines of flight. Thus far, Genet echoes Deleuze and Guattari's lines of flight insofar as the lines in Giacometti's drawings also lead toward 'une destination inconnue'. Yet, unlike in *Mille plateaux*, Genet does gesture to precedence within that unknown destination, the 'lignes qui semblent fuir' imbued with the power to mobilise what is hidden and disclose what is unseen 'derrière la toile'. Genet interprets Giacometti's lines as more than the formal elements of a painting, asserting that 'il va de soi que je tente surtout de préciser une émotion, de la décrire, non d'expliquer les techniques de l'artiste' [it goes without saying that I am trying to pinpoint an emotion, to describe it, not to explain the artist's techniques] (*AAG*, pp. 66; 61). Genet's term, 'lines of flight', thus presents the line as a conduit to an affect he encounters in Giacometti's portraits *behind* the canvas, when the painter pulls signification back from what is represented to what is felt. This shift away from representation returns us to Deleuze and Guattari, whose lines of flight do not represent the depth of the artwork but provide the very conditions of a representation out of which such depth of meaning develops. In *Mille plateaux*, they tell us that 'loin que les lignes de fuite soient faites pour représenter la profondeur, ce sont elles qui inventent par surcroît la possibilité d'une telle représentation qui ne les occupe qu'un instant, à tel moment' [far from being made to represent depth, themselves invent the possibility of such a representation, which occupies them only for an instant, at a given moment].[28] These lines carry the artwork away from what it describes, mobilising a depth of emotion that cannot be inscribed directly onto the canvas. The lines of Giacometti's work are so affective precisely because they carve out a territory of intangible proximity that beckons to be touched, and yet which recoils and regresses to the horizon and beyond. Genet reads Giacometti's lines of flight as visible but cultivating a meaning which can never be fully apparent: the wrought discomfort of their presence gives form and vantage to an intimate, infinite unavailability.

The centrality of the face in such abstraction brings to mind Levinas's ethical reading of the face as also a site of infinity, a site which is infinitely foreign, which we can approach but never fully access.[29] For Levinas the face operates as a border at which the other may manifest himself to me, but he is unable to encroach on that border, he will always remain radically and infinitely foreign. Seán Hand explains such an idea as 'the face emerges as the emblem of everything that fundamentally resists categorization, containment or comprehension. Levinas therefore describes it as being '"infinitely foreign" or as manifesting the Other's inviolability and holiness'.[30] Genet sees in the lines of Giacometti's faces precisely such inviolable foreignness. For him, the face is a locus of infinity both foreign in the sense that it is alien, unknown and foreign, also because its lines of flight can have no territory nor belonging because they are constitutively detached. Levinas's and Genet's responses to the face are thus similar: infinite, foreign, uncontained, ungraspable, the face manifests itself in a disconcerting familiarity which is nonetheless de-familiarised in the process of looking. Those lines of flight that diverge from the face posit a form of relation mired in boundless estrangement: Genet's round face made straight offers a pertinent metaphor for this location of meaning in the distortion of what is most familiar.

Although philosophically Levinas's transcendent and Deleuze's immanent approaches are at odds, Genet's description of Giacometti's facial lines of flight seems to bring them into dialogue. To return to Genet's description of the tangle of lines that compose the face of the portrait, we find lines that impose themselves, traversing the onlooker, subsiding into him and then retreating into an abstraction forever out of reach. Unlike the figure of the point, which exposed the solitude embedded in Giacometti's figures, here the figure of the line promotes relation along a continuity that it disrupts — a relation that depends on disrupted continuity. The face *finds* its onlooker, seeks him out, engages in an imperceptible contact and then abandons any cohesion. The 'relief terrible' that radiates from Giacometti's canvas, for Genet, is one which has not so much actively severed connection, but which represents rupture itself: the lines' own severance, the harshness of their uncompromising jutting, angular contours, forge a model of connection based on the *joint* recognition of our disconnection, even of our rejection of connection. Looking at Giacometti's figures as not simply pursuing the path of a line of flight, but embodying it entirely, we can reframe the model of relation in *L'Atelier d'Alberto Giacometti* in a strikingly positive way: not as a rupture to be remedied, or repaired, but rather as finally *achieving* this rupture, finally realising, like Levinas's 'visage étranger', our infinite foreignness and making it the basis for our relational engagement.

How are we to compare, if at all, Genet's lines of flight with the definitive rupture promised by Deleuze and Guattari's abstract 'ligne de fuite'? If 'une ligne est un homme', then is Genet offering a proto-version of Deleuze and Guattari's deterritorialised subjectivity or not? Let us turn to Deleuze's and Guattari's lengthy description of this abstract line:

Dans la rupture [...] on est devenu soi-même imperceptible et clandestin dans
un voyage immobile. Plus rien ne peut se passer ni s'être passé. Plus personne
ne peut rien pour moi ni contre moi. Mes territoires sont hors de prise, et pas
parce qu'ils sont imaginaires, au contraire: parce que je suis en train de les
tracer. Finies les grandes ou les petites guerres. Finis les voyages, toujours à la
traîne de quelque chose. Je n'ai plus aucun secret, à la force d'avoir perdu le
visage, forme et matière. Je ne suis plus qu'une ligne. Je suis devenu capable
d'aimer, non pas d'un amour universel abstrait, mais celui que je vais choisir,
et qui va me choisir, en aveugle, mon double, qui n'a pas plus de moi que moi.
On s'est sauvé par amour et pour l'amour, en abandonnant l'amour et le moi.
On n'est plus qu'une ligne abstraite, comme une flèche qui traverse le vide.
Déterritorialisation absolue.

[In rupture [...] one has become imperceptible and clandestine in motionless
voyage. Nothing can happen, or can have happened, any longer. Nobody can
do anything for or against me any longer. My territories are out of grasp, not
because they are imaginary, but the opposite: because I am in the process of
drawing them. Wars, big and little, are behind me. Voyages, always in tow to
something else, are behind me. I no longer have any secrets, having lost my
face, form, and matter. I am now no more than a line. I have become capable
of loving, not with an abstract, universal love, but a love I shall choose, and that
shall choose me, blindly, my double, just as selfless as I. One has been saved by
and for love, by abandoning love and self. Now one is no more than an abstract
line, like an arrow crossing the void. Absolute deterritorialization.][31]

Here rupture is constituted as the basis for the realisation of subjectivity as Deleuze
and Guattari's term 'becoming'. Rupture forms the basis of an unfettered mode
of existence in which we come to define ourselves as an abstract line, and from
there all relation becomes possible in the recognition that no relation is binding.
Subjectivity in this model is entirely autonomous: in fact is not a subject at all, not
subjected to anything or not beholden to what Simon Critchley articulates as 'the
Latin *subjectum* literally "that which is thrown under", thus the subject is that which
is thrown under as a prior support or more fundamental stratum upon which other
qualities, such as predicates, accidents and attributes may be based'.[32] Instead, as an
abstract line, all classifications are rejected, all territories subside as life formalises
into the pure pursuit of carving out or establishing a unique path *ex nihilo*. Unlike
the figure of the point which we read as perforating and atomising, and creating a
serial singularity, here Deleuze and Guattari's line of flight is a figure of connective
rupture that abandons all pre-destined, prescribed interactions to establish a relation
whose conditions are mutual effacement, mutual separation. Rather than losing
oneself in the self, here one forsakes the self in order to engage with the other:
a literal ef*face*ment, a de-facing or loss of the face, in which an abandonment of
the self allows the self to enter into a love, amity, friendship; connection through
disconnection. The abstract line in the Deleuzo-Guattarian rendering thus carries
the theoretical potential of relation, while always separating relation from any fixed
markers.

Treading a Fine Line: *Le Funambule*

The lines of flight that make Giacometti's sculptures seem both familiar and foreign are made flesh six years later. Moving from the written page to live witness, Genet describes beholding the corpse of his lover, half-Algerian, half-German acrobat Abdallah Bentaga, in a Paris morgue in late February 1964. His words that are hauntingly mimetic of that disconnected relation he theorises in *L'Atelier d'Alberto Giacometti*, and in an unpublished text from the 1980s he remembers how:

> De son visage au mien, il y avait cette distance en mouvement, sans cesse en mouvement. C'était une pierre que j'aurais pu ramasser et tenir dans mes mains et c'était au même moment un minéral très loin dans l'espace et même dans le temps, indifférent à mon examen, ignorant totalement le monde. Et, en regardant ce visage d'Abdallah mort, je reconnus le très proche et l'incalculablement, scandaleusement lointain des sculptures de Giacometti.
>
> [There was a distance that was in motion between his face and mine, ceaselessly in motion. He was a stone I might have picked up and held in my hands and he was at the same time a mineral far away in space and even in time, indifferent to my examination or rather totally unaware of the world. In looking at the face of Abdallah dead, I recognize from close up and incalculably, scandalously from afar the sculptures of Giacometti.][33]

The language of stone seems initially to transform Abdallah into a sculpture. His inert body is monumentalised not just as a rock to be held onto, but as the mineral matter from which the object itself is carved. The geological metaphor thus moves Abdallah away from the material world entirely — the mundane stone in Genet's hands is now transformed into the immaterial, incorporeal ore that both precedes and exceeds his gaze. The image feels eschatological: Genet returns Abdallah's body to the earth and finds himself forced *out* of relation, desperately trying to measure the distance that separates the sentient from the mineral. Yet that distance, a linear form of space, simply alienates Abdallah in a way that makes any measurement impossible, his loss of proximity etched on to 'ce visage d'Abdallah mort' in a way that sacrifices the Levinasian face that remains absolutely in a relation. This distance seems to break the space-time continuum, such that the line that once served as a ruler able to measure space and time, now becomes the sign of a discontinuity that alienates Genet by attaching him to the ultimate detachment of death itself. Trapped in a unilateral gaze, Genet drifts into the terrifying interstice he describes between Hebrew letters, which 'sépar[e] un cadavre de l'œil du vivant qui le regarde' [separates the corpse from the living eye] (*CA*, pp. 365; 310), as though only a spatial imaginary is able to conjure the radical estrangement that collapses language. This 'distance en mouvement' recalls the mathematical metaphor for parted lovers consecrated by John Donne's compass, which I analysed in Part I. Genet, too, tries to keep hold of Abdallah by imagining their separation not as a 'a breach, but an expansion'.[34] But his words defy the containment offered by Donne's idealised circumference; here, we are closer to Giacometti's remote vision of intimacy, a geometric form of being and relating where 'une ligne est un homme', perhaps because lines, like man, are forever poised between estrangement and connection.

Genet's horror at encountering Abdallah in his apartment in the rue de Bourgogne in 1964 perhaps explains his reluctance to speak about either the acrobat — 'Abdallah fait partie de ma vie tellement intime que je préfère ne pas parler de lui devant la caméra' [Abdallah is so much a part of my inner life I prefer not to speak about him in front of the camera] (*ED*, pp. 219; 188) — or the text, *Le Funambule*, written in homage to him and to the 'perils faced by the artist' in 1957.[35] As Jean-Bernard Moraly tells us, Genet refused the republication of this essay in 1966 when the furore surrounding the infamous staging of *Les Paravents* at the Théâtre de l'Odeon called for a return to all of his writing on art, aesthetics and the dangers of the creative act.[36] In March 1957, Genet told his editor Marc Barbezat that he had 'pas touché au Funambule. Je le laisse croupir' [I'm letting it rot].[37] His methodology presages the spectrality of his subject matter as he lets his manuscript languish, symbolically decomposing what he has already composed. To allow the text of *Le Funambule* to stagnate, to exist half-way between composition and completion, becomes almost a self-fulfilling prophesy that presages the decay of Abdallah's own body seven years later.

Yet, while Abdallah may have served as muse for *Pour un funambule* (as it was originally published in the *Revue Preuves* in September 1957), the silence that follows his death only further reinforces Genet's message in the text itself: that the artist is constitutively separated from the world of the living. Drawing on the analogy of the high wire, Genet imagines that poets and artists must navigate what Rosi Braidotti will later characterise in feminist theory as the 'precarious conceptual geometry' of disrupting safe, established pathways of thought, channelling the energy of the 'acrobat who steps onto the tightrope without a safety net [...] run[ning] the risk of a fall into the void'.[38] However, *Le Funambule* offers an aesthetic rather than political vision of art: Genet appeals to the artist's capacity to transcend the public eye and perform the suspension of real space and real time. The precarious conceptual geometry that Genet must navigate throughout *Le Funambule* is how to honour the daringly anarchic detachment promised by the poetic gesture, on the one hand, and how, on the other, to celebrate the *fil* as a linear cord that is deeply bound up with ideas of filiation and connection that remain forever elusive, and painfully fragile, in his writing.

Filiation

Abdallah, the corpse walking on a high wire, becomes a spectre of a filial bond that Genet is constantly reworking into his texts.[39] Genet's close friend, the Spanish writer Juan Goytisolo, claims that the inspiration for *Le Funambule* was precisely to concretise that imagined filiation:

> La relation entre eux est de père à fils. Genet a décidé d'en faire un grand artiste et inventé pour lui des tours de saltimbanque qui exigent un entraînement patient et rigoureux, un admirable texte poétique *Pour un Funambule* sera le résultat de la conjonction de leurs volontés. Abdallah se lance avec enthousiasme dans la tâche, Genet a l'air très satisfait de ses progrès, leur amitié irradie une glorieuse beauté morale.[40]

[They had a father-son relationship. Genet decided to turn him into a great artist, inventing demanding acrobatics that required patience and rigour. *Pour un Funambule* was the admirable poetic text that resulted from their union. Abdallah threw himself enthusiastically into the task, Genet seemed satisfied by his progress, and their friendship radiated with a glorious, moral beauty.]

Goytisolo perceived Genet's relation to Abdallah as an imagined filiation in which Genet is positioned as Creator, the father who makes of Abdallah the artist he becomes. As surrogate father to Abdallah, any genetic filiation is displaced; lineage becomes a construct that displaces the roots of the family tree and which iterates Genet's own missing lineage as a ward of the *assistance publique*. Asserting himself in place of his own paternal lack, Genet's relationship to the tightrope walker in Goytisolo's reading would fill in the gap that, as Dominique Eddé explores, is coincidentally left by the blank of his father who 's'appelait Blanc' [surname was 'Blanc'].[41] *Blanc*: a blank space inhabited by a paternal absence given presence through the blank signifier which replaces that gap, the surname reifying the *blancs* that are often fetishised by Genet's writing.[42] If *Blanc* signifies a paternal absence that cannot signify, then the lines of Genet's texts seem to seek to reclaim that gap by embedding it within his texts. Albert Dichy contests Genet's awareness of the surname, while Cixous insists on the impossibility of this poetic coincidence, stating that 'il ne se serait jamais appelé Blanc. Le père lui restera inconnu' [he could never have been called Blanc. The father will always remain unknown to him].[43] *Blanc* too neatly reinforces the gap left by the unnamed, unknown father and, instead, Cixous seeks to move away from the proper name to the symbol, stating that 'à la place du nom du père, un blanc' [in the place of the paternal signature, a gap].[44] Genet's textual identity is governed, however symbolically, by the heritage of an absent filiation. The *blanc* replaces the father in order to preserve the trace of absence left by that lineage, such that as a symbol the *blanc* is no longer able to be filled.

'*Pour un Funambule* est un hymne au fil' [*The Funambulists* is a hymn to the wire [*fil*]], argues Derrida in *Glas* (G, pp. 114b; 99b). But it is also a paean to Abdallah and Genet's filiation, offering a poetic reverie on the nature of a filial ligature that Cixous claims Genet strives to untie:

> Il faut introduire le détachement partout où un peu de lien se forme, s'il tient à un fil comme le funambule, on devra couper le fil, précipiter la chute (mais une mort, on la retournera en gloire, on ramasse le soleil dans le caniveau et on le relance au ciel). Après des années de désert, il se sera constitué de nouveau captif et de nouveau amoureux de sa captivité dans l'enchevêtre des fils du texte (de soi). Il va de soi qu'il veut tout perdre y compris le fil, jusqu'au reste. Aller au terme. Marcher à la mort.[45]

> [One must introduce detachment anywhere a slight bond is formed. If he holds on to a thread like the tightrope walker does, we will have to cut the thread, precipitate a fall (but the death that follows will be glorified, just like we pick up the sun from the gutter and throw it back to heaven). After many solitary years, he will once again be held captive and fall in love with his own captivity in the tangle of threads of the text (of the self [silk]). It goes without saying that

he wants to lose everything, including the thread, up until the last remainder.
Go to full term. Walk towards death.]

While the *fil* of the tightrope might be considered a line of flight which uproots and suspends any ligature, for Cixous, it is a thread that binds Genet to a relationality he radically seeks to eschew. It re-entwines itself within his texts to cast a perennial attachment, an inescapable affiliation between this signifier and his writing as though the it becomes the literal matter that produces the textile of his texts. We return to the materiality of the *fil* in the next section, but here I am interested in how Cixous states that he wants to untangle himself from this thread 'jusqu'au reste'. Relation always creates a remainder in Genet's writing, the terms that Cixous uses to relate the *fil* to the 'reste' recalling Genet's own recollection of himself in *Journal du voleur* as a 'fils' whose 'père *reste* inconnu'. The *fil* in Cixous's interpretation connects us to a father and son, this truss materially binding us to a filiation which is itself held in suspense: the father is unknown to the son, he is a figure that can only be anticipated in a suspense that mirrors the physical suspension of the tightrope.

Goytisolo's reading of Genet and Abdallah's filiation is liberated from any such genealogical bondage. Perhaps that is why their filial bond diffuses a glorious moral beauty that resonates with Levinas's moral consciousness as giving access to an other who is necessarily separate from me.[46] Their shared morality posits the intrinsic separateness at the heart of their affiliation, Genet's symbolic adoption both attaching him to, and disconnecting him from, Abdallah. The radiance Goytisolo attributes to this moral union further endorses their illusory lineage if we think of Johan Faeber's term 'trans-parent-cy' which he describes as 'la seule famille de Genet, oserait-on dire, serait celle du trans-parent, du parent invisible ultime, du parent à travers' [we might dare to say that the only family Genet has would be that of the trans-parent, the absolute invisible parent, the transversal parent].[47] In the spectre of a non-existent filiation, Genet creates a lineage which is transversal, trans-parent, moving beyond the verticality of biological father-son relations, he responds to his own spectres of filiation by conceiving a horizontal connection with the tightrope walker that defies the very notion of descent. For Denis Provencher, in his reading of Genet's legacy of 'transfiliation', which highlights the queer diaspora that Genet has inspired across the Maghrebi world, he speaks of 'usher[ing] in new forms of heritage and transmission [...] across linguistic, cultural, and temporal-spatial boundaries', the notion of transfiliation 'reaching across generations and [being] transgressive because of its potential to reverse the direction of the transfer of knowledge, tradition and symbolic heritage between parent and child'.[48] Transfiliation fractures the hierarchical verticality of lineage to produce more sinuous lines of connection that are transnational and intergenerational in scope, akin to Genet's own imagined filiation as the white son to a black father, David Hilliard, thirty years his junior (*CA*, pp. 352; 300). In its pure elevation, then, the *fil* of the tightrope transposes the filial into a horizontal mode of exchange, a process we find echoed in *Journal du voleur* when Genet construes his relation to Stilitano as transforming the direction of the filial bond: 'j'étais un enfant que son père conduit avec prudence. (Aujourd'hui je suis un père que son enfant conduit à l'amour)' [I was a child being carefully led by his father. (Today I am a father led to love by his child)] (*JV*, pp. 47; 57). Both child and father, Genet's filiation operates a relation of substitution in which each takes turns to carry the other, to lead the other, in a bearing that reverberates throughout the filial signifier in *Le Funambule*.

In ten fragments of the text, it is the line that takes centre stage as Genet's acrobat coaxes the *fil* into consciousness, animating its limp objectivity into a sentient form: 'Cet amour [...] que tu dois montrer à ton fil, il aura autant de force qu'en montre le fil de fer pour te porter [...] le fil était mort — ou si tu veux muet, aveugle — te voici: il va vivre et parler' [This love [...] that you must show for your wire, will have as much strength as the metal wire has to carry you [...] The wire was dead — or if you like, mute, blind — but now that you are here, it will live and speak] (*F*, pp. 9; 98). The agency is complicated here, as the *fil* occupies the privileged position of being both the child — the *fils* of this renaissance that the tightrope walker encourages — and the bearer, the parental body that carries or supports the tightrope walker. Genet's high wire is thus no ordinary *fil*: it is the anthropomorphising of its own shape, a vector which is both geometrically linear, and a 'veho vect', a vehicle or conveyor which physically carries the subject that balances on it. This iron wire carries the acrobat to his full term, the cord almost umbilical in its parental bearing. Yet, Genet lambasts such a term in *Miracle de la rose* when arguing that 'il m'en coûterait de dire que les hommes sont mes frères. Ce mot m'écœure parce qu'il me rattache aux hommes par un cordon ombilical, il me replonge à l'intérieur d'un ventre' [it would pain me to have to say that men are my brothers. The word sickens me because it attaches me to men by an umbilical cord. It thrusts me back into the womb] (*MR*, pp. 268; 114). The umbilical cord is abject for Genet, a thread that binds him to the claustrophobia of the womb. Such is the contrast to the tightrope that represents an exteriority, a liberation that defies the binds of the ground below. The tightrope may offer a physical carriage, but its support is nonetheless affective: energised by love, the *fil* is a figure brought to life through nurture, reciprocity, and in a desperate tenderness that Genet cannot achieve through a maternal line to which he seems vulnerable. As a conduit, the *fil* leads out of the physical body — away from the maternal cord that yokes and binds the subject — toward an emotive space of love which Genet denies being grounded in the body at all, any such corporeality linked to injury where 'je ne serais pas surpris, quand tu marches par terre que tu tombes et te fasses une entorse. Le fil te portera mieux, plus sûrement qu'une route' [I would not be surprised, when you walk on earth, if you fall and sprain something. The wire will carry you better, more safely, than a road] (*F*, pp. 11, 100). Almost as though actualising Deleuze and Guatarri's ultimate goal of deterritorialisation, Genet's *fil* takes flight from all forms of groundedness. He shuns the road as a form of fixed entrenchment that threatens to sprain the subject, his tightrope moving away from paths already trodden to form a carriage that is not immured in an essentialising or determined set path.

The line of the *fil* in *Le Funambule* brings the anti-essentialist epistemology of post-structuralist and feminist theory to an aesthetic stage. Genet seems to anticipate the kind of nomadic thinking Braidotti proposes in the 1990s and 2000s, in which subjectivity is not composed of fixed attributes that are inherited, or lineal, but is constituted in a 'becoming' comprised of assemblages with the human and non-human.[49] The material *fil* allows Genet to imagine the acrobat's coming into being beyond the yoke of biological lineage or determinism; this linear signifier echoing the geometric analogy of an anti-essentialist selfhood proposed by feminist theorist, Teresa de Lauretis, who compares the folly of trying to pin down monolithically the 'essence' of woman to the attempt to determine the essence of a triangle.[50] However, *Le Funambule* seeks no such philosophical or rational logic in the drama of becoming that it stages. Amidst a contextual backdrop of 1950s absurdist theatre, Genet creates a vocabulary in which to express a search for the self that is not restricted by reality, but realised and *liberated*, through pure illusion. In the realm of spectacle alone, the *fil* allows the self to become enacted, rather than born, right before our eyes. Genet orientates the acrobat's entire choreography towards the illumination of the *fil*, in a gesture that replaces the theatre of representation with a purist theatre of self-discovery:

> Tes bonds, tes sauts, tes danses [...] tu les réussiras non pour que tu brilles, mais afin qu'un fil d'acier qui était mort et sans voix enfin chante. Quel fil étonnant! Comme il soutient son danseur et comme il l'aime! A son tour le fil sera de toi le plus merveilleux danseur.

> [Your leaps, your somersaults, your dances [...] you will execute them successfully, not for you to shine, but that a steel wire that was dead and voiceless will finally sing What a surprising wire! How it supports its dancer and how it loves him! In its turn, the wire will be the most amazing dancer of you.] (*F*, pp.10; 99)

Both acrobat and wire are symbiotic here: neither exist without the play of the other. The activity of the tightrope walker in his boundless twists and turns creates an identity based on elevation, detachment from anything outside an artistry based on suspension: a relation that creates unto itself a commonality that requires the other to come into being insofar as the conditions of his being are unthinkable in any normative framework. Indeed, Genet perceives this coming into being not as an evolution, but as a realisation: a fulfilment of a unique presence brought about by a play of pure mobilities. This is the very theatre of becoming, a practice which responds to the Deleuzo-Guattarian formulation in which 'devenir n'est pas une évolution, du moins une évolution par descendance et filiation [...] une ligne de devenir a seulement un milieu. Le milieu n'est pas une moyenne, c'est un accéléré, c'est la vitesse absolue du mouvement' [becoming is not an evolution, at least not an evolution by descent and filiation [...] a line of becoming has only a middle. The middle is not an average, it is fast motion, it is the absolute speed of movement] (*F*, pp. 291, 360; 263, 323). The tightrope is inherently medial, it is by definition stretched across as a line which is not a means but an end in itself: 'cet étroit chemin qui vient de nulle part et y va' so that 'le dépaysement soit plus grand' [this narrow path that comes from nowhere and goes nowhere so that the change of scene may be greater] (pp. 24; 113). Like Deleuze's line of becoming, Genet's tightrope suspends all goal-orientated activity; its straight line is an aimless movement interested only in the uprooting all grounded, fixed points of anchorage.

Genet refers to this non-evolutionary presence as a death throughout *Le Funambule*, as though the goal of this coming to being in the aesthetic act offers a temporal reversal of birth, origins or beginnings. Instead, the acrobat aims for spectrality, the *danse macabre* of a subject who dies before appearing on the wire, absenting themself from life in the etymological sense of an absence as *ab-esse*: being away from essence, moving away from being as essence to embody 'ce bloc d'absence que tu vas devenir' [this block of absence that you are going to become] (*F*, pp. 14; 102). Becoming is thus associated with the achievement of a non-essentialisable position, a status mediated on and by a *fil* that figuratively engenders the acrobat and delivers him to his becoming: 'à devenir tel qu'il se voudrait, tel qu'il se rêve' [to this becoming what he would like to be, how he dreams himself] (pp. 15; 103). Becoming takes shape in the artistic act as volition, promise, purpose; a process which is symbiotic insofar as tightrope and acrobat formalise and lend function to the other, just as Stilitano and Genet do as father and son in *Journal du voleur*. Where for Deleuze and Guattari becoming and filiation are mutually exclusive such that 'le devenir ne produit rien par filiation, toute filiation serait imaginaire' [becoming produces nothing by filiation; all filiation is imaginary], the filiation we are privy to in *Le Funambule* is decidedly imaginary in that it is conjured through signifiers that Genet imagines and brings to life in the text.[51] Genet even draws attention to how the *fil* evokes a sense of nostalgia — the very practice of re-imagining — by asking 'qui donc avant toi avait compris quelle nostalgie demeure enfermée dans l'âme d'un fil d'acier de sept millimètres?' [who before you ever understood what nostalgia rests enclosed in the soul of a seven-millimetre steel wire?] (*F*, pp. 10; 99). The *fil* that enables deterritorialisation thus also facilitates restitution, homecoming; Genet's line forging a lineage that is rooted to the imaginary space of memory and which is thus extricated from the repressive roots that Deleuze and Guattari associate with filiation. For Deleuze and Guattari, such nostalgia invalidates and contradicts their notion of becoming, which is defined as '*une anti-mémoire* [...] le souvenir a toujours une fonction de reterritorialisation' [antimemory [...] memories always have a reterritorialization function].[52] Yet, for Genet, such an opposition is defunct since the nostalgia to which *Le Funambule* refers lacks any concrete terrain. Genet gestures, instead, to the evanescence of this memory and to its refusal to be located, such that all points of reference hold within them their own mode of escape: 'pour le funambule dont je parle [...] son regard triste doit renvoyer aux images d'une enfance misérable, inoubliable, où il se savait abandonné' [his sad gaze [...] has to reflect images of an unforgettably wretched childhood in which he knew he was abandoned] (*F*, pp. 13; 102). Because it is anchored to abandonment, reterritorialisation in *Le Funambule* reasserts its own flight insofar as the memories of childhood that reclaim Abdallah do so in a manner which replays the jettison from that childhood. Genet evokes a childhood in images that lack either place or rootedness, projections that are mercurial, unfixed and which reject any stable return because as an image that childhood becomes spectral and unable to belong to a specific locale.

We might recall Tom Conley's discussion of how images in Genet's writing 'becom[e] an event that at once captures and evacuates our most intense feelings of life at the instant a quantum of space is gained and lost'.[53] Genet imagines the image of Abdallah's 'regard triste' as recalling the image of an unforgettable childhood lost in its own being forgotten. These layered images stage the event of an abandoned childhood that lacks any territory, the image ratifying what Conley notices in Deleuze's brief reference to Genet in *L'Image-mouvement* as 'an image [that] remains forever in an immediacy of motion. It is not static, and by its very nature it never reifies or fixes into place what it seems to represent'.[54] As the simulacra of an event which is forever deferred and hidden in the perpetual slippage produced by its own manifestation as an image, these images are the unstable catalysts that inspire Genet's texts. Motivated by the imagery of nostalgia, mediated by the *fil* of a spectral filiation, these are texts haunted by memory which in an interview in 1983 he confirms is part of an ideology in which 'créer c'est toujours parler de l'enfance. C'est toujours nostalgique' [creating always means speaking about childhood. It's always nostalgic] (*ED*, pp. 277; 239). His writing is always signed by nostalgia, by a time signature of *le fil, le fils*, filiation or, as Hélène Cixous remarks, so too do all of his texts 'exploite[nt] le filon, les fils, les fils, la fliction' [exploit the vein, the threads, the sons, the *affliction*].[55] It is the *fil* as a tightrope which foregrounds a lineage without territory, without roots, a vestigial space which need not contradict the anti-arborescence that Deleuze and Guattari champion. Where for Deleuze and Guattari deterritorialisation is opposed to any lineage because this would re-anchor the subject, Genet foregrounds a spectral lineage in *Le Funambule* that affirms its roots as being founded in the ephemeral rather than the concrete. He imagines a filiation that is relational without being shackled to physical roots or generational progress, positioning the acrobat amidst a line of spectral relics who are all leftover from the social organisation of a family orientated towards futurity. Instead:

> Vous êtes les résidus d'un âge fabuleux. Vous revenez de très loin [...]. Dehors, c'est le bruit discordant, c'est le désordre; dedans, c'est la certitude généalogique qui vient des millénaires, la sécurité de se savoir lié dans une sorte d'usine où se forgent les jeux précis qui servent l'exposition solennelle de vous-même qui préparent la Fête. Vous ne vivez que pour la Fête. Non pour celle que s'accordent en payant, les pères et les mères de famille. Je parle de votre illustration pour quelques minutes.

> [You are the remnants of a mythical age. You come from very far away [...]. Outside is discordant noise, disorder: inside, it is the genealogical certainty that comes from millennia, the security of knowing one is connected in a sort of factory where precise rules are made that serve as the solemn exposition of yourselves, who prepare the Show. You live only for the Show. Not the one that fathers and mothers treat themselves to by paying. I'll speak about your drawing for a few minutes.] (*F*, pp. 25; 115)

Moraly reads the scene as a homage to the metaphysical possibilities offered by the 'spectacle du cirque [...] image naïve, odorante, d'un ancient paradis' [circus show [...] a naïve, redolent image of a bygone paradise].[56] Arguably, Genet's nostalgia is not angled towards reconstructing a lost Eden where the artifice of theatre provides solace from a discordant reality; rather, his tightrope walker grants us access to a different organisation of ancestry. One that is nomadic, atemporal and defined by a commitment to the poetic act that is divorced from the world outside. Genet speaks of the 'sécurité', 'certitude' and 'précis[ion]' of an age-old rejection of the social sphere and its logic, as the *fil* makes visible the mechanics of a filiation that relates individuals not via biological succession, but on a factory belt where one is not born, but made. Dystopian? Perhaps, but Genet is exploring how creative gestures and patterns might build a community that directly defies the inherited postures transmitted through familial models. Like Provencher's transfiliation, the line of the tightrope thus cuts through the noise, chaos and dissonance of the political space beyond the theatre, and offers a coherent form of geometric order and relation that allows the self to reach their apotheosis.

Genet eschews the familial lineage of parents who finance the artistic scene, abstracting that lineage in a way that brings to mind the sculptures of Louise Bourgeois and her use of wires and lines to represent the family network. For her, 'solid geometry [i]s a symbol for emotional security. Euclidean or other kinds of geometry are closed systems where relations can be anticipated and are eternal'.[57] For Bourgeois, relations are fortified by the rigour of order, the formality of geometry allowing for connections to be consolidated. Like Genet's tightrope which traverses the void, Bourgeois's geometry navigates the in-between to forge relations it then encloses, keeping hold of them through an abstraction that renders them eternal. If we think of the immortal, or rather post-mortal, spectre of Genet's tightrope walker who rejects the localised 'pères et les mères de famille' and venerates those 'millénaires' whose ancestry is legendary, we can see a similar pattern emerge in *Le Funambule*, where order and abstraction formalise a lineage that is never accessible — thus never limiting — but whose restructuring is made possible in the creative space offered by the text.

That Genet moves directly from this discussion of genealogy to the geometric sketch he finds in Abdallah's wallet (the only direct reference to Abdallah in the text according to White) forces a textual connection between geometry and filiation.[58] Rifling through Abdallah's wallet, he tells us:

> Je trouve une feuille de papier pliée où il a tracé de curieux signes: le long d'une ligne droite, qui représente le fil, des traits obliques à droite, des traits à gauche — ce sont ses pieds, ou plutôt la place que prendraient ses pieds, ce sont les pas qu'il fera. Et en regard de chaque trait, un chiffre. Puisque dans un art qui n'était soumis qu'à un entraînement hasardeux et empirique il travaille à apporter les rigueurs, les disciplines chiffrées, il vaincra. Que m'importe donc qu'il sache lire? Il connait assez les chiffres pour mesurer les rythmes et les nombres.

> [I find a folded piece of paper on which he has drawn curious signs: a straight line, which represents the wire, with slanting marks to the right and left — those are his feet, or rather the place his feet would take, it is the steps he will take. And opposite each mark, a number. Because he works to bring rigors, quantitative discipline, to an art that had been subject only to a haphazard and empirical training, he will conquer. What do I care, then, if he knows how to read or not? He knows figures well enough to measure the rhythms and numbers.] (*F*, pp. 11; 100)

Genet reads Abdallah as an image, the *fils* who walks along the *fil* abstracted to a series of gestural lines and footsteps. It is the quantitative nature of Abdallah's calculation, his measurement, that is both surprising and beguiling; Abdallah is able to gauge and weigh up that 'distance en mouvement' that Genet is unable to thirty years later on beholding Abdallah's dead body. Genet attributes success to this mathematic approach, which concretises the transient contact between the body and the wire; these geometric lines offering, as Bourgeois suggests, a solid mode of symbolising relations which resist formalisation. There is a different type of visibility afforded by this numerical system that stands in place of those footprints which are invisible when up in the air, that codifies the tightrope walker's trajectory and transforms it from a pathway into a formula. The numbers, however, do not hold any specific value. They are described only as 'chiffres', or *cifra* meaning zero. There is thus the quantification of an impulse which has no inherent value but which is nonetheless present; a way to index a movement towards a nothing or non-entity which Genet heralds throughout the text as an apparition, an 'image dont je parle, qu'un mort habite' [an image of which I speak, inhabited by a dead man] (*F*, pp. 14; 103). As a clever mathematician (a 'subtil calculateur', p.14), Abdallah is codified as just such a present absence: his own spectral status on the wire is imprinted and safeguarded by being turned into a geometric keepsake, a sign which attests to his need to pin down the reality of his flight. I am reminded of Victor Hugo's account of the barricade erected at the Faubourg du Temple in *Les Misérables*, which he describes as 'une apparition mystérieuse. C'était juste, emboîté, imbriqué, rectiligne, symétrique et funèbre [...] on sentait que le chef de la barricade était un géomètre ou un spectre' [a mysterious apparition. It was slightly tailored, stacked, imbricated, rectilineal, symmetrical and deadly. [...] You felt that the chief of this barricade was either a geometer or a spectre].[59] Except that instead of a barrier, the diagram here positions the tightrope as a horizon, a line which maps the possibility of exceeding any boundary. Indeed, Genet's and Hugo's terms may resonate, but their outlook is somewhat different: the connection between geometry and spectrality mirrored by the etymological proximity of the tightrope as a *funis*, or cord, and the spectre as a *funus*, or dead person. In *Le Funambule*, this spectral geometry is not an image of terror or obstruction as in Hugo's description, but more the ability to figure the spectre in a concrete space, to materialise what denies physical expression.

Abdallah's drawing is significant because it constitutes an artistic becoming in geometric terms. Through mathematic precision, Genet explores how Abdallah abstracts his lived persona to become the image of the artist at once spectral and animate: 'c'est en toi-même enfin que durant quelques minutes le spectacle te change. Ton bref tombeau vous illumine. À la fois tu y es enfermé et ton image ne cesse de s'en échapper' [it is into yourself, finally, that for a few minutes the performance changes you. Your brief tomb illuminates you. You are enclosed within it while at the same time your image keeps escaping from it] (*F*, pp. 26; 103). While the image is imagined, the split subjectivity that is enabled by the line permits an imagined lineage between artist and ego, the tightrope forging a connection between the subject and his specular image. The process has all the trappings of a Lacanian mirror stage — but without the attempt to unify subject and image, nor the desire to assume a single self. Rather what Genet lingers on is what Lacan sees as the asymptotic relation between the subject and his becoming: 'l'instance du *moi* [se situe] dans une lignée de fiction, à jamais irréductible pour le seul individu — ou plutôt, qui ne rejoindra qu'asymptotiquement le devenir du sujet' [the agency known as the ego [is situated] in a fictional direction that will forever remain irreducible for any single individual or, rather, that will only asymptotically approach the subject's becoming].[60] This asymptote is a line that does not converge with the object with which it comes into contact, but which falls alongside it. The tightrope forms just such an asymptotic line insofar as it denies the subject's convergence with its image, the acrobat dancing for his or her own image in a narcissism that Genet defends as being death itself. The acrobat may dance for his or her own image, but it is the solitude of death that is ultimately sought. Abdallah's emergence on the wire differs from Lacan's inchoate infant who is given unity through the cohesive image it encounters in the mirror; rather the tightrope walker for Genet is moving in the opposite direction not into life but out of it, above it. His apotheosis visually enacts the Lacanian discrepancy between a present and ideal self, but Genet reverses the process such that the tightrope walker, divested of any lived reality, realises himself through his engagement with the image as a spectre.

There is no image that stands before the subject in *Le Funambule*. Rather, the acrobatic spectacle disinters the double sites of the self to give rise to a spectre which comes from within not without. This image leaks from the subject, and what the *fil* enables for Genet is the exposition of precisely these double, interconnected but separate, sites of selfhood. The tightrope is able to fulfil what Deleuze would see as 'la ligne de fuite active et créatrice, ET... ET... ET' [active and creative line of flight, AND... AND ... AND], the line of flight characterised not by its being, its *est* or *être*, but by its homonymic addition, *et*.[61] The line of flight thus mediates being as adding, being as fragmented and relational, Genet's tightrope forming a literal line of flight that dramatises this very division since it is the unstable form that dances around image and acrobat: 'ce n'est pas toi qui dansera, c'est ton fil' [it is not you who will dance, it is the wire] (*F*, pp. 12; 101). It is the line, the *fil*, that embodies the subject's becoming on the wire as fragmented. The line forms the deterritorialised platform that realises the multiplicity of the acrobat's subjectivity.

Abdallah thus fulfils the 'no-thing-ness', the not one, of the sketch he proposes. As a geometer and a spectre, he negotiates those 'chiffres' or zeros on the page in the same manner that he does on the high wire, moving from one spectral site to another. The tightrope may form a single line, but it resists any singularity thereafter; it formalises a process of attachment to no concrete terrain, a connectivity wrought out of being cut off, a present yet phantasmal relation between Genet the father and Abdallah the son, between wire and tightrope walker, between image and spectre. Such relations are abstracted by the tightrope, purified in this suspended gap between concrete points where the artist is liberated in its deterritorialisation, a nascent ghost which exists both before and beyond any fixed evolution. Spectrality in *Le Funambule* offers potential, its infinite intervallic power taps into a value system Genet explores two decades before this essay in a letter to his friend Ibis in 1933. In describing the tightrope as 'six mètres de long [qui] sont une ligne infinie et une cage' [its six metres' length are an infinite line and a cage] (*F*, pp. 24; 113), Genet yokes the *fil* to a site of infinity that is both productive and entrapping: 'L'infini pour moi, c'est l'incréé. Et le créé ne peut être — raisonnablement — dans ce qui n'est pas. Écoutez, je ne suis pas très d'humeur à philosopher et je m'y prends toujours fort mal, mais je ne crois en Rien' [For me, infinity is the uncreated. And the created cannot be — reasonably — in what does not exist. Listen, I'm not really in the mood to philosophise and I always take to it so badly anyway, but I believe in Nothingness].[62] As the not yet created, Genet's infinity is full of the possibility promised by 'nothingness'. The acrobat's infinite wire is thus not nihilistic in that it vaunts the annihilation of existence; rather, it asserts the hope of new creation that can only be found in an uncodified, inexistent *rien*. If Genet's creation is always about childhood, about the nostalgia of a filiation now absent, then the signifier of an infinite *fil* in an essay on Abdallah the *fils* serves to sublimate the promise of a filial connection that cannot be lost by never coming into being. Filiation may be defined as 'the relation of one thing to another from which it may be said to be descended or derived; position in a genealogical classification' (*OED*), but Genet's spectral filiation forges the conditions that make unbound relations possible, prior to and above descent.

Like Nietzsche's celebration of the rope-dancer in *Thus Spake Zarathustra*, the wire enables an overcoming of oneself and the transfiguration of 'the narrow confines of a stable subjectivity', because it puts the risk of falling into the void above the 'natural' or accepted order of the world that warns against that danger.[63] When a jester appears and the acrobat falls, Nietzsche does not take this as the inevitability of suffering, death or even nihilism, but the corollary of a vocation that puts creation and creativity over the self. The rope-dancer thus dramatises the transformative potential of the creative act, which harnesses disorder to realise a higher realisation of existence bound towards the nothing, or the not yet created:

> Man is a rope stretched between the animal and the Superman — a rope over an abyss. A dangerous crossing, a dangerous wayfaring, a dangerous looking-back, a dangerous trembling and halting. What is great in man is that he is a bridge and not a goal, what is lovable in man is that he is an *over*-going and a down-going.[64]

Genet's own ambitions in *Le Funambule* are undeniably resonant, and as Derrida noted in *Glas*, Genet's essay reads as a 'lecture à peu près complète, littéralement littérale, de *Zarathoustra*' [an almost complete, literally literal rereading of Zarathustra] (*G*, pp. 118b; 102b). Moreover, at the height of his relationship with Abdallah, Genet wrote to his publisher, Marc Barbezat, on 24 June 1961 asking for him to 'apporte[r] avec vous tout Nietzsche: *Zarathoustra*, *Par delà le bien et le mal* | *Gay savoir* | *Ecce homo*] [Bring everything you have on Nietzsche: *Zarathoustra*, *Beyond Good and Evil* | *Gay Science* | *Ecce Homo*] (*LMOB*, p. 214). Genet may have been unwittingly inspired by the metaphor of the tightrope that offers a way to abandon the world and its subjective order, his own essay also foregoing the ontological models that root the subject in evolution or derivation. But where Nietzsche imagines man as the tightrope itself, a bridge between two states of selfhood, Genet pushes the poetic possibilities of his own creation in *Le Fumambule* to invest the linear geometry of the tightrope with an accurate, precise recalculation of filiation that need not be bound by origins or teleological futurity. On his *fil*, we relate only to the transversal, trans-parent, an 'over-going' and never a vertical descent.

No Strings Attached: The Line as *lien*

Having met Genet in the 1970s, Dominique Eddé contests the utility of comparing Nietzsche to Genet since she finds their political philosophies wildly opposed. Where Nietzsche's nihilism seeks to destroy the current to invest in the new, Eddé argues that Genet 'n'a que faire de la transfiguration de l'homme' [has no interest in the transfiguration of the human].[65] To sublimate the individual would be to contribute to a new kind of future, which, however utopian, is anathema to Eddé's claim that Genet's seeks absolute withdrawal from humanity:

> Sa mission 'positive' c'est d'être, en soi, moyen et fin confondus, un modèle de cassure avec l'ordre des hommes [...] contrairement à l'Allemand, il est coupé de toute filiation, de toute généalogie. Et cependant, durant l'enfance, l'église restera non seulement son plus fertile creuset de métaphores, mais aussi, avec la figure de la trinité, le plus puissant lieu de transfert de sa naissance orpheline.[66]

> [His 'positive' mission is to be, in and of himself, means and ends confused, a model of rupture from the social order [...] unlike the German, he is cut off from all filiation, all genealogy. And yet, throughout childhood, the Church would become not only the most fertile source of metaphor, but along with the Trinity, the most powerful site of transference for his orphan birth.]

Nietzsche's desire to reinvent the human derives from his crusade against a Lutheran upbringing whose Christian morality, he argued, kept the individual down rather than allowing them to attain their highest potential. By contrast, Genet's original rupture from the family forms the basis for a wider disinterest in human improvement or generational progress, Eddé arguing that he is fixated more on the myth of impossible filiation that is hallowed by the Christian model of the Trinity. That triangular relation between father and son, infinite and finite, mediated by the Holy Spirit, offers a powerful fiction that is nonetheless divorced from actual familial kinship, allowing Genet to fetishise the fantasy of filiation without being trapped by heterosexual futurity. In an interview in 1983, he even professes to being 'tout à fait détaché de tout sentiment familial' [completely detached from all family feeling] (*ED*, pp. 298; 258), which Kadji Amin analyses as being 'more wish than fact' since Genet is so prone to replicating the filial relation that 'reproduce[s] his place on its eroticised margins'.[67] For Sartre, this imitation means Genet lacks what he deems the 'virile', forward-marching energy capable of reproducing a new social landscape. Unlike Rimbaud or Nietzsche's humanist energy, which maps out the lines of social change ('*trace* les lignes et elles sont par le mouvement qui les trace'), Sartre critiques the passivity of Genet's work, which:

> Le jette au milieu d'un monde tout fait où les lignes et les courbes luttent contre la dispersion et l'émiettement à l'infini [...] incapable de se *tailler* une place dans l'univers, il *imagine* pour se persuader qu'il a créé le monde qui l'exclut.

> [Thrusts him into a ready-made world in which the lines and curves struggle against the dispersion and splintering *ad infinitum* [...] incapable of *carving out* a place for himself in the universe, he imagines in order to convince himself that he has created the world which excludes him.] (*SG*, pp. 520; 468)

Sartre deploys the language of geometry here in an entirely embodied manner: to re-imagine the socio-political map is virile, masculine; whereas Genet's apparent femininity subjugates him to the world as is. Where the figure of the line promises pioneering change — able to redefine the borders that are fixed and entrenched by systems of oppression — Sartre argues that Genet is simply compliant to the ready-made geometries that promote social cohesion rather than the disruption Nietzsche renders productive. The argument is not only misogynistic, but it suggests that Genet's exclusion from the world is part of his own failure to reshape it. Incapable of occupying the role of creator that Sartre endows upon the philosopher, Genet the poet simply disconnects. His imagination thus becomes a form of self-delusion in Sartre's interpretation, as though the geometric contours we find throughout his poetic imaginary keep the world together in order to keep himself out of it. If he were to explode it as Nietzsche might hope, then he becomes part of the debris, and thus still attached to a world he radically rejects.

Here, geometry is yoked only to cartographies of domination and re-organisation, Sartre offering a far too brittle exposition of the ways in which the line might be able to construct a more supple form of relation in Genet's writing. I argue against criticisms that position Genet as detached, anti-communal or anti-connective, and develop his poetics of the *fil* as an insistent ligature in his writing.[68] Genet's strings, cords, filature, construct a more flexible kinship than the linear topographies to which Sartre claims he is beholden. By drawing on Derrida's analysis of the silkworm and the verdict in 'Un ver à soie', and Nancy's ontology of being as tying, I consider how the *fil* materialises as an elastic connection that ties Genet to a span of time in his childhood that produces the very verdict to which he holds himself captive. Genet endlessly reties the threads of a filiation that might recapture a time once frayed, and recasts it as a renewed bond.

In a letter from 1944, Genet compares the *fil* to his writing instrument: 'me donner du papier, c'est comme si dans la rue une boutique de luthier s'ouvrait pour donner à un musicien pauvre qui joue, un jeu de cordes de violon' [giving me a piece of paper is like a luthier's shop opening just to give a poor musician a set of violin strings] (*LMOB*, p. 40). It is as though the base material, the parchment of his text, were as elemental as those strings whose reverberations give function and sound to the vessel that supports them. Genet's simile lends proximity to paper and strings as the constitutive forms that enable composition. Without these, his work has no form; as though the 'cordes de violon' form the lines on the page where he sets his writing, these strings give voice to the text. This symbolic reliance on violin strings crops up as similarly constitutive in *Notre-Dame-des-Fleurs* when Genet recounts a childhood memory:

> Culafroy entrait dans sa chambre [...] il arrache un violon grisâtre qu'il a confectionné lui-même [...] avec la couverture cartonnée de l'album d'images, avec le morceau du manche d'un balai et quatre fils blancs: les cordes. C'était un violon plat et gris, un violon à deux dimensions, avec seulement la table d'harmonie et le manche ou filaient quatre fils blancs, géométriques, rigoureux sur l'extravagance, un spectre de violon. [...]. Culafroy ne savait, par ses formes torturées, qu'un violon inquiétait sa sensible mère et qu'il s'en promenait dans ses rêves en compagnie de chats souples, dans des coins de murs, sous des balcons où des filous se partagent le butin de la nuit, ou d'autres apaches s'enroulent autour d'un bec de gaz, dans des escaliers qui grincent comme des violons qu'on écorche vifs. Ernestine pleura de rage de ne pouvoir tuer son fils [...] Culafroy fabriqua l'instrument, mais, devant Ernestine, jamais plus il ne voulut dire le mot commençant par viol.

> [Culafroy would enter his room [...] he pulls out a grayish violin which he himself has made [...] with the cardboard binding of the picture album, the piece of broom handle and four white threads, the strings. It was a flat gray violin, a two-dimensional violin, with only the soundboard and the neck, and four white strings, geometric and rigorous, spanning the extravagance, a phantom violin [...]. Culafroy did not know that a violin, because of its tortured lines, could upset his sensitive mother, and that violins moved about in her dreams in the company of lithe cats, at corners of walls, under balconies where thieves divide the night's loot, where other toughs slouch around a lamppost, on stairways that squeak like violins being skinned alive. Ernestine wept with rage at being unable to kill her son [...] Culafroy made the instrument, but in front of Ernestine never again would he utter the word that begins with the same syllable as violate.] (*NDF*, pp. 75–76; 178)

Culafroy's make-shift violin — constructed in two-dimensions and thus devoid of any actual musical function — is but a frame for the strings stretched across it. As a pure image, it harks back to the filial spectres we explored in *Le Funambule*, Genet eager to make the 'fils blancs' present, to foreground them as more than the constitutive matter of the instrument but as cords which are attached, fretted, slotted in. The emphasis here is on the pervasive presence of geometric lines that, unlike their shell, must be visible at all costs; their dysfunctional purpose being the simulation of vibrations that agitate his mother, the tortured lines of these 'fils' only present to quite literally wind her up. The 'fil' metamorphoses throughout the scene, such that Ernestine's desire to kill her 'fils' slips into the strings that aggravate her; those 'filous' who partition their spoils remind her of the 'fil' that tears apart her nerves; the 'fils blancs' recall the idiom *cousu de fil blanc*, or predictable, as though Genet is bound not only to fabricate the 'fil', but to render it a torturous line. In this double fabrication, the 'fil' is poised at a symbolic junction between a linear attachment that the 'fils' is desperate to forge, and a violation that the mother attributes to the etymological form of this 'viol', these strings forcing a relation upon her that she is desperate to sever. Culafroy's childhood memory refracts Genet's own: the linear bond engineered by the son is experienced by the mother as a violation; the 'fil' tied to an ersatz filiation that Genet's text cobbles together.

Genet reinstates the 'fils perdu(s)', the lost threads or sons, in a manner that recalls Derrida's analysis of filiation in 'Un ver à soie'. Turning from one childhood memory to another, Derrida recounts how:

> Dans les quatre coins d'une boite à chaussures, donc, on m'y avait initié, j'hébergeais et nourrissais des vers à soie [...] cette petite vie silencieuse et finie ne faisait rien d'autre, là-bas, si près, sous mes yeux mais à une distance infinie, rien d'autre que cela: se préparer soi-même à se cacher soi-même, aimer à se cacher en vue de se produire au dehors et de s'y perdre, cracher cela même dont le corps reprenait possession pour l'habiter en s'y enveloppant de nuit blanche [...] pour rester auprès de soi, l'être qu'il avait été en vue de se réengendrer soi-même dans la filature de ses fils ou de ses filles — au-delà de toute différence sexuelle ou plutôt de toute dualité des sexes et même de tout accouplement.

> [In the four corners of a shoebox, then, I'd been shown how, I kept and fed silkworms [...] this little silent finite life was doing nothing other, over there, so close, right next to me but at an infinite distance, nothing other than this: preparing itself to hide itself, liking to hide itself with a view to coming out and losing itself spitting out the very thing the body took possession of again to inhabit it, wrapping itself in white night [...] with a view to re-engendering itself in the spinning of its filiation, sons or daughters-beyond any sexual difference or rather any duality of the sexes, and even beyond any coupling.][69]

Derrida's nostalgia for these silkworms, hatched in his youth and whose 'fils' are emblematic of that childhood, centres on his fascination for their natural, internal production of threads which have long been appropriated by philosophical discourses of the 'veil' or 'shroud'. This is a text which grapples with what Geoffrey Bennington calls 'veils, veiling, and unveiling [...] the whole tired Western way with truth and untruth [...] the striptease of truth called philosophy'.[70] Filature becomes a process devoid of any exteriority, detached from the veil that has been appropriated by discourses of revelation and unveiling: it is instead a natural process that belongs solely to the silkworm that spins them. Secreting this fine thread, Derrida describes the foreign familiarity of the silkworm which gives birth to a *fil* at the same time as it loses itself within this continuous filament, unable to cut itself off from it. These fibres cloud the distinction between product and producer, self and other, since both are intertwined in a paradoxically singular filiation. Generated in and by the silkworm, these *fils* are both sons *and* threads, sons *as* threads, filaments which are never wholly part of or different from the self that produces them.

This filature recalls a Kristevan abjection in which 'je *m*'expulse, je *me* crache, je *m*'abjecte dans le même mouvement par lequel je prétends *me* poser' [I expel myself, I spit myself out, I abject myself within the same motion through which 'I' claim to establish myself].[71] But where Kristeva's subject is defined in opposition to that which is jettisoned, Derrida's silkworm is established within both the process of expulsion and the product of secretion. Derrida's sites of filature are multiple and defiantly present, the silkworm primed to embody its own secretions in a homophonic play between *cacher/cracher* such that *le fil* which is discharged forms the shelter of the self, an abjection which re-engenders the self by never being entirely disconnected from it. This *filature* generates a filiation that is never wholly other, but whose externalisation is necessary to generate a sense of self: 'il projetait au dehors ce qui procédait de lui et restait au fond, au fond *de lui*: hors de soi en soi et près de soi' [it projected outside what proceeded from it and remained at bottom at the bottom of it: outside itself in itself and near itself]; this *fil* both an inherent part of the self and contiguous to it, the silkworm at work to expel that *soie* [silk] which constitutes its own *soi* [self].[72] The silkworm is an avatar of a filiation which is thus wrapped up in itself, this *fil de soie* a cipher for the *fil* of the self, as a self, such that the filature that spins this thread also externalises a self which gives birth to itself, the line of the *fil* providing the symbolic conduit through which the *soi(e)* is engendered, the self in both signifier and signified.

The line of the *fil* thus promulgates a complex fabric of attachment in Derrida's 'Un ver à soie'. It entwines the time of childhood with a filiation of the self unto itself, transforming the linear signifier of the *fils* into an abject son and self. Culafroy's alliance to the geometric violin strings evinces a similarly self-referential filature: the urgency to define himself by these *fils*, to defiantly position them as the lines that violate the mother and thus break the normative cord that binds her to the son, testifies to a desire to replace the bond of lineage with a new filiation that is tied to the self alone. Yet, Genet's filature poses a problematic politics of connection. This silk-thread, or *fil(s) de soi(e)* whose play of signifiers Derrida literalises in 1998, is actively dramatised by Genet a decade previously in *Un captif amoureux*:

> '*Étrange séparation*', plutôt réprobation glacée m'interdisant l'approche des autres. Au moins cinq ans loin d'eux, comme si, femme musulmane enveloppée d'une mousseline de granit le regard nu, plus vif que profond, je cherchais dans le regard des autres le mince fil de soie qui devait nous relier tous, indiquant une continuité de l'être, repérable par deux regards abandonnés l'un dans l'autre mais sans désir.

> [A 'strange separation', or rather a cold reprobation, kept me from approaching other people. After at least five years away from them, like a Muslim woman in a veil of stone, with a naked gaze more lively than profound, I sought in other people's eyes the thin silk thread that ought to link us all, the sign of a continuity of being that two gazes intertwining without desire should be able to detect.] (*CA*, pp. 424; 361).

The personal becomes the ethical here, as Genet moves away from the solitude of his early works towards a renewed hope of solidarity inspired by the Palestinians. Seemingly, the solace Genet finds with the fedayeen helps build a more generalised utopian communitarianism. His metaphor of the 'fil de soie' strives to materialise a continuum that *ought* to exist between people, that ought to enable the self to be established through its relation to the other, just as one might expect in the Lacanian Imaginary where the gaze of the other engages me in a relation, and both affirms and alienates me in the process. For Laroche, this scene allows Genet to break down the punitive dialectics that once governed his political interventions and seek a renewed alliance with the other, metamorphosing the 'chaînes de la prison — acier,

matière fécale, courant d'air — en ce mince fil de soie de l'échange des regards'
[the prison chains — iron, fecal matter, air currents — into the thin silk thread of
exchanged glances].[73] Yet, from the bondage of imprisonment comes a much more
fragile bond that Genet lends its own kind of weight. Although the time-frame is
slightly ambiguous, the implication is that when Genet travelled around Japan, the
United States and the Middle East from 1967–72, he finds himself newly awakened
to the possibility of a shared gaze that he cannot return; the thin silk thread actually
creating a veil that shuts Genet off. He adopts the posture of a Muslim woman
behind a hijab, the fabric that should be made of gossamer chiffon, experienced by
him as stone, the 'mousseline de granit' operating like a sort of iron curtain that puts
a barrier up to ward off any totalising, reciprocal gaze. Moreover, the idealised fine
silk thread he seeks problematises the notion of alliance by troubling the distinction
of the subjects that are tied, his *fil de soi(e)* cast as a continuous line that abandons
the self into the other.

Genet's *fil* thus constitutes the self *by relation* in a manner that resembles Jean-Luc
Nancy's ontology of the *lien*, which he defines in *Le Sens du monde* as a:

> Politique des nœuds, des nouages singuliers, de chaque un en tant que nouage,
> en tant que relais et relance [...] le lien: ce qui ne comporte ni intériorité ni
> extériorité, mais qui, dans le nouage, fait sans cesse passer le dedans dehors,
> l'un à l'autre ou par l'autre, le sens dessus dessous, revenant sans fin sur soi sans
> revenir à soi.

> [Politics of knots, of singular knottings, of each *one* as a knotting, as a relay and
> reprojection of knotting [...] the link: what is neither interiority nor exteriority
> but which, in being tied, ceaselessly makes each into the other, the outside
> inside, turning back on itself without returning *to* itself.][74]

Nancy's politics of the tie conceives of the subject as constitutively tied to other
subjects, gleaning our own singularity from the fact that it can *untie* itself from
those around it. The tie is necessarily a figure that both joins and separates, it is the
emblem of such coexistence, this 'nouage' echoing Derrida's filature insofar as both
foreground the subject's need to turn to the tie or thread in order to glean its sense
of self. Like Derrida's *fil*, Nancy's tie understands the process of self-production as
inherently relational, but where Derrida's silkworm relates only to itself, a thread
of the self, we might argue that Nancy explains this thread of selfhood as a knot
with other selves, a loop which constitutes that self as such by intertwining it
with others in a motion that is forward not inward. This ontological network of
each individual, 'chacun', or '*chaque un* en tant que nouage' is qualified in his later
Être singulier pluriel as intrinsic to any 'singul*ier*': the individual necessarily a unity
that unites *with* something, the 'singuli ne se dit en latin qu'au pluriel, parce qu'il
désigne l "un" du "un par un. Le singulier, c'est d'emblée chaque un et donc aussi
chacun avec et entre tous les autres' [In Latin, the term *singuli* already says the
plural, because it designates the 'one' as belonging to 'one by one'. The singular is
primarily *each* one and therefore, also *with* and *among* all the others].[75] Each self, each
singular individual, must belong to a wider community from which it is taken to
be given its quantitative *chacun*, it pertains to a part, it establishes a gap from which
relation, or linkage, is made possible.

Such is Genet's own logic in this final text, where a sense of self starts to emerge from behind the muslin cloth whose *fils* create those lines of connection. He muses:

> Pendant cinq ans j'avais habité une invisible guérite d'où l'on peut parler et voir n'importe qui et moi-même ou n'importe quoi étant un fragment détaché du reste du monde [...]. Parfaitement noyé dans mon espèce et mon règne, mon existence individuelle avait de moins en moins de surface ni de volume. Pourtant, depuis quelque temps, je me reconnaissais un. Moi et non n'importe qui ou n'importe quoi. Autour de moi le monde commençait à pulluler d'individus — j'allais écrire d'invendus — séparés, ou dépareillés, séparés, donc capables d'entrer en relation.

> [For five years I'd lived in a sort of invisible sentry box from which I could see and speak to everyone while I myself was a fragment broken off from the rest of the world [...]. I was completely swamped in the animal kingdom and the human race, and my own individual existence possessed less and less surface and volume. Yet for some time I'd realized I had one. I was me, not just anyone or anything. Around me the world began to swarm with individuals, single or separate, and, if separate, capable of entering into relationships.] (*CA*, pp. 425; 361–62)

Genet's metaphors appear contradictory: he claims both to be sheltered from the world of relation — a detached fragment that echoes the singular seriality we explored in the point — and to be drowned out by a multitudinous ecology. When put together, however, we see that Genet is materialising the self in both instances as geometric space, whose area becomes increasingly hard to measure as he notices the volume and surface of his individuality give way to relation. And while there is an astonishing egalitarianism here, as Genet positions himself as one of many biological categories in the taxonomic rank from 'espèce' to 'règne', there is also the undertone that relation operates like an infectious mass that multiplies singular selves so that they might connect. The process of relating thus becomes one of decoupling: like a cell, individuals are 'dépareillés', isolated or separated, but also, as its homophone suggests, rendered incomplete, as though the individual becomes contingent on the other in order to be affirmed. Is there some cynicism to Genet's slippage between 'individus' and 'invendus' here? His paranomasia reimagines the individual as a remainder, and specifically a textual one as 'invendus' often refers to unsold books, ensuring that a part of the individual is always left over from any relation it enters into. The geometry Genet uses to shape his singularity, the area he defines as 'un' and 'moi', thus enables him to establish the terrain of a selfhood made possible because of a renewed contact with the other, while also facilitating a strange separation from them that helps him cling to that differentiated singularity; the rhetorical shape of the sentence with its double 'séparés' keeping him forever 'dépareillé', isolated, in the middle of any relational continuum. He thus corroborates Nancy's ontology of the tie in which the individual is constituted as such because of the contact granted through relation: 'un sujet unique ne pourrait même pas *se* designer et *se* rapporter à soi comme sujet' [no single subject could even designate itself and relate itself to itself as subject].[76] But he also invokes the post-structuralist image of the remainder to position his subjectivity as a textual trace that cannot be tied down.

Genet orchestrates his own ontology of the tie in this scene, comparing his inability to integrate into the world of subjects and objects to the equivalence between a Pyramid, 'un soulier, un lacet de soulier [qui] n'indiquaient rien de différent sauf qu'une habitude prise dans l'enfance m'empêchait encore de chausser les Pyramides ou le désert' [a shoe lace was no different, either, except that a habit acquired in childhood prevented me from putting the Pyramids or the desert on my feet] (*CA*, pp. 424; 362). Monuments collapse into the humble shoelace as Genet distills his world vision into that modest symbol of a tie, which, even more than the *fil de soie*, is not just a knot, but the acquired skill learned in all childhoods and a nostalgic tie back to that time. Bound to the habits learned in childhood, we see Genet forge a selfhood in the 1980s out of the poetic tie that tethers him back to an early memory of being untied; his 'politique des nœuds' not as interpersonal, then, but as temporal, Genet connected to time where he is disconnected. The volume and surface of his own individuality are not just linked to geometric space, then, but as time. In an interview in *L'Ennemi déclaré* from 1981, he confirms that:

> Une chose est sacrée pour moi — j'emploie bien le mot sacré — sacré, c'est le temps. L'espace ne compte pas. Un espace peut se réduire ou s'augmenter énormément, ça n'a pas beaucoup d'importance. Mais le temps j'ai eu l'impression, et je l'ai encore qu'un certain temps de vie à ma naissance m'était donné [...]. Il a fallu que je travaille ce temps. Il ne fallait pas que je le laisse en jachère [...]. J'ai eu comme préoccupation de transformer ce temps en volume, en plusieurs volumes.

> [One thing is sacred for me — and I knowingly use the word sacred — time is sacred. Space doesn't matter. A space can be reduced or enlarged enormously, it has little importance. But time — I have had the impression, and still do, that a certain amount of time was given to me at birth [...] it has been imperative for me to work this time. I could not leave it fallow, so to speak [...] I have been preoccupied with transforming this time into a volume, several volumes.] (*ED*, pp. 221; 191)

Being tied to time creates the constitutive matter of Genet's writing. Neither successive nor progressive, Genet sacralises time as the temporal totem around which his writing is organised. Time is given body not within his corpus but *as* the corpus: he volumises it, recasting it in material terms as the embodied fabric onto and into which he weaves his text. Time is often obfuscated by Genet's own emphasis on spatial modalities, and yet despite the opposition he seems to draw here between time and space, time is still figured *as* space. The terms which he eschews as spatially capricious, 'un espace peut se réduire ou s'augmenter', are previously described as temporally sovereign when in *Le Bagne* he describes how 'le temps est élastique. Il s'étire, il s'allonge, il rétrécit' [time is elastic. It stretches out and contracts] (*B*, p. 94). Time is figured as a ductile line, an elastic band or thread to exploit the idiom *fil du temps*, a spatial form which stretches, elongates, shrinks, such that any measurement is evacuated and all temporal markers lose meaning. As Hanrahan has astutely noted, Genet is re-working time as space, trans-*forming* it as though it were tangible: a subject that 'matters to him *as matter*'.[77] These temporal volumes (which are also spatial) are not only the matter of his writing, but the matter of his own volume, this time governs his own self as much as it does his texts. Where he drowns in the outside world, his temporal volumes provide a lifeline, a link that saves the self by anchoring it to time as a form that can be re-fashioned *without* becoming a stable or fixed entity.

Genet's 'certain temps de vie à ma naissance [qui] m'était donné' could be read as a signifying a certain amount of time having been allotted to him at birth, a generalised lifespan. But time is so monumentalised in his writing, its threads so ubiquitous, that I read this time 'à ma naissance' as a seminal moment cast at birth to which his writing constantly returns. The time that is woven into his many tomes is not a life-time, but rather a moment in that life, the moment he becomes a *fils* establishing a time of filiation that his texts endlessly re-work and re-figure. Genet describes having to work this sacred time as the constitutive matter of his texts, the 'jachère' needing to be ploughed, farmed, grafted, fostered and worked *into* his writing as a means of not only making present that time at birth, but mimetically re-gifting it back to his texts, the time in which he becomes a *fils* rethreaded through the filial signifiers in his texts which eulogise a filiation otherwise absent. The *fil* reconnects Genet to childhood by making present what he claims in *Un captif amoureux* to in fact be absent:

> Ma vie s'inscrivait en creux, ce creux devint aussi terrible qu'un gouffre. Le travail qu'on nomme damasquinage consiste à creuser à l'acide une plaque d'acier de dessins en creux où doivent s'incruster des fils d'or. En moi les fils d'or manquaient. Mon abandon à l'Assistance Publique fut une naissance certainement différente des autres naissances mais pas plus effrayante qu'elles.

> [When I saw that my life was a sort of intaglio or relief in reverse, its hollows became as terrible as abysses. In the process known as demascening the patterns are engraved on a steel plate and inlaid with gold. In me there is no gold. Being abandoned and left to be brought up as an orphan was a birth that was different from but not any worse than most.] (*CA*, pp. 205; 171–72)

Just as he does not want the time at his birth to be left 'en jachère', as fallow, neither does he want to leave his life as a 'creux', a hollow, his texts creating a filial imprint that is in fact missing. As Edmund White remarks, he compares the shapes of his own life to the process of metal-working, and indulges in the signifier of the *fil* to tie this absence to an absent filiation: these *fils d'or* as golden threads that are homophonic with Genet the *fils d'or*, the absent 'golden boy'.[78] As a *fil(s)*, Genet embodies the very ligature that binds him to the time of his becoming a son, and for Nathalie Fredette, it is this filial moment that marks Genet's whole corpus: 'l'œuvre ne cessera jamais d'être un texte qui s'enchaîne, tissu ou trame, d'où il s'ensuit que l'histoire du "fils" se lit dans la trame secrète du fil (autre filiation)' [his work will never cease to be a text that is linked together, its fabric or weft showing that the story of the 'son' is to be read through the secret weft of thread (other filiation)].[79] Affirming the materiality of Genet's writing, Fredette simultaneously yokes the threads of its fabric not only to time in general — to any *fil du temps* — but to the specific temporality of filiation. Genet's timeless temporal space that we have explored in his prisons, is in his second novel, *Miracle de la rose*, directly linked to the time of childhood:

Il me suffit d'évoquer mes amours d'enfant pour que je redescende au fond du temps dans ses plus ténébreuses demeures, dans une région solitaire, où je ne retrouve plus que la Colonie, formidable et seule. Elle me tire à elle de tous ses membres musclés, avec ce geste des matelots qui lèvent de l'eau un filin, une main se portant devant l'autre au fur et à mesure que la corde s'entasse sur le pont et je retrouve auprès du Divers regagné, une enfance nauséeuse et magnifiée par l'horreur, que je n'eusse jamais voulu quitter.

[I need only evoke my childhood loves to redescend to the depths of time, in its darkest dwellings, in a lonely region, where I find only the Colony, formidable and alone. She draws me to her with all her sinewy limbs, with the gesture of sailors who pull a rope out of the water, placing one hand in front of the other while the rope piles up on deck, and I regress, with the Divers of old at my side, to a nauseating childhood which is magnified by horror and which I would never want to leave.] (*MR*, pp. 313; 110)

Metamorphosed into a 'filin', a life-line, Genet's thread pulls him into the depths of his childhood. Mired in the thick sludge of nostalgia, Genet figures his *fil* as a sailor's rope, sullied with the dregs and residue collected not when being dragged out of the water, but in being dragged in by his childhood memory: *le fil* paranomastically tied to Genet as a *fils* looking to return to this 'enfance nauséeuse [...] que je n'eusse jamais voulu quitter'. Genet's life-line does not provide a route out but a way in, the 'filin' quite literally a line of his life which pulls him in to this temporal prison as magnetic as it is emetic.

Time captures Genet, a labyrinthine space from which he holds no hope of escape, but into which he throws himself: Ariadne in the labyrinth as he imagines himself in *Notre-Dame-des-Fleurs*. Like Ariadne, Genet holds the thread of his own salvation and consequently becomes the guardian of his own prison, revelling in the impossibility of being able to 'tirer le fil du temps qui l'a tissé [l'aveu] et faire qu'il se dévide et se détruise. Fuir? Quelle idée! Le labyrinthe est plus tortueux que les considérants des juges' [to unravel the thread of time that wove [the confession], and to make it unwind and destroy itself. Flee? What an idea! The labyrinth is more tortuous than the summing-up of judges] (*NDF*, pp. 60; 169). For Deleuze, who reads Kant's thinking on time in *Critique et clinique*, time is the very embodiment of this labyrinth and, for him, Kant allows traditional modes of conceiving time to be reversed. Deleuze explains how Kant recasts time from measuring the interval between movements to becoming a line that governs movement:

Le temps devient donc unilinéaire et rectiligne, non plus du tout au sens où il mesurerait un mouvement dérivé, mais en lui-même et par lui-même, en tant qu'il impose à tout mouvement possible la succession de ses déterminations [...]. Ordre du temps vide. Le labyrinthe a changé d'allure: ce n'est plus un cercle ni une spirale, mais un fil, une pure ligne droite, d'autant plus mystérieuse qu'elle est simple, inexorable.

[Time becomes unilinear and rectilinear, no longer in the sense that it would measure a derived movement, but in and through itself, insofar as it imposes the succession of its determination on every possibility movement [...] the order of an empty time [...] the labyrinth takes on a new look — neither a circle nor a spiral, but a thread, all the more mysterious in that it is simple, inexorable, terrible.][80]

No longer is Ariadne's thread able to offer emancipation from the labyrinth; instead, the labyrinth becomes the thread itself. This inexorable *fil du temps*, indivisible and incessant, is given form and space as a void not subject to temporal measures, but a torturous timelessness that becomes the prison Genet is both fettered to and sheltered by. If, following Kant, time is a pure straight line that entangles us, then the hegemony of the line as a form of spatio-temporal entrapment in Genet's writing gathers additional weight. As a thread of time, the line governs Genet's whole corpus: the line of the *fil* unravelling itself as a labyrinthine filiation from which Genet finds no escape. Like Derrida's silkworm which is re-born through its production of threads that symbolically engender new births, new *fils* or *filles* ('se réengendrer soi-même dans la filature de ses fils ou de ses filles' [re-engendering itself in the spinning of its filiation, sons or daughters]), so too does Genet weave his text from a linear thread that not only re-asserts his position as a *fils*, but that re-engenders the filiation to which he is bound.[81]

   To conclude with the linear imagery of 'Un ver à soie', I conceive of Genet's linear time as a Derridean verdict: the ver-dict, or the worm (*ver*) word (*dict*), sewn as a truth or *ver*idiction into his texts. Derrida materially describes the verdict as a 'maillage imprenable', which he then temporally locates as 'ce verdict qui semble avoir été au commencement, comme votre premier mot' [this verdict that seems to have been at the beginning, like your first word].[82] Similarly, I read Genet's time as a material, if ungraspable, unfurling thread that leads to a verdict he creates at his birth. Genet's abandonment to the *assistance publique* marks a filial rupture that his texts all explore. Psychoanalysis may interpret this nostalgic replaying of childhood as constitutive of the writing process: Freud argues for example that 'imaginative creation, like daydreaming, is a continuation and substitute for the play of childhood'.[83] But for Genet writing this time, inscribing and unravelling its *fils*, or lines, its *fils* [son] is not a substitute, but a means of engendering or giving presence to a filiation that is marked by absence throughout Genet's texts. Whether Culafroy's violin strings, the silk thread that makes relation possible, the severance of lineage, or the laceration of lines or *liens* of kinship, Genet creates an interplay between the line and the tie, the *fil* and the *fils*, which illuminates a highly complex construction of a disconnected connectivity. Marty conceives of Genet's linear rupture as a product of his imprisonment, such that 'Genet dissolve les liens dans la mesure où la structure de son monde est métaphysiquement celle du prisonnier. Le monde des prisonniers, comme l'a montré Lacan dans un exemple célèbre, est une multiplicité qui ne peut pas faire lien' [Genet dissolves the links in the sense that the structure of his world is metaphysically the same as the prisoner's. As Lacan has demonstrated in a famous example, the space of the prisoner is one of a mulitiplicity that cannot forge a connection].[84] But this prison is the prison of time: a time to which he is perennially bound, the only link that connects or ties him down. Genet does not dissolve links, rather he is constantly forging connections through the ubiquitous *fil* that tethers him to a filiation materialised as the very fabric of his texts. He may ostensibly champion a 'no strings attached' approach to relation, extricated from Nancy's 'singu*lier*' which constitutes the subject by tying it to other subjects, but Genet's *fils* do bind him. The line connects him to filiation as a moment in time when he becomes relational. As a *fils*, Genet stitches himself into time and binds himself to a filial relation that forms the verdict, the worm-word or veridiction, of his texts.

Notes to Chapter 2

1. Henri Michaux, *Misérable miracle: la mescaline. Avec quarante-huit dessins et documents manuscrits originaux de l'auteur* (Paris: Gallimard, 1972), p. 127; *Darkness Moves: An Henri Michaux Anthology, 1927–1984*, trans. by David Ball (Berkeley: University of California Press, 1997), p. 204.
2. Guillaume Apollinaire, *Le Bestiaire ou cortège d'Orphée* (Paris: La Sirène, 1919), 'Orphée'.
3. Euclid, *The First Six Books of the Elements of Euclid*, p. xviii.
4. Todd May, *Gilles Deleuze: An Introduction* (Cambridge: Cambridge University Press, 2005), p. 171.
5. Mary Bryden, 'Deleuze and Anglo-American Literature: Water, Whales and Melville', in *An Introduction to the Philosophy of Gilles Deleuze*, ed. by Jean Khalfa (London & New York: Continuum, 2003), pp. 105–13 (p. 106).
6. Deleuze and Guattari, *Mille plateaux*, pp. 228; 186.
7. Voltaire, *Questions sur l'Encyclopédie* (Paris: Stoupe, 1792), p. 365. See Clare Siviter, 'Introduction', in *Tragedy and Nation in the Age of Napoleon* (Liverpool: Liverpool University Press, 2020), pp. 19–35, for an excellent precis of the creation of the French canon.
8. Deleuze and Guattari, *Mille plateaux*, pp. 15; 36.
9. Jean Genet, 'Lettre à Léonor Fini', in *Fragments... et autres textes* (Paris: Gallimard, 1990), pp. 45–58 (p. 52); 'Letter to Léonor Fini', in *Fragments of the Artwork*, trans. by Mendell, pp. 8–15 (p. 11).
10. Ibid., pp. 51; 10.
11. Jean Genet, *Le Bagne* (Paris: L'Arbelète, 1994), p. 110 (hereafter referenced in main text as *B*).
12. Deleuze and Guattari, *Mille plateaux*, pp. 208; 170.
13. Bill Martin, *Matrix and Line: Derrida and the Possibilities of Postmodern Social Theory* (Albany: State University of New York Press, 1992), p. 25.
14. Jacques Derrida, *De la grammatologie* (Paris: Minuit, 1976), p. 96; *Of Grammatology*, trans. by Gayatri Chakravorty Spivak (Baltimore, MD: John Hopkins University Press, 2016), p. 71.
15. Ibid., pp. 98; 73.
16. Ian Maclachlan, 'A Hinge', in *Reading Derrida's 'Of Grammatology'*, ed. by Sean Gaston and Ian Maclachlan (London: Continuum, 2011), pp. 74–75 (p. 75).
17. Derrida, *De la grammatologie*, pp. 96; 71.
18. Timothy Mathews, *The Art of Relation* (London: I. B. Tauris, 2013), p. 26.
19. Hadrien Laroche, *Le Dernier Genet: histoires des hommes infames* (Paris: Seuil, 2010), p. 310; *The Last Genet*, trans. by David Homel (Vancouver: Arsenal Pulp Press, 2010), p. 351.
20. Laroche argues that 'dans la terrible discontinuité de la lettre (hébraique), il voit encore l'effrayante continuité du people (élu): procréation, naissance, sperme' [In the terrifying discontinuity of the letter (Hebrew), he sees the frightful continuity of a people (Chosen): procreation, birth, ejaculate] (*Le Dernier Genet*, pp. 310; 351); while Hanrahan claims that 'if the Hebrew writing troubles Genet so deeply, it is because [of...] the impossibility of figuring time directly', 'Sculpting Time', p. 52. See also Bruno Chaouat, 'Out of Palestine', in *Israeli-Palestinian Conflict in the Francophone World*, ed. by Nathalie Debrauwere-Miller (London: Routledge, 2010), pp. 141–62: 'the anxiety triggered by this incised and incisive writing is a death anxiety [...] staring at the face of the dead letter as if by Medusa's head' (p. 150).
21. Hanrahan claims that the discontinuity 'of its letters casts into stark relief the chasm separating it from what it wants to designate' ('Sculpting Time', p. 53).
22. Mathews, *The Art of Relation*, p. 40.
23. Albert Dichy, *L'Échappée belle* (Paris: Gallimard, 2016), p. 113.
24. Deleuze and Guattari, *Mille plateaux*, pp. 224; 221.
25. Genet is not evoked in literary references in either *Mille plateaux* or in Deleuze's *Critique et clinique* (Paris: Minuit, 1993), with its own literary focus.

26. May, *Gilles Deleuze*, p. 137.

27. Deleuze and Parnet, *Dialogues*, pp. 152; 125.

28. Deleuze and Guattari, *Mille plateaux*, pp. 366; 329.

29. Emmanuel Levinas, *Totalité et infini* (The Hague: Martinus Nijhoff, 1961), p. 168.

30. Seán Hand, *Emmanuel Levinas* (London: Routledge, 2012), p. 42.

31. Deleuze and Guattari, *Mille plateaux*, pp. 244; 220–21.

32. Simon Critchley, *Ethics, Politics, and Subjectivity* (London: Verso, 1999), p. 53.

33. Cited in Pierre Constant, *Violon solo: la musique de Jean Genet* (Paris: L'Amandier, 2011), p. 261; and in White, *Genet*, p. 543.

34. Donne, 'A Valediction', l. 23.

35. White, *Genet*, p. 443.

36. Jean-Bernard Moraly: 'Les difficultés rencontrées pendant longtemps pour accéder à ce texte expliquent, sans doute, que jusqu'à present, aucune analyse n'en ait été tentée. Car il est essentiel' [The difficulties in accessing this text perhaps explain why no analysis has been attempted until now]: Jean-Bernard Moraly and others, *Les Nègres au port de la lune*, (Paris: La Différence, 1988), p. 219.

37. Jean Genet, *Lettres à Olga et Marc Barbezat* (Décines: L'Arbalète, 1988), pp. 156, 171 (hereafter referenced in main text as *LMOB*).

38. Rosi Braidotti, *Patterns of Dissonance* (Cambridge: Polity Press, 1991), p. 14.

39. Jean Genet, *Le Funambule*, in *OC*, v, 8–27 (p. 17); *The Tightrope Walker*, in *The Criminal Child*, trans. by Charlotte Mendell and Jeffrey Zuckerman (New York: New York Review of Books, 2020), pp. 98–117 (p. 106) (hereafter referenced in main text as *F*).

40. Juan Goytisolo, *Genet à Barcelone* (Paris: Fayard, 2009), p. 57.

41. Dominique Eddé, *Le Crime de Jean Genet* (Paris: Seuil, 2007), p. 86.

42. As Genet told Leïla Shahid in an interview on his relationship with the Palestinians, 'les espaces comptent beaucoup [...] je voudrais choisir les endroits où j'intercalerai du blanc entre un paragraphe et l'autre' [the spaces are really important [...] I want to choose places where I can insert a gap between one paragraph and another]: Jérôme Hankins, 'Entretien avec Leila Shahid', in *Genet à Chatila*, ed. by Jérôme Hankins (Arles: Solin, 1992), pp. 17–69 (p. 46).

43. See Albert Dichy and Pascal Fouché, *Jean Genet: essai de chronologie 1910–1944* (Paris: Gallimard, 2010), pp. 30, 26.

44. Cixous, *L'Entretien de la blessure*, pp. 10–11.

45. Ibid., p. 41. My own translation toys with the paranomasia of the self, the silkworm, and the veil in Derrida's essay 'Un ver à soie: points de vue piqués sur l'autre voile', in Hélène Cixous and Jacques Derrida, *Voiles* (Paris: Galilée, 1998), pp. 23–85.

46. Emmanuel Levinas, *Difficile liberté* (Paris: Albin Michel, 1976), p. 409. See also Simon Critchley, *The Ethics of Deconstruction* (Edinburgh: Edinburgh University Press, 1999), p. 5.

47. Johan Faeber, 'L'Homme qui marchait dans la douleur', in *Jean Genet*, ed. by Alazet and Dambre, pp. 91–102 (p. 94). For a different emphasis, Jean-Francois Lyotard explores Marcel Duchamp's artwork 'Les Grands Transparents' in terms that resonate with and yet diverge from Genet's, Lyotard exploring the idea of *trans*-formance as *per*formance by using the example of a thread in Duchamp's piece 'Stoppages Etalon' whose suspended objects Lyotard describes ' "[comme] si un fil droit horizontal d'un mètre de longueur tombe d'un mètre de hauteur sur un plan horizontal en se déformant à *son gré* et donne une figure nouvelle de l'unité de longueur". Ce qui est important dans cette opération n'est pas l'acte, la *performance* de M. Marcel Duchamp laissant tomber sa ficelle. Ce qui est important, c'est [...] la projection comme *transformance*' [if a straight horizontal thread one metre long falls from a height of one metre on to a horizontal plane, deforming itself *at its own free will* and gives a new figure of the unit of length'. What's important is not the act, the *performance* of Monsieur Marcel Duchamp dropping his thread. What is important is [...] projection as *transformance*]: *Les Transformateurs Duchamp* (Paris: Galilée, 1977), p. 36; 'Duchamp as a Transformer', in *Duchamp's TRANS/formers*, trans. by Ian McLeod (Leuven: Leuven University Press, 2010), pp. 47–221 (p. 71). Just as Genet propagates a transformation of the performer Abdallah along the *fil*, so too does he transform himself from a *fils* (of an unknown father) to an author (thus father of the text) interested in performing the transformative potential of the signifier '*fil*' into a *fils*. Such is the homonym this chapter explores.

48. Denis Provencher, *Queer Maghrebi French: Language, Temporalities, Transfiliations* (Liverpool: Liverpool University Press, 2017), p. 47.
49. Rosi Braidotti, *Transpositions: On Nomadic Ethics* (Cambridge: Polity Press, 2006), p. 99.
50. Teresa de Lauretis, 'The Essence of the Triangle, or, Taking the Risk of Essentialism Seriously: Feminist Theory in Italy, the U.S., and Britain', *Differences*, 1.6 (Summer 1989), 3–37.
51. Deleuze and Guattari, *Mille plateaux*, pp. 291; 263.
52. Ibid.
53. Tom Conley, 'From Image to Event: Reading Genet through Deleuze', in *Genet: In the Language of the Enemy* (= *Yale French Studies*, 91 (1997)), 49–63 (p. 50).
54. Ibid., p. 51.
55. Cixous, *L'Entretien de la blessure*, p. 25.
56. Moraly and others, *Les Nègres au port de la lune*, p. 207.
57. Louise Bourgeois, interview with Susi Block in 1976 in *The Art Journal*, cited in Louise Bourgeois, *Destruction of the Father/ Reconstruction of the Father: Writings and Interviews, 1923–1997*, ed. by Marie-Laure Bernadac and Hans-Ulrich Obrist (London: Violette, 1998), p. 102.
58. White: 'Almost nothing in this exalted text is *particularly* relevant to Abdallah as an individual except a brief passage near the beginning' (*Genet*, p. 510).
59. Victor Hugo, *Les Misérables*, 10 vols (Brussels: A. Lacroix, Verboeckhoven, 1862), VII, 20; *Les Misérables*, trans. by Julie Rose (London: Random House, 2008), p. 995.
60. Jacques Lacan, 'Le Stade du miroir comme formateur de la fonction du Je', in *Écrits I* (Paris: Seuil, 1949), pp. 93–100 (p. 91); 'The Mirror Stage as Formative of the Function as Revealed in Psychoanalytic Experience', in *Écrits*, trans. by Bruce Fink (New York: W. W. Norton, 2007), pp. 75–81 (p. 76).
61. Deleuze and Parnet, *Dialogues*, pp. 16; 9–10.
62. Jean Genet, *Lettres à Ibis* (Décines: L'Arbalète/ Gallimard, 2010), p. 32.
63. Elisabeth Stephens, 'Corporeographies: The Dancing Body in *'adame Miroir* and *Un chant d'amour*', in *Jean Genet: Performance and Politics*, ed. by Clare Finburgh, Carl Lavery and Maria Shevtsova (Basingstoke: Palgrave Macmillan, 2006), pp. 159–64 (p. 160).
64. Friedrich Nietzsche, *Thus Spake Zarathustra* (Kent: Digireads, 2007) p.17.
65. Eddé, *Le Crime de Jean Genet*, p. 79.
66. Ibid., p. 83.
67. Amin, *Disturbing Attachments*, p. 111. Amin notes that 'Genet took on the fatherly role as a benefactor to his last lover, El Katrani, who even referred to him as père, or "father" and "sponsoring," their heterosexual lives […]. Genet hovers ambiguously between marginalized queer guest, adopted child, and fatherly benefactor, although he never became part of any home' (pp. 111–12).
68. See Lavery, *The Politics of Jean Genet's Late Theatre*, who offers an excellent reading of Genet's commitment to communitarianism and inclusivity through a 'utopian view of revolution, characterised by anti-Statism, aesthetics and radical equality' (p. 3). Bersani (*Homos*), Jérôme Neutre (*Genet sur les routes du sud* (Paris: Fayard, 2002)), Éric Marty (*Bref séjour à Jerusalem* (Paris: Gallimard, 2003)), and Ivan Jablonka *Les Vérités inavouables de Jean Genet* (Paris: Seuil, 2004) have all criticised Genet's anti-relational project, either in relation to queer kinships or to his anti-West politics. I want to ally with Derrideans such as Mairéad Hanrahan, Patrice Bougon and Jean Michel Rabaté who argue that Genet's reluctance to occupy any identitarian position situates him more as a 'friendly enemy', ethically committed and constitutively anti-identitarian.
69. Derrida, 'Un ver à soie', pp. 83–84; 'A Silkworm of One's Own', in *Veils*, trans. by Geoffrey Bennington, (Stanford, CA: Stanford University Press, 2002), pp. 17–93 (pp. 89–90).
70. Geoffrey Bennington, *Not Half No End: Militantly Melancholic Essays of Jacques Derrida* (Paris & Edinburgh: Edinburgh University Press, 2010), p. 158.
71. Julia Kristeva, *Pouvoirs de l'horreur* (Paris: Seuil, 1980), p. 11; *Powers of Horror*, trans. by Leon S. Roudiez (New York: Columbia University Press, 1982), p. 3.
72. Derrida, 'Un ver à soie', pp. 83; 89.
73. Laroche, *Le Dernier Genet*, pp. 128; 127.
74. Jean-Luc Nancy, *Le Sens du monde* (Paris: Galilée, 1993), pp. 174–76; *The Sense of the World*, trans. by Jeffrey Librett (Minneapolis: University of Minnesota Press, 2008), p. 139.

75. Jean-Luc Nancy, *Être singulier pluriel* (Paris: Galilée, 1996), p. 52; *Being Singular Plural*, trans. by Robert D. Richardson and Anne E. O'Byrne (Stanford, CA: Stanford University Press, 2000), p. 32.
76. Ibid., pp. 60; 40.
77. Hanrahan, 'Sculpting Time', p. 43.
78. Edmund White, *The Burning Library: Essays* (London: Vintage, 1995), p. 303.
79. Nathalie Fredette, *Figures baroques de Jean Genet* (Montreal: XYZ; Saint-Denis: Presses universitaires de Vincennes, 2001), p. 76.
80. Deleuze, *Critique et clinique*, p. 41; *Essays Critical and Clinical*, trans. by Daniel W. Smith and Michael A. Greco (London: Verso, 1998), p. 28.
81. Derrida, 'Un ver à soie', pp. 83; 90.
82. Ibid., pp. 26; 23.
83. Sigmund Freud, 'Creative Writers and Day-dreaming', in *The Standard Edition of the Complete Psychological Works of Sigmund Freud*, ed. and trans. by James Strachey, 24 vols (London: Hogarth Press, 1953–74), IX (1959), 143–53 (p. 152).
84. Marty, *Genet*, p. 72. Marty refers here to Lacan's *Le Temps logique* written in 1945, which explores the analogy of intersubjectivity and uses the example of three prisoners who refuse any communication which each other when trying to fathom the colour of disks on their backs for which they require each other's help.

CHAPTER 3

❖

Vectors II — Obliques

Yet consider children's drawings: viewing them vertically usually conflicts with their inner meaning. — Walter Benjamin[1]

To be at an oblique angle to what coheres does matter, where the 'point' of this coherence unfolds as the gift of the straight line. — Sara Ahmed[2]

Disorientation: Child's Play?

Sara Ahmed opens her 2006 text on queer phenomenology by asking what it means to be orientated. How might we find our way in the world? How might we navigate the space we inhabit, and angle ourselves towards or away from different sites of residence? Since orientation is always embodied by the subject who moves, lives, looks, then, as generations of feminist writers have argued, the points at which we stand in our situated dwelling must be politicised.[3] Orientation is thus part of how we are socially conditioned: the postures we take in relation to objects, other individuals, even state actors, or how we read and view the media that helps to express our lived experiences, have all been directed according to the norms of straightness, going along the 'right' lines, or following the well-trodden paths of convention. As Walter Benjamin argued nearly a century prior in his writings on the technologies of human perception, these straight lines are what claim to make the world legible. He explains that 'the substance of the world' — the artistic and textual inscriptions that make it intelligible — is split across a vertical and horizontal axis: 'from the human point of view, the level of drawing is horizontal, that of painting, vertical'.[4] The vertical pole 'seems representational; it somehow contains the objects' whereas 'the cross-section seems symbolic; it contains signs'.[5] To understand what an image denotes, we have been taught to hold it directly in front of us for the meaning to be gleaned straightforwardly; whereas trying to interpret its inner meaning via symbols and semiotics, we know we should read laterally like a text.

Yet, Benjamin reminds us of the arbitrariness of such orientations. Engravings in stone were once read vertically, and thus our habits of reading, seeing and grasping the world of signification are historically determined and prone to change. In 1917, just as the Dadaists were navigating their own new pathways towards disruptive, disorientated kinds of signification, Benjamin demands we think critically about the orientations that fix the world of meaning. After all, it would be anathema to try and interpret children's drawings through that perpendicular schema; their unbridled depictions displacing conventional organisation to liberate a meaning that is free from codification.[6] The child's imaginary — a fertile source of inspiration to surrealists looking to unleash more instinctive forms of expression — rarely sees straight. Their fictions need not toe the line of the socially-conditioned adult; they are free to digress from the upright, the upstanding, and pursue detour as their unwitting starting-point.

In a posthumously published text on Palestine, Genet professes that 'les méandres de l'âme enfantine sont très difficiles à suivre' [the twists and turns of a child's mind are difficult to follow].[7] Nevertheless, he still associates the digressive energy of the child's perspective, its river-like derivations from teleology or straightforwardness, with a candour that cuts right to the heart of his own political posture.[8] He evokes a book of Palestinian children's drawings dealing with the Arab-Israeli Six-Day War, and tells us that:

> Si le feddai était déjà embelli par son courage, le soldat israélien était présenté comme un être terrifiant: lui et son pistolet mitrailleur devenaient une grande ombre cachant le soleil palestinien, obligeant les femmes et les enfants à la fuite et qui desséchait les récoltes.[9]

> [Where the feddayin was already perceived as courageous, the Israeli soldier was presented as terrifying: he and his machine gun became a great shadow obscuring the Palestinian sun, forcing women and children to flee and withering the crops.]

The symbolism here seems unequivocal: as the shadow eclipses the sun, transforming the embodied enemy into a faceless, ominous threat, Genet uses the child's imaginary to exaggerate the political dialectics of control and suppression. The literal slips easily into the symbolic as the machine gun becomes metonymic for an internalised experience of violence. But the meaning of the drawing is not representational, it is affective: it points to a legacy of domination written into the child's body and etched into the autonomous play of their imaginative drift. Only as the child's mind wanders, does Genet *see* the human cost of the brittle lines drawn by political orientations. Within what is ostensibly black and white — the dialectics of *ombre/soleil*, Israeli/Palestinian, bully/victim — Genet perceives a far more insidious truth about the brutality of how we are taught to position ourselves towards one another. These 'méandres de l'âme enfantine' dramatise how the straight lines of political factions, being on opposing sides of a border, or even 'taking up' space in contested geographies, give rise to a bodily experience of obliqueness. Those jettisoned from the horizontal lines of nationhood or the vertical lines of belonging, are forced 'à la fuite'. They become disorientated, out of place, in what Ahmed theorises as being 'oblique [...]. You can feel odd, even disturbed. Experiences of migration, or of becoming estranged from the contours of life at home, can take this form'.[10]

In this section, I explore how Genet harnesses the estrangement, deviance and drift of the diagonal as a way to imagine new political futures beyond what is fixed, given or normatively 'in line'. The generative, but errant play of obliquity helps Genet to move away from the horizontal and vertical vectors against which perception is governed and policed, helping him take flight from what is often lent social, epistemic and political visibility. Both textually and personally, he allies himself to the mobile geometry of the oblique as a means of straying away from 'upstanding' sites that jettison those who fall outside their borders. Genet's own restless wandering, his 'déambulation sans repos',[11] has received extensive critical commentary and continues to attract biographical interest.[12] There is an irresistible attraction to read his art through the prism of his personal legend, prompting a psychoanalytic urge to unearth the reasons why he may advocate on behalf of 'ceux qui cherchent un territoire bien que je refuse d'en avoir un' [those who seek a territory although I refuse to have one] (*ED*, pp. 282; 218). Rather than essentialise Genet's errancy as purely a feature of his personal narrative, I argue that Genet's proclivity for going astray offers more of a social rather than personal form of displacement. This analysis sits alongside Carl Lavery's reading of Genet's oblique form of committed art and Albert Dichy's claim that Genet's 1950s theatre offers 'une attaque non plus frontale, mais oblique. Léger déplacement: son œuvre théâtrale ne profère plus son drame personnel' [a (societal) attack which is no longer direct, but oblique. A slight displacement: his theatrical works no longer dramatise his own personal drama].[13] Indeed, Genet's 'détachement total à l'égard d'une région particulière' [total detachment with regard to any particular region] as he states in 'Cathédrale de Chartres — "Vue cavalière"' (1977) offers a performative practice of flow, of rootlessness, or obliquity that establishes new conditions of political visibility for the invisible, the dead, and the absent (*ED*, pp. 194; 66). Intersecting with queer directionalities (Foucault, Ahmed), the post-structuralist pursuit of equivocation (Derrida), and the mythologised figure of the 'drifter' adopted by the SI *dérive*, this section traverses the deliquescence and delinquency that haunts the etymology of the oblique in a bid to reckon with a revolutionary future.[14]

A Diagonal *Démarche*

It is perhaps unsurprising that it took Genet until his final interview, broadcast on BBC2 on 12 November 1985, to assume an asymmetrical posture towards society. He had spent a lifetime dodging political persuasions; yet, six months prior to his death, with no time left for slippage or equivocation, he embraces the oblique head on:

> Ma démarche par rapport à la société est oblique. Elle n'est pas directe. Elle n'est pas non plus parallèle, puisqu'elle le traverse, elle traverse le monde, elle le voit. Elle est oblique. Je l'ai vu en diagonale, le monde, et je le vois encore en diagonale, plus directement peut-être maintenant qu'il y a vingt-cinq ou trente ans. Le théâtre, en tout cas, le théâtre que je préfère, c'est justement celui qui saisit la société en diagonale.
>
> [My approach to society is oblique. It's not direct. It's also not parallel, since it intersects and crosses through society, it crosses through the world, it sees the world. It's oblique. I saw the world from an angle, and I still see it from an angle, though perhaps more directly now than twenty-five or thirty years ago.

The theater, in any case the theater that I prefer, is precisely the kind that grasps the world from an angle.] (*ED*, pp. 303; 262)

Genet's geometric vocabulary plots a spatial map of his relations to a world with which he is radically out of line. Imagining the world topographically, he invites us to envisage the linear pathways and contours along which conformity is channelled, while creating a series of anaphora — 'traverse', 'oblique', 'diagonale' — to emphasise his own deviation. The heteroclite properties of the oblique are first evident in its geometric form, which 's'écarte de la perpendiculaire (à une ligne donnée)' [distances itself from the perpendicular, from a given line], the prefix *ob-* deriving from the Latin for 'over', 'against', or 'inverse', such that the oblique always transgresses a fixed axis. Yet, being poised at a different angle to the horizon, being off-centre, nevertheless brings the oblique to bear on questions of social aberration.[15] Moreover, the oblique is constitutively in flux: in anatomical terms, it refers to the muscles that bend away from the core axis of the body, and thus galvanises movement (revolution?), departure (rebellion?) and traversal (resistance?) (*OED*). Genet is drawn to the deviant autonomy promised by this diagonal *démarche*, which both faces the world, traversing it in a frontal act of displacing that which is considered axiomatic, normative, upstanding; while also slipping away from it, standing apart from the value systems to which it does not belong. Because the oblique line drifts through the world at an angle, it provides a new vantage point from which to see the world, its indirection suggesting that any straightforward perception is actually blind. To perceive is also to grasp — vision leading to action — and indeed Genet presents an engaged practice of obliquity that sees the world precisely by seizing a meaning otherwise imperceptible. His slanted diagonal world-view grasps hold of a social order to which it is peripheral and undermines its normative stability, implying that being stuck within the world is to be limited to its ignorance. There is something unsettling about the oblique's dual perspective — its diagonal drift *through*, and its sloping inclination *away* — and it is even experienced as a physical precariousness in Merleau-Ponty's phenomenology, which states that every object has:

> Une distance optimale d'où il demande à être vu, une orientation sous laquelle il donne davantage de lui-même [...] l'orientation oblique de l'objet par rapport à moi n'est pas mesurée par l'angle qu'il forme avec le plan de mon visage, mais éprouvée comme un déséquilibre, comme une inégale répartition de ses influences sur moi.

> [An optimum distance from which it requires to be seen, a direction viewed from which it vouchsafes most of itself [...] an oblique position of the object in relation to me is not measured by the angle which it forms with the plane of my face, but felt as a lack of balance, as an unequal distribution of its influences upon me.][16]

Not only does Genet harness just such a sensation of imbalance in his theatre, and in his work at large, but he turns that feeling of unevenness, of asymmetry or displacement, into its very political foundation. Genet's oblique perspective of the world stands against the very idea that there is an 'optimal' way of seeing, and that the world and its objects can ever be formalised by one fixed position.

Genet's writing often positions himself at an angle to the object of his gaze. For example, when contemplating Rembrandt's self-portrait in the Fine Art Museum in Cologne, he advises that:

> Il faut se placer en diagonale, dans un angle. C'est de là que je l'ai regardé, mais la tête en bas — la mienne — retournée, si l'on veut. Le sang me venait à la tête, mais que ce visage qui riait était triste!
>
> [You have to take a diagonal view, from an angle. That is how I looked at it, but head down — my head — turned around, if you like. The blood rushed to my head, but how sad that laughing face!][17]

The command is instructive, not accusatory: Genet obliges us to join him in diverging from the straightforward ways of seeing that render us spectators of a world we consume rather than confront. Anathema to any passive reception of the world that the SI reproached as a capitalist 'society of spectacle' throughout the 1960s, in which being was degraded into having, and having into appearing, Genet actively seeks to disrupt the visual encounter to move beyond the illusions of direct perception.[18] François Bizet reads Genet's discomfort as a sign of his commitment to art's capacity to revitalise a new outlook, his 'corps à l'oblique, renversé, congestionné [...] acceptant les exigences de l'œuvre' [oblique, tilted body, flushed face [...] accepting the demands of the artwork].[19] The oblique thus operates physically on the body to impose a new interpretive framework, and as Genet moves back for a retrospective second-look at the portrait, at Rembrandt's own sense of self, we realise that it is not to bring the initially imperceptible into sight, but to expose the undecidability of perception itself. The two halves of the binary 'ria[nt]' and 'triste' are bound together in Genet's oblique gaze, troubling their division into opposites by revealing the simultaneous presence of both. The legibility of the artwork is thus derived from its conflicting dualisms, the role of this angular perspective to make such multiplicity visible. Challenging a dialectic model in which terms are defined by their opposite, Genet dissolves the veracity of one into the other — residing neither in the entirely true, nor the entirely false (as such ideas presuppose a sovereign judgement), but in an oblique intersection that becomes a metaphor of interpretation par excellence.

However, I want to gamble that Genet's oblique self-positioning in the museum extends beyond his own visual quirks or beyond even the quest for an alternative hermeneutic. It appeals to a wider political practice that looks to bend the reader's own ways of looking at the world. Genet's oblique approach to the artwork, or to the theatre, dramatises an active mode of seeing that is not directly made available. Any spectacle that grasps the world from an angle diverges from the commodification that Debord and the Situationists attributed to the culture of the spectacle, in which the individual is a 'prisonnière d'un univers aplati, borné par l'écran' [imprisoned in a flattened universe bounded by the *screen*].[20] Genet's transversal approach destabilises these suffocating, two-dimensional planes of endless spectacle in which life, relations and existence can be quantified, packaged into consumable goods and then mediated by an image through which we consume reality. Representation thus becomes totalising. Indeed, this is what Genet explores in his posthumously published play, *Elle*, when he toys with the layers of artifice that surround the Pope. As Genet's 'Pape' bemoans his fate as an iconic simulacrum ('dans tous les lieux du monde, et à chaque seconde, des millions de fidèles font de mon image une consummation invraisemblable' [in every place across the world, every single second, millions of followers consume my image in unbelievable quantities]), Genet dissolves the pretence of him as an image by replacing the figure of the Pope with a sugar cube (a parodic interpretation of the host) that melts away in the hot cups of coffee, milk, camomile tea in which his image is imbibed daily.[21]

Genet's tendency to saturate the image with excessive theatricalisation means that we are prevented from following the false hope that there will be any accessible reality beneath.[22] In substituting one symbol for another, he will not reify one image into any stable or real essence, and thus he obliquely incites the audience to engage with precisely that which *resists* visualisation. Indeed, Genet encourages us to recognise that the insincerity of the spectacle does not hide a fixed truth; rather, it reveals an absence that cannot come directly to the fore. Meaning is found in what cannot be made present in the realm of representation. This is at the heart of Genet's paradox in 'Ce qui est resté d'un Rembrandt':

> Seulement ces sortes de vérités, celles qui ne sont pas démontrables et même qui sont fausses, celles que l'on ne peut conduire sans absurdité jusqu'à leur extrémité sans aller à la négation d'elles et de soi, c'est celles-là qui doivent être exaltées par l'œuvre d'art [...] l'œuvre de Rembrandt n'a de sens — au moins pour moi — que si je sais que ce que je viens d'écrire était faux.

> [A work of art should exalt only those truths which are not demonstrable, and which are even 'false', those which we cannot carry to their ultimate conclusions without absurdity, without negating both them and ourself [...] Rembrandt's entire work has meaning — at least for me — only if I know that what I have just written is false.][23]

There is no transcendental meaning here that hides behind the artwork, no truth behind the fallacy of a representation that could be gleaned in the process of unveiling. Rather, Genet invites us to recognise that any representation should dramatise our very inability to understand the world we seek to depict. The falseness of the image provides an imaginative site of reinvention: a pointing beyond itself towards an absence or void that cannot be gleaned head-on because it slips from the grasp of codification. Structurally, the text iterates that equivocation through an oblique *mise-en-page* that demands we piece together a signification derived from parts whose content in fact refuses the totality this jigsaw might promise. Signification that can be demonstrated, verified, is only ever false for Genet who dissolves the integrity — both its wholeness and its credibility — of any claim that does not lead to its own negation. Genet undercuts his own assertions by venerating non-truth precisely because it is equivocal. The artwork has an impact because it is always two-faced, diagonal, deceiving the spectator by showing what it is not.

Genet's practice of obliqueness is thus more than an aesthetic destabilisation of the hegemony of the image; it is a politically charged endeavour that demands that we see past the inauthenticity of what is put before our eyes to locate meaning in the off-centre, the inaccessible, the unseen. His affirmation in *L'Ennemi déclaré* that 'toutes mes pièces [ont] une façon un peu oblique d'aborder la politique' [all of my plays [...] address politics obliquely] (*ED*, pp. 285; 242) suggest that there is more truth in his creative play with reality, in his oblique displacement of it, than in any direct confrontation. Carl Lavery develops the complexity of this position when he explains that:

> Genet's oblique notion of engagement is to see it as a form of theatre, which, grounded in historical actuality, points beyond itself to a place or void that is radically atemporal. Obliqueness, then, is a method for puncturing the realm of appearances; its objective is to reveal emptiness, and through that revelation to instigate a new political sequence.[24]

Genet's oblique deviation offers a much more radical interpretation of the drift that Debord and the Situationists develop in their resistance to an overly accessible culture of image and hypervisibility. This is precisely because it seeks to transform the spectacle into an exhibition of absence.

Genet exploits the diagonal drift as a means of staging that emptiness which cuts through the realm of appearances, as is demonstrated by an extra footnote that he adds to the L'Arbalète edition of *Les Bonnes* in 1968:

> Les metteurs en scène doivent s'appliquer à mettre au point une déambulation qui ne sera pas laissée au hasard: les bonnes et Madame se rendent d'un point à un autre de la scène, en dessinant une géométrie qui ait un sens. Je ne peux dire lequel, mais cette géométrie ne doit pas être voulue par de simples allées et venues. Elle s'inscrira comme, dit-on, dans le vol des oiseaux, s'inscrivent les présages, dans le vol des abeilles une activité de vie, dans la démarche de certains poètes une activité de mort.

> [The producers should make sure they develop a drift (*une déambulation*) that will not be left to chance: the Maids and Madame must move from one side of the stage to the other by mapping out a geometry that has a direction. I cannot say which way this will be, other than that this geometry must not be simply the product of casual comings and goings. It should be inscribed in what we call the flight of birds carrying an omen, in the flightpath of bees going about their life, in the approach of some poets who move towards death.][25]

Nineteen years after the first publication of *Les Bonnes*, Genet returns to his original text to ensure that 'une géométrie qui ait un sens' — a geometry with both direction and meaning — is fully evident on the stage of what had, by that point, become a frequently performed and infamous play. The characters must drift with direction: their 'déambulation' is configured as a gait that should amble indirectly across the stage, moving not from A to B, but plotting a trajectory that follows the same elusive path as an omen, a poet trying to grasp at expressing death, or the unmappable, unpredictable routes of bees darting around. None of these drifts can be reduced to one direction, nor containable image, nor clear teleology. Each stages a sensation of displacement, a moving towards an unknown that is beyond human control. The *déambulation* performs that feeling of being out of reach and dramatises a destabilising sense of not being able to predict what is ahead. Genet's drift has none of the liberty or the 'comportement ludique-constructif' [playful-constructive behaviour] that characterises the critically informed walking practice of Debord's *dérive*.[26] Instead, Genet inscribes an almost Jansenistic predestination that forces his characters to walk as though straying towards an undiscovered territory, perhaps what Ian Magedera has called the 'premonition of death in movement'.[27] However, if the movement of the Maids is only a dramatic ploy to presage the death that occurs at the end of the play, then the spectator becomes part of a goal-oriented plot that is controlled by a master director. I would argue that the sensation that Genet's *déambulation* hopes to elicit in the spectator is a journey into abstraction. The geometric lines of these pathways map a cartography of indirection that diverges from everything that can be quantified in the world of appearances; Genet's drift enables a becoming clandestine, or fugitive. Augurs trying to plot the course of birds carrying an omen; scientists doggedly trying to fathom the random directions of bees' flightpaths; poets all drawn towards a void that silences their voice: these are the heterogenous, oblique mysteries that Genet's *déambulation* seeks to dramatise.

We might note that this footnote is an oblique textual form: a paratext that strays away from the main narrative to illuminate what cannot be seen directly by it. Gérard Genette describes the paratext as a:

> *Seuil*, ou — mot de Borges à propos d'une préface — [...] un 'vestibule' qui offre à chacun la possibilité d'entrer, ou de rebrousser chemin. 'Zone indécise' entre le dedans et le dehors, elle-même sans limite rigoureuse, ni vers l'intérieur (le texte) ni vers l'extérieur (le discours du monde sur le texte).

> [Threshold, or — a word Borges uses apropos of a preface — a 'vestibule' that offers the world at large the possibility of either stepping inside or turning back. It is an 'undefined zone' between the inside and the outside, a zone without any hard and fast boundary on either the inward side (turned toward the text) or the outward side (turned toward the world's discourse about the text.][28]

Drifting between diegesis and exegesis, between what we might consider representation and explanation, the indeterminacy of the paratext serves to destabilise the certainty of the reader's understanding of the main text or the play staged in front of us. We turn to the paratext for answers, but, just like Genet's oblique vision of the world, this 'undefined zone' troubles the dominance of a definitive epistemology, a dominant text, an optimal direction of sight. It shows that our engagement with the world directly before us is never total, nor totalisable by a neat opposition between spectacle and reality, truth and fiction. Genet's additional footnote is not incorporated into his other paratext, 'Comment jouer *Les Bonnes*', which sits at the doorway to each edition of the play. Rather, he inserts it as a liminal text within the play, so that the reader's eyes drift away from the 'spectacle' towards the mechanics of its production. We thus perform the physical drift we will see acted out on stage, whilst experiencing our own movement towards uncertainty as we struggle to determine what can be directly gleaned from the text.

Genet's pursuit of indirection seeks precisely to confound any reader operating from within the totalising Enlightenment values of the French establishment, whose promises of universalism only expose the borders that cleave between in and out. Indeed, it is this wilful aesthetico-political practice of deviation that allows him to escape from society's insatiable desire to produce and reproduce the world as it is. The oblique geometry that allows the maids to err contributes to Genet's wider political poetics of the outlaw's drift away from the social, epistemic and political values of straightness, which, as Ahmed tells us, get 'attached to other values including decent, conventional, direct, and honest'.[29] The politics of Genet's *démarche oblique* thus play out at the symbolic level of the drift through the tropes of walking, pacing, marching and meandering that he uses to differentiate conformism from resistance. Take *Journal du voleur*, for example, when his narrator describes his nostalgia for the sound of footsteps:

> En cellule quand je rêvais l'esprit vague, au-dessus de moi un détenu tout à coup se lève et marche de long en large, d'un pas toujours égale. Ma rêverie reste vague aussi mais ce bruit [...] me rappelle que le corps qui la rêve, celui d'où elle s'échappe est en prison, prisonnier d'un pas net, soudain, régulier [...]. Mon talent sera l'amour que je porte à ce qui compose le monde des prisons et des bagnes. Non que je les veuille transformer, amener jusqu'à votre vie, ou que je leur accord l'indulgence et la pitié: je reconnais aux voleurs, aux traîtres, aux assassins, aux méchants, aux fourbes une beauté profonde — une beauté en creux — que je vous refuse.

> [As I lie dreaming in my cell, my mind idly drifting, suddenly a convict in the cell above gets up and starts walking to and fro, to and fro. My reverie is also adrift, but this sound reminds me that the body dreaming it, the one from which it has escaped, is in prison, prisoner of a clear, sudden, regular pacing [...]. My talent will be the love I bear to that which makes up the world of prisons and penal colonies. Not that I want to transform them or bring them round to your kind of life [...] I recognize in thieves, traitors and murderers, in the ruthless and the cunning, a deep beauty — a sunken beauty — which I deny you.] (*JV*, pp. 123; 49)

The convict's imprisonment is accentuated by his restless stride. He is a prisoner of his own steps, limited to the futile regularity of a gait that can only circulate around a cell separated from the world of the socially living. Much like in the enclosure of a theatre, so these steps can go nowhere, a stark contrast to the boundless freedom of the narrator's imaginative drift. Yet, Genet is not nostalgic for the escapism of the daydream. Rather, he wants to relive that metronomic sound of pacing back and forth that ruptures his mental drift, in order to channel his mental wanderings into a poetic resolution. Instead of drifting from the reality of his confinement, or disavowing the segregation that caused it, he directs his 'esprit vague' into an engaged poetics that aims to speak on behalf of those who are marshalled into conformity and thus to 'donner un chant à ce qui était muet' [giv[e] song to that which was dumb] (*JV*, pp. 123; 49). His oneiric drift — with its 'rêverie', 'nostalgie', 'esprit vague' — is funnelled into a discourse that will speak out of the 'hollow language' of those who are separated from life, to recall Judith Butler's formulation of the ethics of a liveable life (in which life is not about endurance, having 'life left' or 'living on', but about making the conditions of subjectivity intelligible so that they can become liveable), mining their 'sunken beauty' by refusing to redirect them or 'bring them round' to the straight lines of social orthodoxy.[30] The transitive 'amener jusqu'à votre vie' should construct a point of contact between these two worlds, between reader and inmate. Instead, Genet's language constructs 'your kind of life' as a border that is fortified against any kind of infiltration. His spatial language refuses to go 'jusqu'à' ('up to', 'to the point of') that straight norm. Nor will it ever seek to be assimilated by the kind of life that will always prevent entry. Genet's tribute to deviance and deviants, replete with their etymological proximity to the *dériviste*, is reflected in his own poetic detour away from the reader who belongs to the 'kind of life' he eschews. Directly accused in the scornful second person, we, like the convicts, are cut off and coldly set apart from the journeys we read. We are lined up in a similar pattern of conformity, forced to toe a line we have not chosen but which positions us in the normative and axiomatic role of 'other'; 'votre vie' makes us the anonymous enforcer of regulated forms of behaviour, as well as the outsider who is outcast from a world never written for us. After all, just as Sartre states (metatextually citing Genet's *L'Enfant criminel* so that his own candour becomes oblique), 'ce poète "nous parle en ennemi"' [this poet 'speaks to us as an enemy'] (*SG*, pp. 636; 545).

Yet, despite the antipathy of his address, Genet's devious poetics are always contiguous to the world they seek to displace. They collide with it, not in a frontal manner, but in a practice of obliqueness that moves us by throwing upstanding values off-kilter. As Sartre comments: 'mon casier judiciaire est vierge et je n'ai pas de gout pour les jeunes garçons: or les écrits de Genet m'ont touché. S'ils me touchent, c'est qu'ils me concernent; s'ils me concernent, c'est que j'en peux tirer profit' [I have no police record and no inclination for boys. Yet Genet's writings have moved me. If they move me that means they concern me. If they concern me, that means I can profit from them].[31] Of course, there is a problematic hinge on which Sartre recognises the ethical value of his writing here: his 'yet' reinforces the primacy of a straight axis from which Genet strays, and which only serves to further enhance the poignancy of a relation between two worlds positioned so wildly far apart. However, what if we consider the political value of 'being moved' more literally? What if we reinterpret the 'profit' we may derive from engaging with Genet's work not as a static lesson we can exploit to learn about an alternative form of behaviour and, *ipso facto*, our own ontological experience, but rather, as a way to make all fixed positions by which we seek to identify ourselves — and which thus immobilise us — drift?

To do so would be to rethink our own relationship to the world in a radical manner: to open ourselves up to the troubling forms of engagement pursued by Genet when he states that what he 'cherche, ou recherche, ou voudrait découvrir, ne le jamais découvrir le délicieux ennemi très désarmé, dont l'équilibre est instable, le profil incertain' [seeks, or goes in search of, or would like to find — or never to find — [is] the delicious disarmed enemy whose balance is off, whose profile is vague] (*ED*, pp. 9; 1). His position is confrontational, but only obliquely so, as what he seeks is a way to push any fixed identity or political standpoint off-balance. His enemy can have no membership to a clearly identified group, nor can it exist as a real figure: it must be vague, unstable and disarming; providing the catalyst that mobilises a pure form of resistance. Seeking the enemy but never finding it thus becomes a kind of oblique *dérive* in itself. It becomes a form of existence that displaces the stable grounds of affiliation in order to search for everything that is *not me*. In this anti-identitarian epistemology, Genet tells us in *Journal du voleur* that 'on ne me ramenera pas dans la voie droite' [I will not be brought back to the path of righteousness] (*JV*, pp. 218; 89). His excoriation of the unwavering path of moral rectitude is less a transgression of the straight and narrow lines of governance, and more a deviation from a static path that demands fidelity to any regulated pattern of existence.

Such is Genet's refusal to ontologise a political posture that he even evacuates his *démarche oblique* of its disruptive potential. Building on the mordant apostasy of the 'antisocial' prison imaginary in *Journal du voleur*, Genet argues in the 'Introduction à *Les Frères de Soledad*', the published prison letters of Black Panther, George Jackson, that 'un livre écrit en prison [...] s'adresse peut-être davantage à des lecteurs non reprouvés, qui jamais n'ont été et n'iront en prison, et c'est pour cela que d'une certaine manière un livre pareil s'avance d'une démarche oblique' [A book written in prison [...] is addressed perhaps above all to readers who are not outcasts, who have never been and will never go to prison, and that is why in some sense such a book proceeds obliquely] (*ED*, pp. 67; 52–53). The oblique seems to construct a diplomatic bridge between the all-seeing or panoptic space of social acceptability and the hidden space of the outcast, whose exclusion shores up the social order in a Girardian mechanism of scapegoating.[32] Yet, Genet seeks no such negotiation between these spaces, and even his equivocal phrasing seems to drag its heels. His contingencies, 'd'une certaine manière', 'peut-être'; his relative clauses that qualify any previous assertion; his apophasis, negatively gesturing to those 'non reprouvés' as a way of bringing the social insider into contact with the pariahs they revile — all Genet's techniques of oblique prison writing are orientated towards social conformity. To write obliquely thus seems problematically dialectical, as though the prisoner must deviate away from the abjection of their lived experience in order to flatter the straightforward message of the masses. Genet's criticism echoes Derrida's own anxiety towards the oblique as a form that is too derivative, too much of a short cut between the well-trodden, demotic horizontal and the hierarchical, corporate vertical that remind us of Michel de Certeau's schematics in his 1984 essay on urban space (to which we will return shortly). Derrida argues that:

> L'oblique reste le choix d'une stratégie encore frustré, obligée de parer au plus pressé, un calcul géométrique pour détourner au plus vite et l'abord frontal et la ligne droite: le plus court chemin présumé d'un point à un autre [...] ce déplacement paraît encore trop direct, linéaire, économique en somme.

> [The oblique remains the choice of a strategy that is still crude, obliged to ward off what is most urgent, a geometric calculus for diverting as quickly as possible both the frontal approach and the straight line: presumed to be the shortest path from the one to another [...] this displacement still appears too direct, linear, in short, economic].[33]

The oblique may have offered Derrida a temporary fix for side-stepping prescriptive forms of meaning, he laments how ultimately its geometric form diverts from straight axes in such a way that simply re-embeds their orthodoxy. The oblique would have first to *accept* the social axes it sought to displace, just as Genet's oblique prison narratives have to fit around already existing social narratives in order to be considered palatable. The oblique thus becomes a utilitarian instrument for the propagation of dominant social narratives precisely because it threatens to operate only inside the borders of the status quo.

Certainly, this resonates with Genet's frustrations in 'Introduction à *Les Frères de Soledad*', where he beckons us to see behind the obliquity of prison writing, which becomes an imprisoning schema in itself. Through pursed lips, he remarks:

> Il est donc prudent que tout écrit qui nous arrive de ce lieu infernal nous en arrive comme mutilé, élagué de ses ornements trop tumultueux. C'est donc derrière une grille, seule acceptée par eux, que ses lecteurs, s'ils l'osent, devineront l'infamie d'une situation qu'un vocabulaire honnête ne sait restituer, mais derrière les mots admis, discernez les autres!

> [It is therefore prudent that any writing that reaches us from this infernal place should reach us as though mutilated, pruned of its overly tumultuous adornments. It is thus behind bars, accepted only by them, that its readers, if they dare, will guess at the infamy of a situation that a forthright vocabulary could never reconstruct: but behind the permitted words, learn to hear the others!] (*ED*, pp. 67; 53)

Genet now stands both on the side of the *nous* reading Jackson's prison narratives and outside the *eux* who take them literally. He dares us to circumvent the *oratio obliqua* that is made necessary by the self-congratulatory virtue of 'honest' speech, and gets around any derivative geometry by displacing both indirect and direct language so that truth can lie only in deception. For Genet, oblique discourse is truncated, disfigured, stripped of its baroque branches that might utter too poetically 'les mots interdits, maudits, les mots ensanglantés, les mots crachés avec la bave, déchargés avec le sperme, les mots calomniés, reprouvés, les mots non écrits — comme l'ultime nom de Dieu' [the forbidden and accursed words, the bloody words, the words spit out in a lather, discharged with sperm, the slandered, reprobate words, the unwritten words — like the ultimate name of God] (*ED*, pp. 67; 43). Yet, Genet's oblique takes us directly to these omitted words that are jettisoned as the remnants of a discursive hygiene; behind the sanitised, find the smut, Genet tell us. In its etymology, the oblique is just such a remainder: deriving from the Latin term *limus*, to mean both 'askance' and 'faeces', 'mire' or 'filth'. Genet's obliquity sits contiguous to this abjection: it points out the experiences stained by saliva, sperm, blood or even silence, that are damned or removed by the social body. Yet because the words of the marginalised few *'s'avance d'une démarche oblique'*, they will forever endure, irrigated by a language of malediction that chases them out of an upstanding centre, but moving forwards as an indelible mire that derives from the very social order it threatens.

The oblique as *limus* is perhaps the answer to Derrida's critique of its linear geometric form, which just reasserts an already limiting system. In *Passions*, he claims that we must 'se servir d'une autre figure, absolument aporétique' [to make use of another figure, absolutely aporetic] to address the limits of our understanding.[34] Yet, he nonetheless asserts the oblique as a figure of that inconceivable aporia twenty years prior in the introductory essay to *Marges de la philosophie*, 'Tympan' (1972), when he considers the lack of centre, the din that resounds in a philosophical thought that nevertheless believes its own ability to master the limit of understanding. In this dual column text that precedes *Glas* (1974), but follows Genet's 'Ce qui est resté d'un Rembrandt' (1967), Derrida argues that the constitutive threshold for philosophy, the limit of our processes of harnessing knowledge into some sort of sense, is not a fixed border 'de forme droite et régulière de la limite' but rather '[c]omme tout *limus*, le *limes*, chemin de traverse, signifie l'oblique' [a straight and regular form of the limit [...] Like every *limus*, the *limes*, the short-cut, signifies the oblique].[35] In moving toward its own limit, Derrida wonders if this *limus*, both qua limit and remainder, defines and escapes any philosophical system of knowledge. Frontal discourse imposes itself within the boundaries of epistemology, deciding what something *is* insofar as it can be assumed to be known. But Derrida's oblique *limus* troubles any such knowable threshold, operating not as a horizon to be reached but as a limit that is already oblique, already transgressive by nature, its traversal operates at the vertex of a 'limite/ passage' which renders both such terms inoperative.[36] Such ambivalence is fitting for an equivocation that both problematises the possibility of direct interpretation, while also offering itself as an interpretable object that stages this absolute undecidability. When remapped onto the obliquity Genet ascribes to prison writing, we might reconsider how this discursive *limus* gestures to the overflowing of philosophical thought, a mode of competing with enlightenment narratives to nudge us to think about the outside of a codification that numbs experience through exegesis.

Transversal Lines of Resistance

From the performer's gait to the contorted Rembrandt spectator, the prisoner's imaginary drift to indirect prison writing itself, Genet's oblique approach drives us away from the epistemic conditions by which the world is said to make sense. Arguably, the political implications of such indirection reaches its apotheosis in 'L'Étrange Mot d'...', Genet's controversial treatise on the place of theatre in the urban landscape. He frames the text almost paratextually, launching arguments already made about the purpose of theatre in 'Comment jouer *Le Balcon*' (1962), 'Comment jouer *Les Bonnes*' (1958), and 'Jouer *Les Nègres*' (1979). Yet, its reach is more fundamental, more structural, than that peripheral form implies, echoing experimental Situationist texts like Ivan Cthetchglov's 'Formulaire pour un urbanisme nouveau' (1953) or Michel de Certeau's now canonical essay on urban geography, 'Pratiques de l'espace, marches dans la ville' in *L'Invention du quotidien* (1990), that also seek to displace the vertical monoliths of capitalist institutions that govern everyday life. Couched in the meandering 'nonchalance active d'un enfant' [active nonchalance of the child], Genet dreams of reorganising the urban map that lends prominence to upstanding establishments (including courts of justice, cathedrals, parliament, government headquarters) and notoriety to clandestine ones (such as the black market), in order to make way for a theatre that will stage the ultimate evasiveness of death itself.[37] In a bourgeois society ensnared in the pursuit of forward-marching progress, materiality and visible development, Genet proposes that the role of the theatre is to 'montre[r] le vide' [illuminate the void] that reminds us not only of our mortality, but of an ontological reality that escapes from the grasp of urban geographies of total domination.[38] Genet modulates Debord's rejection of 'l'urbanisme de la ville fonctionnaliste constituent la prise de possession de l'environnement naturel et humain par le capitalisme' [urbanism [as...] capitalism's method for taking over the natural and human environment], by proposing a new urban architecture that stages the indirect play on the oblique.[39] He imagines reclaiming the cemetery that has been marginalised to the outskirts and relocating it into the heart of the city; a beacon of resistance to any political structure that attempts to control space and time. While Debord and the Lettrist International collective campaigned for the elimination of cemeteries as 'hideous remnants' that serve as propaganda for a fixed 'past filled with alienation', Genet resuscitates the cemetery as a living site of performance; indeed, it is his ideal locus of theatre.[40]

Genet's theatre-cemetery should be situated 'le plus près possible, dans l'ombre vraiment tutélaire du lieu où l'on garde les morts ou du seul monument qui les digère' [as close as possible, in the truly tutelary shade of the place where the dead are kept, or in the shadow of the only monument that digests them].[41] The ceremonial presence of absence, loss and death are put centre stage, as Genet imitates Ancient Egyptian theatre and casts his play with the ephemeral shadows of non-being. His theatre is situated in a space of transience: located in the drifting shade cast by these monuments of death, but never immobilised by them. The drift of the shadow is more than an itinerant figure: its aim is to leave an impression of darkness on the spectator, which can never be enlightened by the reductive 'luminosity of analysis' that Genet associates with a modern culture obsessed with proof, exegesis and revelation. If this theatre hopes not only to glorify shadow, but to 'découvrir une ombre fraiche et torride, qui sera notre œuvre' [discover a fresh and scorching shadow, which will be our work], then perhaps it is in order to foreground the searing, inexplicable obscurity of death and to dramatise its uncertainty on stage.[42] The symbol of the shadow protects us: paradoxically revealing a nothingness to which we will all return; rather than blinding us and our now 'transparent eyelids' with the bright, artificial lights of a science that vaunts sterile clarity over poetic affect.

In practice, of course (and this differs radically from the SI's excoriation of theatre), Genet's theatrical vision is wildly disturbing. His insistence on merging the entertainment spectacle with live funeral rites, thus juxtaposing the staged artifice of one with the reality of another, can certainly be seen as an incendiary mockery of the ritual of mourning. However, what his cemetery theatre does achieve is an absolute deterritorialisation of space and time: the theatre becomes the ultimate locus of transversality. The spectator deviates from linear chronology, crossing over into the space of the non-living whilst they are still a sentient being watching a performance. The cemetery already blurs the strict borders between life and death in what Foucault calls a 'strange heterotopia': an interstitial place to which each living individual is connected through an ancestor residing there; and a site that ruptures temporal finitude by showcasing both 'la perte de la vie' [the loss of life] and 'cette quasi éternité où il ne cesse pas de se dissoudre et de s'effacer' [the quasi-eternity [of...] dissolution and disappearance].[43] But the theatre is also heterotopic, Foucault describing it as a locus in which real bodies enter a real space to conjure multiple imagined spaces: 'en un seul lieu réel plusieurs espaces, plusieurs emplacements qui sont en eux-mêmes incompatibles' [in a single real place several spaces, several sites that are in themselves incompatible].[44] Genet's cemetery-theatre is thus a double heterotopia, which intersects with actual time and space, while glimpsing into the virtual beyond the lived world. By displacing time, space, appearance and reality, the cemetery-theatre resists the Aristotelian appeal to dramatic mimicry and affords a disconnection from any metrics seeking to quantify living in terms of its material progress. There is a total liberation at play in this theatrical drift that recalls Debord's own interest in ludic non-consumability; both Genet and the SI disavowing any value structure that insists on constant evolution and commodifiable understanding.

One figure in Genet's urban architecture stands out in particular for defying the forward-marching narrative of social development. In the textual structure of 'L'Étrange Mot d'...', just off-centre from the twenty-one fragments that compose the text, is an oblique image. Genet stipulates that his ideal theatre would be 'tout près du four crématoire, à la cheminée raide, oblique et phallique' [quite close to the crematorium furnace, to the stiff, tilting, phallic chimney].[45] While the phallus is a symbol of life-giving futurity, here, as a crematorium chimney, it only brings death. Life and death are thus forced together on stage in a stark reminder of the finitude of our life-cycle. Samuel Weber reads the chimney as a metonym for the broader derangement of time we find in the crematorium more generally, arguing that 'the timeless architecture of the crematorium chimney [...] challenges the temporal perspective informed by that "mythical or controversial event also called the Advent" which promises the triumph of life over death'.[46] Where the Western notion of progress sets up history as the promise of resurrection, Weber positions Genet's theatre as its antithesis, seeking instead to confront us with the drama of mortality itself.

However, look closer at Genet's chimney. It is anything but the classic column that might signal a universal death. Rather, it is erected as an oblique phallus, poised not for procreation but for an eroticised sterility that is tilted away from all goal-orientated activity. The image invites a queer reading, reminding us that the 'oblique' is a cognate of the German *quer* to mean 'transverse, crosswise, obstructive (of things), going wrong, (of a person) peculiar, (of a glance) directed sideways, especially in a surreptitious or hostile manner, (of opinion and behaviour) at odds with others' (*OED*). Etched into its very etymology is an enmity towards straightness, a knowing look of hostility cast towards the masses whose notions of progress have been conditioned by the reign of capital whose productivity forces us onto the linear factory belt of existence. Genet's phallic chimney echoes what Lee Edelman has coined the 'queer death drive' that defies 'the consensus by which all politics confirms the absolute value of reproductive futurism'.[47] Inside the cemetery-theatre, Genet stages a way of being that is radically resistant to the inexorable march forward of capitalist reproductive politics. It is not a place of productivity, nor progress, but a site whose deviation towards non-futurity, and what might be seen as an 'anti-life' from this queer perspective, offers a way of harnessing that death drive as a political resistance to being governed by a 'reproductive futurism' that strives for eternal life and always creates the same.

If Edelman imagines queerness in *No Future* as being anti-life — when life is lent meaning only in the forward-marching time of hetero-reproductivity — then he also gestures to the possibility of ontological renewal in the wake of a strictly heteronormative way of living. He argues that because queerness exposes the 'obliquity of our relation to what we experience in and as social reality', because it deviates away from the nuclear family by which existence is thought to be made possible, then it is also privileged to envisage another reality.[48] Queer theory more generally is shored up by Foucault's own optimistic reading of what these diagonal social and sexual relations might achieve. In his 1981 interview, 'De l'amitié comme mode de vie', Foucault argues that the spatial marginalisation of the homosexual, positioned at a diagonal to the tyranny of a straight norm, actually enables a vibrant nexus of non-institutionalised ways of being in the world:

> L'homosexualité est une occasion historique de rouvrir des virtualités relationnelles et affectives, non pas tellement par les qualités intrinsèques de l'homosexuel, mais parce que la position de celui-ci 'en biais', en quelque sorte, les lignes diagonales qu'il peut tracer dans le tissu social permettent de faire apparaître ces virtualités.

> [Homosexuality is an historic occasion to re-open affective and relational qualities, not so much through the intrinsic qualities of the homosexual, but due to the biases against the position he occupies; in a certain sense, diagonal lines that he can trace in the social fabric permit him to make these virtualities visible.][49]

Kadji Amin is hesitant about Foucault's redemptive utopianism here, arguing that the specific context of pederasty to which he is referring in early 1980s France actually resurrects the same kinds of domination as the heteronormativity that makes an outcast of the gay subject. Yet, while Amin eschews Foucault's age-structured homosexual coupling as a product of modern Western (post-) colonial powers, I would argue that Foucault is alluding to the revolutionary potential of this geometric vision of queer subjectivity.[50] Rather than essentialise a gay identity that can be re-integrated, Foucault suggests that queerness is inherently transversal, cutting across the gridded mesh of a social fabric in which relations are mapped vertically onto lineage, or horizontally onto heterosexual reproduction. Instead, the oblique lines that traverse these tightly woven relational structures offer a way to displace rather than repeat the power play that marginalised the gay individual in the first place. Foucault appropriates the imposed liminal space of the homosexual who is ostracised for being at odds, or 'en biais', with social norms, and uses this divergence as the optimal site from which to disorientate the fixed systems of relation that enslave us to conformity.

For Deleuze, Foucault's entire philosophical project is motivated by seeking social and political mutability via the 'lignes transversales de résistance et non plus des lignes intégrales du pouvoir' [transversal lines of resistance and not the integral lines of power]; he argues that Foucault's desire to 'cross the line', rather than re-entrench centres of power, is motivated by a need to escape from the re-stratification that comes with all attempts at resistance.[51] Arguably, this is where Foucault's oblique figuration of homosexuality becomes most insurgent. The social fabric that binds us together becomes a veil that obscures new relational 'virtualités', and Foucault privileges queer modes of feeling and interacting as able to dis-align, slip away or open up new angles through that mesh of interaction.[52] As a diagonal, queerness thus makes visible what has not yet been instrumentalised by systems of power. The social reality that consigns it either to death or to political invisibility in Foucault's reading also liberates queerness from the *actual* and allows it to think from the position of the *virtual*. Queer obliquity thus moves beyond the 'what is' of essentialism, beyond 'les qualités intrinsèques de l'homosexuel', towards a kinetic way of life that peeps behind the social veil towards the potential of alternative modes of being together.

Genet's own transversal lines of queer resistance seem to anticipate Foucault's, albeit less optimistically. Under the aegis of the oblique phallic chimney, perhaps we might re-read Genet's self-flagellating queer subjectivity in *Fragments*, which is pummelled by a death-drive, as actually a source of revitalising politics:

> La pédérastie comporte son système érotique propre, sa sensibilité, ses passions, son amour, son cérémonial, ses rites, ses noces, ses deuils, ses chants: une civilisation, mais qui, au lieu de lier, isole, et qui se vit solitairement en chacun de nous [...] elle ne construit que d'apparents tombeaux.

> [Pederasty comprises its own erotic system, its sensibility, its passions, its love, its ceremonial, its rites, its weddings, its mourning rituals, its songs: a civilization, one that, instead of connecting, isolates, and that is lived solitarily in each of us [...] it constructs only apparent tombs.][53]

Genet stages queerness as a drama to be enacted among the 'apparent tombs' of a socially-imposed death. We are almost catapulted into his cemetery-theatre here, replete with the rites and rituals of real bodies who act out imagined worlds. Genet, like Foucault, will not ontologise a gay subject; rather, he introduces us to queer actors whose shared performance practices bind them together in a virtual community. And while Genet is at pains to assert the lived reality of this queer kinship — his possessive anaphora; the language of civilisation; the inversion of sociality as connective — by situating it in the graveyard of straightness, as an atomising, entombing practice, he never actualises it as socially liveable.[54] Instead, he reaches out to Foucault's own ambition for new possibilities of affect and relation: imagining a queer civilisation built on the effervescence of eroticism, desire, love and passion that keeps relations alive, by *not* integrating them into the unfeeling of society. His queer citizen confronts civilisation as a linear path towards human improvement and enlightenment, and obliquely swerves to hail the individual. Even his sentence diverges: he faces the faceless conformity of 'lier' and then bifurcates towards the individuated 'isole', 'chacun', 'nous', constructing queer kinship as a way to champion non-assimilation. If, as Ahmed astutely reads in phenomenological terms, 'what makes things "queer" for Merleau-Ponty is in that moment when they become distant, oblique, and "slip away"', then Genet's queer retreat from the social relation opens up an irrecuperable space of kinship that cannot be actualised, or subordinated, by the hegemonic centre that first alienated it.[55]

As Michael Hardt's extraordinary essay on Genet's time tells us, Genet's writing is entangled in this 'pure virtuality', in what is 'real without being actual, ideal without being abstract'.[56] As such, I read his oblique experience of queerness not as a denunciation of 'the hell of homosexuality', as White argues, nor as an exile from the living, as his insistence on death might imply, but as a revolutionary posture towards the openness of becoming.[57] For Hardt:

> Genet will betray any purpose or fixed identity but will pursue unendingly a process of constitution, a becoming, a ceremonial [...] Genet's ceremonials are always ceremonials of love [...] Genet abandons himself (and any notion of self) in his equal immersion or participation in the ceremonial.[58]

The ceremony that grants Genet's queer system its sense of community does so by opening out onto a virtual space in which egalitarian relations can be rehearsed. That ritual not only safeguards the individual by helping them to 'disidentify' with the role ascribed to them in the 'real' world, but it acts as a vector that transports us into an oblique space of politics where, as Lavery has eloquently argued, 'new utopic possibilities for collective life can be embodied *and* lived out'.[59] In these terms, Genet's vision of queerness in *Fragments* appears less concerned with sexuality, or corporeality, and more with the emancipatory geometry it engenders. Queerness generates the oblique lines of resistance that contribute to Genet's more fundamental, ahistorical and perhaps even asexual project of total social evasion.[60]

By way of a conclusion, we might recall how *Les Paravents* experiments with the more universalist project of imagining an oblique politics that bypasses the living entirely. In his first letter to Roger Blin prior to the play's performance on 21 April 1966, Genet anticipates his cemetery-theatre by addressing a perilously contemporary play on the Algerian War to 'le monde des morts' [the world of the dead] and to the posterity and nostalgia this implies.[61] He has no volition to act within the hegemonic frames of power and society that spawned the colonial backdrop of the play, nor to 'troubler l'ordre du monde' [disrupt the world order] in a revolutionary upheaval that threatens renewal. Rather, Genet wants the poetic event of the play to make death active, to use language like a chemical reaction whose 'déflagration poétique' [poetic combustion][62] will catalyse the virtual and explode the reality we have been blindly living. As Hardt describes it, 'death might be imagined as this virtual state of being outside time',[63] such that the pure and unliveable liberation Genet seeks is only possible from an asymmetrical position to a world he has no direct interest in changing. That macro project is embodied by the nearly 100 characters in the play, whose cosmetics, he tells Blin, must be 'très violents, mais tous *asymétriques*' [extremely violent, but all asymmetrical].[64] Cosmetic excess highlights the artifice required to escape from the empiricism and reason that defines the putative reality of the dominant culture. Instead, by visualising obliquity across each face, Genet leaves Western culture alone and literalises asymmetry as an inviolable political project: 'leurs maquillages, en les rendant "autres", leur permettront toutes les audaces: cessant d'avoir une responsabilité sociale, ils en auront une autre, à l'égard d'un autre Ordre' [their make-up will, by transforming them into 'others', enable them to try any and every audacity: as they will be unencumbered by any social responsibility, they will assume another, with respect to another Order].[65] To return to the question with which we began this chapter, what does Genet seek in his oblique approach to the world? Perhaps simply a way to envisage the alterity that cancels out any social debt, or to collapse responsibility to the social order entirely. The oblique is invested in a different kind of social and ethical commitment: one that dares to slip away from the constraints of a centre-margin and dance in the play of illusions where the world can be refracted and disorientated. After all, Genet's obliquity is a *démarche* that never stands still.

Notes to Chapter 3

1. Walter Benjamin, 'Painting and the Graphic Arts', in *Selected Writings*, ed. by Marcus Bullock and Michael W. Jennings, 4 vols (Cambridge, MA, & London: Belknap Press of Harvard University Press, c1996–2003), I, 82.
2. Ahmed, *Queer Phenomenology*, p. 172.
3. See Audre Lorde, *Sister Outsider: Essays and Speeches* (Trumansberg, NY: Crossing Press, 1984); Donna Haraway, *Simions, Cyborgs, and Women: The Reinvention of Nature* (New York: Routledge, 1991); Adrienne Rich, *Blood, Bread, and Poetry: Selected Prose, 1979–1985* (New York: Norton, 1986).
4. Walter Benjamin, *Gesammelte Briefe*, ed. by Christoph Godde and Henri Lonitz, 6 vols (Frankfurt: Suhrkamp, 1995–2000), I, 388–97 (untitled fragment from 1917 on painting and graphics, cited in 'Painting and Graphics', in *The Work of Art in the Age of Its Technological Reproducibility, and Other Writings on Media*, ed. by Michael W. Jennings, Brigid Doherty and Thomas Y. Levin, trans. by Edmund Jephcott (Cambridge, MA: Harvard University Press, 2008), pp. 195–218 (p. 197).
5. Benjamin, 'Painting and the Graphic Arts', p. 219.
6. Walter Benjamin, 'Dream Kitsch', in *The Work of Art in the Age of Its Technological Reproducibility*, ed. by Jennings, Doherty and Levin, pp. 236–39 (p. 236).
7. Jean Genet, 'Les Palestiniens', in *Genet à Chatila*, ed. by Hankins, pp. 87–150 (p. 87).
8. Note that 'les méandres' derives specifically from bends in the river, echoing the etymology of *dé-rive* as an undoing what is riveted. See Libero Andreotti and Xavier Costa, 'Pour une lexique lettriste', *Potlatch*, 26 (7 May 1956); 'Towards a Lettrist Lexicon', trans. by Gerardo Denis, in *Theory of the Dérive and Other Situationist Writings on the City*, ed. by Libero Andreotti and Xavier Costa (Barcelona: Museu d'Art Contemporani de Barcelona, ACTAR, 1996), p. 60.
9. Genet, 'Les Palestiniens', p. 87.
10. Ahmed, *Queer Phenomenology*, p. 170.
11. Emmanuelle Lambert, 'Préface', in *Jean Genet, l'échappée belle*, ed. by Emmanuelle Lambert and Albert Dichy (Paris: Albums Beaux Livres/ Gallimard, 2016), pp. 1–2 (p. 2).
12. Most canonically: the existential reading of 'l'élément désintégré, vagabond à l'individu errant qu'est Genet' [the disintegrated, vagabond element, the wandering individual who is Jean Genet] (*SG*, pp. 290; 258); Genet's anti-Western, anti-imperialist sentiment (Edward Said, 'On Genet's Late Work', in *Imperialism and Theatre*, ed. by J. Ellen Gainor (London: Routledge,

1995), pp. 230–42; Hédi Khélil, *Figures de l'altérité dans le théâtre de Jean Genet: lecture des 'Nègres' et des 'Paravents'* (Paris : Harmattan, 2001)); his anti-Semitism (Marty, *Genet*; Jablonka, *Les Vérités inavouables de Jean Genet*); his deterritorial epistemology (Félix Guattari, *Cartographies schizoanalytiques* (Paris: Galilée, 1989); *Schizoanalytic Cartographies*, trans. by Andrew Goffey (London: Bloomsbury, 2013); Michael Hardt 'Prison Time', *Yale French Studies*, 91 (1997), 64–79; Michael Hardt and Antonio Negri, *Empire* (Cambridge, MA: Harvard University Press, 2001)). Consider also the exhibition 'L'Échappée Belle', Musée des Civilisations de l'Europe et de la Méditerranée (April-July 2016).

13. Lavery, *The Politics of Jean Genet's Late Theatre*, p. 9; Albert Dichy, 'Genet, écrivain?', *Europe*, 808–09 (August-September 1996), 4–5.

14. Foucault, 'De l'amitié comme mode de vie'; Ahmed, *Queer Phenomenology*; Jacques Derrida, *Passions* (Paris: Galilée, 1993).

15. 'oblique', *Centre national de ressources textuelles et lexiques* <https://www.cnrtl.fr/etymologie/oblique> [accessed 19 January 2021].

16. Maurice Merleau-Ponty, *Phénoménologie de la perception* (Paris: Gallimard, 1945), p. 349; *Phenomenology of Perception*, trans. by Colin Smith (London: Routledge, 1996), p. 302.

17. Jean Genet, 'Ce qui est resté d'un Rembrandt déchiré en petits carrés réguliers, et et foutu aux chiottes', in *OC*, IV, 19–31 (p. 27b); 'Something Which Seemed to Resemble Decay...', trans. by Bernard Frechtman, *Arts and Literature*, 1–3 (March 1964), 83–90 (p. 85).

18. Guy Debord: 'la dégradation de l'être à l'avoir et de l'avoir au paraitre' [the degradation of being into having and [a generalized sliding] from having into appearing]: *La Société du spectacle* (Paris: Buchet & Chastel, 1972), p. 17; *The Society of the Spectacle*, trans. by Ken Knabb (London: AK Press, 2005), p. 10.

19. Bizet, *Une communication sans échange*, p. 381.

20. Debord, *La Société du spectacle*, pp. 142; 118.

21. Jean Genet, *Elle*, in *TC*, pp. 447–69 (p. 465).

22. For further exploration of Genet's analysis of the glorification of image and reflection, see 'Comment jouer *Le Balcon*', in *TC*, pp. 257–60 (p. 260).

23. Genet, 'Ce qui est resté d'un Rembrandt', pp. 21–28; 77–86.

24. Lavery, *The Politics of Jean Genet's Late Theatre*, p. 85.

25. Jean Genet, *Les Bonnes*, in *TC*, pp. 125–64 (p. 136).

26. Debord, 'La Théorie de la dérive'.

27. Ian Magedera, *Jean Genet: Les Bonnes*, Glasgow Introductory Guides to French Literature, 42 (Glasgow: University of Glasgow French and German Publications, 1998), p. 25.

28. Gérard Genette, *Seuils* (Paris: Seuil, 1987), pp. 7–8; *Paratexts: Thresholds of Interpretation*, trans. by Jane E. Lewin (Cambridge: Cambridge University Press, 1997), p. 5.

29. Ahmed, *Queer Phenomenology*, p. 70.

30. Judith Butler, *Undoing Gender* (New York: Routledge, 2004), p. 30.

31. Ibid.

32. René Girard, *La Violence et le sacré* (Paris: Grasset, 1972), pp. 139–40. Girard explores how the prisoner becomes the victim of anthropophagy: scapegoated, consumed and regurgitated to ensure the stability of the majority.

33. Jacques Derrida, 'L'Offrande oblique', in *Passions* (Paris: Galilée, 1993), pp. 5–35 (p. 30); 'Passions: "An Oblique Offering"', in *On the Name*, ed. by Thomas Dutoit, trans. by David Wood (Stanford, CA: Stanford University Press, 1995), pp. 3–34 (p. 14).

34. Derrida, *Passions*, pp. 40; 40.

35. Jacques Derrida, 'Tympan', in *Marges de la philosophie* (Paris: Minuit, 1972), pp. i–xxv (p. x); 'Tympan', in *Margins of Philosophy*, trans. by Alan Bass (Brighton: Harvester Press, 1982), pp. ix–xxix (p. xvii).

36. Ibid., p. i.

37. Jean Genet, 'L'Étrange Mot de...', in *TC*, pp. 879–88 (p. 880); 'That Strange Word', in *Fragments of the Artwork*, trans. by Mendell, pp. 103–12 (p. 104).

38. Ibid., pp. 883; 107.

39. Debord, *La Société du spectacle*, pp.169; 95.

40. *Theory of the Dérive and Other Situationist Writings on the City*, ed. by Libero Andreotti and Xavier Costa (Barcelona: Museu d'Art Contemporani de Barcelona, 1996), p. 57.

41. Genet, 'L'Étrange Mot de...', pp. 880; 104.

42. Ibid., pp. 886; 110.

43. Michel Foucault, 'Des espaces autres', *Architecture, Mouvement, Continuité*, 5 (October 1984), 46–49 (p. 48); 'Of Other Spaces', trans. by Jay Miskowiec, *Diacritics*, 16.1 (1986), 22–27 (p. 26).

44. Ibid., pp. 47; 25.

45. Genet, 'L'Étrange Mot de...', pp. 884; 108.

46. Samuel Weber, *Theatricality as Medium* (New York: Fordham University Press, 2004), p.12.

47. Edelman, *No Future*, p. 2.

48. Ibid., p. 6.

49. Foucault, 'De l'amitié comme mode de vie', pp. 985; 311.

50. Amin, *Disturbing Attachments*, p. 15.

51. Gilles Deleuze, *Foucault* (Paris: Minuit, 1986), p. 94; *Foucault*, trans. by Séan Hand (London: Continuum, 1999), p. 78.

52. Ahmed, *Queer Phenomenology*, p. 172.

53. Genet, *Fragments... et autres textes*, pp. 79; 24.

54. This contests Bersani's influential reading of Genet's homosexuality as 'declining to participate in any sociality at all' (*Homos*, p. 168).

55. Ahmed, *Queer Phenomenology*, p. 171.

56. Hardt, 'Prison Time', p. 71.

57. White: 'the most religious of zealots could not have denounced the "hell" of homosexuality with more vigour' (*Genet*, p. 335).

58. Hardt, 'Prison Time', pp. 74–76.

59. Lavery, *The Politics of Jean Genet's Late Theatre*, p. 11.

60. Elizabeth Stephens elegantly reads Genet's queer solitude as a refusal of any collective activism that is recuperable by the dominant culture: *Queer Writing: Homoeroticism in Jean Genet's Fiction* (Basingstoke: Palgrave Macmillan, 2009), p. 75. Genet thus anticipates one of queer theory's key moves by achieving what Michael Warner states, that queer sexuality 'opposes society itself', resisting 'not just the normal behaviour of the social but the idea of normal behaviour': *Fear of a Queer Planet* (Minneapolis & London: University of Minnesota Press, 1993), p. 10.

61. Jean Genet, *Lettres à Roger Blin* (Paris: Gallimard, 1966), p. 11; 'Letters to Roger Blin', in *Reflections on Theatre and Other Writings*, trans. by Richard Seaver (London: Faber & Faber, 1972), pp. 7–60 (p. 11).

62. Ibid.

63. See Timothy Mathews's chapter on this letter in *Literature, Art and the Pursuit of Decay in Twentieth-century France* (Cambridge: Cambridge University Press, 2000), when he claims that the play addresses death and the ruination even of itself so as to prevent confirmation and entrenchment of the social world it seeks to displace: 'stage and staging will move audiences and will cause foundations to tremble — but only if the world ("le monde") that has spawned these scenes is left in peace, is allowed to remain the same' (p. 154).

64. Genet, *Lettres à Roger Blin*, pp. 50; 51. For the importance of colour and make-up in Blin's production of *Les Paravents*, see *Jean Genet*, ed. by David Bradby and Clare Finburgh (London: Routledge, 2012).

65. Genet, *Lettres à Roger Blin*, pp. 12; 12.

CHAPTER 4

❖

Planes

Dans ce drame de la géométrie intime, où faut-il habiter?
[In this drama of intimate geometry, where should one live?]
— Gaston Bachelard[1]

De la forme géométrique morte — rectiligne et plane —
l'artisanat s'élève à la 'rondeur animée'.

[From the dead geometric form — rectilinear and plane —
the artisan class raises itself to 'lifelike roundness'.]
— Jacques Derrida[2]

Saint Genet and *Glas*: Squaring the Circle

In 1952 and 1974 respectively, two of the twentieth century's most prodigious philosophers published seminal tomes on Genet. Rather than eulogising his writing *post facto*, both Sartre's *Saint Genet* and, what Christina Howells perceives as Derrida's ensuing parricidal attack on it, *Glas*, draw on Genet's living corpus to exemplify their own working theories about how to break with dialectical reasoning, and thus how to attain epistemological freedom.[3] In this chapter, I examine how Sartre and Derrida adopt two geometric figures — the circle and the square — as the interpretative lenses through which to read Genet's texts as exemplary of that freedom. I ask how incidental these shapes are to two philosophers who draw on such a plethora of images throughout their writing on Genet, curious about why circles and grids prove such productive figures for an existentialist and a post-structuralist to imagine Genet's escape from the bonds of fixed meaning. I then bring Sartre and Derrida's geometric hermeneutics to bear on the squares and circles we find throughout Genet's prison texts, examining how he constructs spaces of shelter for the subject in physical and poetic prisons that will always defy absolute containment.

Both Sartre's and Derrida's panegyrics were read by Genet with a conflicted mixture of approval, reticence and disgust. On finishing Sartre's manuscript, he admitted in an interview with Madeleine Gobeil in 1964 that:

> Je suis l'illustration d'une de ses théories de la liberté. Il a pu connaitre un homme qui, au lieu de subir, revendiquait ce qui lui a été donné, le revendiquait et était décidé à le pousser à son extrême conséquence.

> [I am the illustration of one of his theories of freedom. He has found a man who,

instead of submitting, has vindicated what has been given to him, vindicated it and was resolute in pushing it to its extreme consequences.] (*ED*, pp. 22; 12)

To attempt to summarise Sartre's monumental biographical analysis, he claims that Genet frees himself from the shackles of ontological pre-determination by adopting the character of the thief that society foists upon him. He internalises the alterity of his social image as a pariah and claims this fiction as the foundation of his own subjectivity. Genet's self-alienation locates him in the world of falsehood, trickery and imagination, rather than in the world of truth-claims, fact or what is present or affirmative in the eyes of society. Yet, Genet does not represent an example of bad faith; rather, Sartre sees him as becoming fully the imagined figure of evil that society maligns. His being is thus forged out of a nothingness, an empty 'Mal' which Genet explains that he lives 'de telle façon que vous ne soyez pas récupéré par des forces sociales qui symbolisent le Bien' [in such a way that you are not recuperated by the social forces that symbolise Good] (*ED*, pp. 14; 8). Sartre argues that Genet's only refuge is rejection; since only outside the system can he escape from the binary validation of social codes.

Although Genet accepted the socially transgressive thrust of Sartre's analysis, being reified as an icon of existential freedom by this totalising text nevertheless forced him into a six-year period of silence from 1949 to 1955. Genet lamented being 'mis à nu sans complaisance. Il parle de moi au présent de l'indicatif' [stripped [...] bear without mercy. He speaks of me in the present tense] (*ED*, pp. 21; 12), as though Sartre's imperious voice buried him alive, fossilising him in a present continuous that asserts what is, rather than what might be. Sartre's grammatical certainty proves as claustrophobic and binding as the social truths Genet disavowed. Genet's resistance to being 'exposed' by Sartre's text testifies to a desire to remain uncodified and unrecognised by words that provide a form of dissimulation in his writing. For Sartre, Genet dresses himself up in language, wearing it as a disguise that affords absolute freedom: its transformative potential changes the visible into the unforeseen, converting 'les matières réputées viles en matières acceptées comme nobles' [transforming subjects taken to be vile into subjects accepted as noble] (pp. 14; 8). The danger of Sartre's authoritarian discourse, then, is that it fixes Genet to a position or truth that runs completely counter to his non-totalisable poetics.

Glas lies in the wake of what Derrida calls Sartre's 'projet d'explication maîtrisant qui emprisonnait de nouveau Genet dans sa vérité, dans une vérité qui aurait été inscrite dans son projet originaire' [project of explanatory mastery that again imprisoned Genet in his truth, in a truth supposedly inscribed in his originary project].[4] Derrida visually explodes the possibility of any such truth when it comes to reading Genet's texts. The riven, interrupted form of *Glas* borrows from Genet's own *mise en page* in 'Ce qui est resté d'un Rembrandt', pitting two texts against one another in a confrontation between Hegel's pursuit of absolute knowledge and Genet's poetic resistance to being totalised by any concept from which a dominant truth could be gleaned. *Glas* offers none of the thematic criticism or psychologising exegesis that we find in *Saint Genet*; rather, it concentrates instead on showing how Genet's prose offers a foil to Hegelian dialectics.[5] *Glas* opens with a rather coy invitation to look to Genet to understand the limits of Hegel's approach to knowledge. Whispering to us from a spy-hole that juts out of the Hegel column — thus thwarting any monolithic commentary — Derrida tells us that 'reste à penser: ça ne s'accentue pas ici maintenant mais sera déjà mis à l'épreuve de l'autre côté' [remain(s) to be thought: it [ça] does not accentuate itself here now but will have already been put to the test on the other side] (G, pp. 7a; 1a). What still remains to be thought, or is left over, from Hegel's thesis, antithesis and synthesis, can never be imagined within a dialectical approach; those unthinkable remainders accumulate instead in Genet's writing, defiantly poised in the opposite column. However, the temporality of Derrida's instructions are complex: he will have already highlighted the gaps in Hegel's absolute knowledge by the time he goes back to analyse it, seemingly aware that what falls from a dialectic also becomes its very founding condition.

Derrida thus reads Genet's poetics not just as a celebration of what is discarded from a system of total understanding *post facto*, but as the very origin of an exclusion that can never be incorporated into any epistemological structure. Because Genet never flatly celebrates any single, concrete remainder, but rather uses his language to produce that which throws all dialectical knowledge out of kilter, he becomes the perfect example of Derrida's post-structuralist project. Yet, unlike Sartre's essentialising approach, Derrida's mimetic homage to Genet's imaginative, textual freedom in *Glas* saves Genet from becoming an archetype precisely because, as White states, 'this method of sinking into a subject rather than dominating it would become Genet's own in his last book, *Prisoner of Love*'.[6] Whether Derrida is writing on Genet, or Genet on the Palestinians, both produce a syncretic approach to writing on a subject, encouraging multiple voices to bleed into the narrative to prevent any authoritarian exegesis. Perhaps that is why Peeters notes that 'après la parution de *Glas*, Derrida sera très touché que Genet lui en dise quelques mots amicaux, de manière presque furtive, mais il évitera soigneusement de lui en reparler' [after the publication of *Glas*, Derrida would be very touched when Genet said a few friendly words to him on the subject, almost furtively, but he took great care never to mention it to him again].[7]

The *tourniquet* and the Matrix: Two Geometric Hermeneutics

Despite clear formal differences, both Robert Harvey and Christina Howells note that *Saint Genet* and *Glas* are united in portraying Genet as the rival to Hegel's 'overweening truth-claims'.[8] Sartre and Derrida are:

> Confounded, like Hercules, in their attempts to behead the Hegelian hydra. Genet seems to slip the net of recuperative dialectics precisely because he has no interest in Hegel, absolute knowledge, or even truth, and refuses to enter the debate except in parodic mode [...] [however,] he perhaps succeeds, by dint of lateral prestidigitation, like Lolaus who decapitated the Hydra with fire not sword.[9]

The allusion to this Greek myth not only pays tribute to Derrida's own reference in *Glas* (*G*, p. 118a), but figures continental philosophy as caught in a classical, epic battle against the logic of dialectical reasoning, which conquers contradiction and resolves it as higher truth. Curiously, I find that Sartre and Derrida turn to another Greek invention — geometry — as a means of showing how Genet decapitates Hegel. For Sartre, Genet's poetics are circular, every assertion he makes turning in on itself to prevent a conclusion; for Derrida, they are gridded, his words forming a matrix that draws attention to the gaps in meaning that it refuses to capture. Both geometries dramatise the freedom of Genet's writing, which, as this chapter will argue, is made all the more acute when it is imprisoned. By inhabiting 'un univers si bien clos' [so closed a universe], Genet revels in being amputated from 'communicatio[n] avec le monde habituel' [communicat[ion] with the usual world] (*MR*, pp. 286; 78). Unencumbered by a normative symbolic order, Genet's carceral imagination exploits its egress from society to transform 'chaque objet de votre monde [qui] a pour moi un autre sens que pour vous. Je rapporte tout à mon systeme où les choses ont une signification infernale' [each object in your world, which has a meaning different for me from the one it has for you. I refer everything to my system, in which things have an infernal signification] (pp. 286; 78). Speaking to us not just as an enemy, but as a poet, Genet loosens language from any familiar frame of reference or structure of logic, to construct a system of 'infernal' reasoning that operates beneath the ethical values attached to affirmative discourse and action. In this underworld of the symbolic in his early prison narratives, Genet swaps the dialectics of rule and transgression, crime and punishment, for an altogether more liberal vision of language disinterested in moral justice or truth. He swaps Aristotle's utopian understanding of rhetoric as the pathway to verity, for a system of meaning that never comes to rest in putative fact.[10] And for Sartre, this is what shapes the 'cercle infernal' [infernal circle] of Genetian thought whereby:

> La progression dialectique [...] s'infléchit en mouvement circulaire [...] il tourne en rond, il ne peut se maintenir qu'en tournant toujours plus vite, passant d'un Mac à un autre Mac, d'une étreinte à une autre étreinte, de l'essence à l'existence et de l'existence à l'essence, de la glorification poétique à la lucidité corrosive, s'il s'arrête, il est mort.

> [The dialectical progression deviates into a circular movement [...] he goes round in circles, he can keep his balance only by moving faster and faster, going from one pimp to another pimp, from one embrace to another embrace, from essence to existence and from existence to essence, from poetic glorification to corrosive lucidity. If he stops, he is dead.] (*SG*, pp. 171; 148)

Sartre ontologises Genet's circular thinking to present his very selfhood as inscribed in and enacted through his writing. As his poetic system dizzyingly rotates around non-fixed identitarian, relational and discursive positions, so Sartre imagines his subjectivity to be forged in a cyclical form of departure and return: moving from the position of essentialised outlaw foisted on him by society to the existential hero who parodies that essence, adopting it despite knowing it to be meaningless. Genet cannot settle; to do so would not only be to imprison himself in a static label with which he never identifies, but to fossilise all being into something attainable and already in existence. Through his infinite rotations, Genet produces a mode of becoming that operates in the negative for Sartre, allowing him forever to shake off determinacy by pursuing 'le Pire [qu'il] fait exister par-delà de son impossibilité même, comme l'ombre d'un idéal, et qu'on se pose en face de l'être, de la vie et des hommes comme une insatisfaction infinie, comme une exigence irréalisable' [the Worst [that] he makes exist beyond its very impossibility, like the shadow of an ideal, and that he confronts being, life and men as an infinite dissatisfaction, as an unrealizable exigency] (SG, pp. 193; 169). Genet would be able to escape the shackles of right and wrong by spiralling downwards away from all positivity — since 'le moment *positif* reste ce qui est chez les Justes: conformisme, aveugle soumission' [the positive moment remains what it is among the Just: conformism, blind submission] — running after what is inexorably worse to ensure the dialectical bonds of good and bad are jolted (pp. 377; 338). Such is his quest for freedom that in this Sisyphean circularity Genet keeps alive all ontological possibility — being, life, even humanity itself — by looping back round on himself to refuse realisation, and therefore death.

There is a radical kind of independence in this non-Manichean way of thinking. Language becomes elastic as Sartre investigates how Genet starts to think against the evident, challenging what is accepted as natural, all the while revelling in his failure to establish an alternative. But that is just the point: in this circular hermeneutic, Genet is able to reach a kind of epistemological liberation by speeding up the gyrations of any dichotomy so that opposites blur into one another. Sartre treats the circle temporally rather than spatially, accelerating it like a carousel in a rotation so that Genet 'fondrait les deux contraires l'un dans l'autre: ainsi les teintes de l'arc-en-ciel s'interpénètrent lorsqu'on fait tourner assez vite un disque multicolore; résultat: du blanc. J'ai nommé *tourniquets* ces agencements' [merges the two opposites, just as, when a multicolored disk is spun quickly enough, the colors of the rainbow interpenetrate and produce white. I have called these devices whirligigs] (SG, pp. 371–72; 333). Sartre's image of the 'tourniquet', a revolving door or turnstile, could easily be read as a point of entry into a way to think beyond binarity. However, this transformative logic is also read as pure negation by Sartre whose image of revolution turns into a kaleidoscopic distortion that produces a nothingness, the 'blanc' both whiteness and gap. So, as Genet's language curves back round on itself, it also brings into focus a void that collapses all synthesis and thwarts the possibility of fulfilment.

Problematically, then, Sartre's *tourniquet* situates Genet on the side of a lack. Trapped in 'cette prison circulaire' [this circular prison], which 'parfois il l'appelle une tombe' [at times he calls it a tomb] (SG, pp. 379; 348), Sartre fears that Genet has immured himself into a cycle that resists onward progression and futurity. The circle becomes the epitome of nihilism in *Saint Genet*, despite Sartre straining to see the freedom of thought that such negativity might offer. He never dares to delve into that void, however, always repositioning Genet back at the surface level of a false circular unity whose suffocating totalisation looks to unify that lack through an image of wholeness. Jean Cocteau's revulsion towards Sartre's book is directed precisely towards such re-appropriations, as he lambasts his 'noblesse de clinicien' [clinician's high-mindedness], the 'franchise' [directness] and 'la rectitude de ce livre' [straightness of this book], telling Genet that 'son livre est davantage le portrait de Sartre que le tien' [his book is more his portrait than yours].[11] Cocteau's reproach is based on the linearity, the uprightness and the quantifiable metrics that Sartre imposes on Genet throughout his text. Being more mirror than critique, *Saint Genet* has to recuperate Genet's infernal, downward significations back into a forward-marching logic simply to allow Sartre to make sense of his own being in the world. Ultimately, Sartre's geometric *tourniquets* only seem to formalise Genet's failure to reach the closure that Sartre himself seeks; his phenomenological approach to ontology will always drive him to reveal and bring the nothingness of consciousness into being.[12]

Perhaps this is where Derrida succeeds in escaping from such dialectical reasoning in *Glas*. He contests Sartre's insistence on exegesis in *Saint Genet*, dismissing it as simply part of the didactic conventions of 1950s French philosophy that sought to expound the 'leçons d'ontologie phénoménologique de l'époque, à la française' [phenomenological ontology of the epoch, in the French style] (*G*, pp. 20b; 13b).[13] Not only does Derrida disavow the rigid constraints of the French dissertation as a cultural institution, but he also derides the philosophical conventions that sought to make sense of existence through the empirical and the present. Indeed, Sartre sermonises to us in *Saint Genet* that being hurled around Genet's *tourniquets* makes the reader understand 'la véritable fonction du verbe *être*: puisqu'il doit *irréaliser* le Non en Oui, transformer le fait en valeur et le réel en apparence, son mouvement figé reproduit l'apparition vertigineuse et néantisante de la Beauté' [the true function of the verb *to be*: since it must derealise the Nay into the Yea, it must transform the fact into value, and the real into appearance, its frozen movement reproduces the dizzying and annihilating apparition of Beauty] (*SG*, pp. 445; 399). He salvages Genet's tendency towards nothingness by aestheticising it, cancelling out the negative with the positive gesture of writing and thus recuperating the lack that Genet experiences in 'le non, le fait, le réel' as a visible, textual beauty. This circularity becomes a way to save the reader, and even Genet himself, from the free-fall of the void; the 'being there' of his writing mitigating against *actual* nihilism. For Derrida, however, this ontological interpretation tries to fix — and thus destroy — the disruptive potential of Genet's poetics that 'tournent à vide' [whirl about idly] (*SG*, pp. 306; 329). He chastises Sartre's clumsy stabilisation of the 'disparition vibratoire' [vibratory disappearance] of meaning in Genet's writing as 'un mallarméisme vague' [a vague Mallarméism]; as though the transcendental void that Sartre's so-called poet of nothingness, Mallarmé, gestures to in poetry, is also essentialised by Genet's poetics (*G*, pp. 21b; 14b).

Derrida must open up the totalising closure of Sartre's circular reading by taking literally how Genet 'turns around a void'. For the second time, Genet's texts are lent geometric form as Derrida maps his language onto the partial geometry of the grid, or matrix, that celebrates the gap they cannot salvage. Analysing a scene from *Notre-Dame-des-Fleurs*, in which Genet recounts how the newspapers would report

Notre Dame's murder trial, Derrida highlights the geometric framework behind
Genet's imaginary:

> Dans l'espacement de l'écriture, pendant le procès du récit, les lignes verticales
> (cravate, pluie, glaive, canne ou éperon du parapluie) coupent les lignes
> horizontales du journal ou du livre, des ailes ou des baleines du parapluie. Le
> langage coupe, décolle, décapite. Les phrases s'enroulent autour d'une direction
> comme des lianes le long d'une colonne tronquée.
>
> [In writing's spacing, during the trial of the narrative [*récit*], the vertical lines
> (necktie, rain, glaive, cain or umbrella tip [*éperon*] cut the horizontal lines of the
> newspaper or the book, of the wings or the spokes of the umbrella. Language
> cuts, decollates, unglues, decapitates. The sentences coil around a direction like
> liana along a truncated column.] (G, pp. 87b; 74b)

Derrida is sensitive to the geometric abstraction at the heart of Genet's most visceral
descriptions. Here, Genet is envisaging how the press will bay for Notre Dame's
blood after killing an old man. He is salacious about the brutal potential of those
'minuscules lignes des faits divers [...] les "Barrios Chinos" des journaux' [tiny lines
of the short crime items [...] the 'Barrios Chinos' of the newspapers] (*NDF*, pp. 176;
338), their *mise en page* beckoning us towards the seedy downtown of journalism
where we go to quench our thirst for transgression and violence. Newspapers
become the guillotine, or revolutionary scaffold for Genet, 'remplis que de colonnes
de faits divers, colonnes sanglantes et mutilées comme des poteaux de torture' [filled
only with columns of crime news, columns as bloody and mutilated as torture
stakes] (pp. 176; 338). As we walk around the rougher neighbourhoods of Genet's
1940s tabloids, we find ourselves directed towards neither the descriptions nor the
judgements of this newspaper copy, but towards a spatial geography that gestures
away from the mainstream and towards the liminal. His meta-textuality takes on
spatial importance as he invites us to consider language as less based on concrete
foundations or reference, but more as a social architecture whose monolithic columns
cleave the normative from the transgressive. The ten lines that will be dedicated to
Notre Dame's trial will be 'assez espacées pour laisser l'air circuler entre les mots
trop violents' [widely enough spaced to let the air circulate between the overviolent
words] (pp. 176; 338). Genet lets words fall into geometric formations that demand
all readers contemplate the unspoken; his interstices leaving enough room for the
social super ego to sound out in its deafening judgement. Amidst the sensationalism
of these intersecting lines and columns, Genet's textual axes invite us to think
beyond violence or intensify it without the risk of codification; his linguistic
geometry allows us to organise meaning altogether differently. As Derrida finds in
Genet's metatextual reading of the newspaper in *Notre-Dame-des-Fleurs*, words are
scaffolded onto a vertical and horizontal axis: our eye moving down the torture
pole of textual condemnation and along sentences loaded with silent verdicts that
'firent battre tous les coeurs' [quickened the hearts] (pp. 176; 338), to drum up affect
more than fact. What Genet's gridded language seems to bring into focus, then,
is both a frame of meaning and its outside. As Derrida's analysis suggests, it is this
contradiction that allows him to break away from the dialectical process of pursuing

knowledge towards a more material response to language as pliable matter that makes meaning through agglutination, decapitation, or intersection.

Derrida directs Sartre's aimless *tourniquets* by coiling Genet's prose around the past, figuring his gridded prose as interested less in growth than in entropy. Indeed, rather than going round in circles, Derrida claims that to understand Genet, 'il faut tout relire à l'envers' [everything has to be reread in reverse]. We must travel down his vertical columns, back to 'un berceau: ce que je suis, c'est toujours l'Immaculée Conception' [a cradle: what I am (following) is always the Immaculate Conception] (G, pp. 87b; 74b). Playing on the homophony of *suis* as both an ontological and a directional term, Derrida suggests that to understand who Genet 'is' ('ce que je suis') is to follow the sign of the absent mother — in this case, both Ernestine, Divine's mother who is glued to the crime news, and Notre Dame's own virginal aura that cries out 'Je suis l'Immaculée Conception' [I am the Immaculate Conception] (NDF, pp. 178; 342). In Derrida's reading, being detached from the mother charges the heavy air that circulates between Genet's words; returning to her absence becomes the void around which his writing turns. He seeks the right metaphor through which to read Genet's texts, careful not to cannibalise him as Sartre had done by avoiding the language of comprehension. He dodges the suffocating circularity we find in *Saint Genet* by eschewing a hermeneutic in which he might feel 'entortillé' [entwined], associating that mode of critical 'encircling' with a parasitic death that constricts Genet 'comme une colonne, dans un cimetière, mangée par un lierre' [like a column, in a cemetery, eaten by an ivy] (G, pp. 228b; 204b). The vertical image seems to spite the monumentalism of *Saint Genet*, figuring Genet himself as the monolith gnawed away at by Sartre's criticism.

Instead, Derrida 's'introduit en tiers entre sa mère et lui' [worm[s] his way in as a third party between his mother and him] (G, pp. 228b; 204b), presenting his own critical approach as the arbiter between the abstract geometric tropes in Genet's writing and an endless return to the maternal. He proposes to read Genet through the figure of the matrix as both a grid and a womb, asking:

> Ai-je construit quelque chose comme la matrice de son texte? A partir de laquelle on pourrait le lire, c'est-à-dire le re-produire? Non, je vois plutôt (mais c'est peut-être encore une matrice ou une grammaire) une sorte de machine à draguer [...] je recommence à racler, à gratter, à draguer le fond de la mer [...] la matrice dentée ne retire que ce qu'elle peut, des algues, des pierres. Des morceaux, puisqu'elle mord. Détachés. Mais le reste lui passe entre les dents, entres les lèvres. On ne prend pas la mer. Elle se reforme toujours. Elle reste, là, égale, calme, intacte, impassible, toujours vierge. Et puis je ne vais surprendre son texte avec une matrice dentée. Il n'écrit, ne décrit que cela: matrice dentée. C'est *son* objet.

> [Have I constructed something like the matrix, the womb of his text? On the basis of which one could read it, that is, re-produce it? No, I see rather (but it may still be a matrix or a grammar) a sort of dredging machine [...]. And I begin again to scrape (*racler*), to scratch, to dredge the bottom of the sea, the mother (*mer*) [...]. The toothed matrix [*matrice dentée*] only withdraws what it can, some algae, some stones. Some bits [*morceaux*], since it bites [*mord*]. Detached. But the remain(s) passes between its teeth, between its lips. You do not catch the sea.

She always re-forms herself. She remains. There, equal, calm. Intact, impassive, always virgin. And then I am not going to surprise his text with a toothed matrix. He only writes, only describes that: toothed matrix. It is *his* object.] (G, pp. 229b; 204b)

There are several competing ideas woven through Derrida's metaphor. The matrix as grid offers a mimetic form of reproduction, its own repeated square patterns providing Derrida with a scaffold of Genet's spatial writing and the tools to unpick, or 'scrape away' at his text in order to 'produire' or show it in *Glas*. But he puns on the (re)productive gesture of such exegesis. The matrix qua womb would also engender Genet's writing; Derrida seeking not to *surprendre*, to overtake or consume the text, but to give life to new epistemological possibilities nascent therein. The matrix-womb would have to contain the text to produce it, chronologically positioning Derrida as the mother who spawns Genet the son. Eager to collapse the messianic connotations of that critical gestation, Derrida perforates his matrix to show off the intrinsic partiality of his interpretation. The matrix is a net, or 'machine à draguer', that only captures fragments of a larger whole it never brings into focus. Derrida's metaphor grasps at the algae and stones, the concrete signifiers of Genet's writing, in a sort of textual geology that also lets the signified, the homophonous *mer/mère*, fall from the mouth. For Derrida, the ineffable mother is brought into relief by the grid that sublimates her elusiveness, dividing her into parts that are ubiquitous throughout Genet's texts while never essentialising her into one static form.

The matrix thus flaunts the undecidable in Genet's writing. Derrida calls it 'une matrice *ou* une grammaire', an incubator *or* a filter that lets go of what it claims to produce; using the internal contradiction of his textual object to disrupt any reproductive chronology in which Genet could be totalised by an authoritarian philosophical parent. The matrix, 'c'est *son* objet'. Aesthetically, this evokes Genet's posthumously published text, *La Sentence*, whose *canevas* [framework] of red and black squares makes manifest the question that plagues all of his texts: 'les mots écrits laissent passer quoi s'ils filtrent?' [what do written words let through if they filter?].[14] Confronting the binding nature of a judge's sentence, Genet imagines what it would mean for language to be a gauze that sifts through the non-said, words forming a framework that only points to a loss they cannot contain. Structured as a mesh, his language is visibly distanced from the binding discourse of the judge's verdict; rather, Genet's words usher in the remainders that stay unspoken, his French *laisser passer* implying a guest pass or invitation to contemplate the other side of any statement. He builds a logic in which 'dire que... est-ce afin de ne pas dire... et même de ne pas dire que?' [to say that... is it in order to not say... and even to not say that...?] (S, p. 28), collapsing dialectical reasoning (say/not say) to produce an undecidable grammar of contingencies and ruptures. Genet does not suggest that expression eclipses meaning, rather he wonders how writing can lead to any closure that draws words together to form a ruling decree that condemns or exonerates the individual. As he writes in this text, his own clauses inch us closer to the uncertainty of any such affirmation: as his monosyllabic words slip from *dire*, *ne pas dire*, *ne pas dire que*, he seems to frame a deconstructive *différance* that feels uncannily post-structuralist.

Yet, while *La Sentence* may seem to mirror *Glas* structurally, just as *Glas* imitates 'Ce qui est resté d'un Rembrandt', it is highly unlikely that Genet was influenced by Derrida's text at the time of drafting since his manuscript was only 'confié [...] aux Editions Gallimard au milieu des années 1970' [entrusted to the publishers in the middle of the 1970s] (*S*, p. 7).[15] Moreover, Derrida reads the matrixial structure of Genet's language less as an endless play of *différance* — less focused on a process of differentiation and delayed meaning — than on a journey towards a specific telos. Through *Glas*, he claims that Genet writes in the place of missing objects, scattering his signature, the proper name, as a *gênet* or flower to replace the absent mother.[16] The matrix and the filter offer ways to frame that absence, producing a mode of writing and reading that can sign without reification. So, unlike Hegel's repression of difference in the dialectic, Derrida's matrix invites us to consider the mother as what circulates around the pillars of Genet's texts, without ever being caught by concrete or univocal reference. Derrida argues that in Genet's text, 'on ne prend pas la mer'; we cannot take the sea/mother because 'elle reste, là, égale, calme, intacte, impassible, toujours vierge' (*G*, pp. 229b; 205b). The mother slips through Genet's grasp like water which falls from the terms that try to contain her; her matrix, her womb, always virginal insofar as it is untouchable. Derrida plays with this model of non-containment by figuring the matrix as 'dentée', a serrated or jagged mechanism that can only partially capture, or a toothed womb inflected with the full metaphorical weight of Freud's *vagina dentata* in which 'the female genitals [are portrayed] as a trap, a black hole, which threatens to swallow [men] up and cut them to pieces'.[17] The mother castrates, her womb a black hole that cannot contain Genet's text, but which eats into it, fragmenting any wholeness by detaching herself from all definitive forms. As a black hole, the full roundness of the mother collapses in on itself to reveal a matrix that vacates rather than fills, the mother revealed to be a geometric grid whose presence can only produce absence. The maternal matrix does not digest Genet the son; she can only disintegrate him, breaking him down into morsels that never reach any synthesis since her womb, like the *enceinte* of the prison that we will proceed to analyse, only ever gestates the inchoate child that never comes to term. The matrix that *mord*, or bites, is a homophone of *mort*, such that in a reversal of the life-giving process, the matrix delivers death. The matrix is thus never fully *enceinte*, neither fully pregnant nor fully enclosed. Rather, as a gridded womb, it incubates a remainder that 'passe entre les dents' (*G*, pp. 209b; 205b), between speech or discourse itself, and which threatens any discursive stricture that tries to restrain it.

The *palais de justice*: A Matrix of Judgement

If Genet's language is structured like a grid, it is both to allow him to escape from the dialectical judgement, and to bring forth an intimate absence that sits within an un-totalisable vision of selfhood. The former returns us to *La Sentence*, wherein Derrida's reading of Genet's gridded language as a toothed matrix echoes Genet's own description of 'les bouches [des juges] qui prononcent la sentence' [the mouths [of judges] who give the verdict] (*S*, p. 28). In an increasingly excited play with the paranomasia of *palais de justice* — as both the justice court and the palate or mouthpiece through which that justice is pronounced — Genet collapses the institutions of judgement found in buildings and in punitive language. He pictures judges vomiting justice from their *palais*: the verdicts that bind the individual to a life sentence nevertheless spew forth from mouths that are 'édentés' [toothless], incomplete and un-whole. The unequivocal discourse of the judge now originates from a space of partiality and fissure, as Genet imagines 'les palais artificiels des magistrats sont armés des dents de jeunes nègres' [the false teeth/ artificial palaces of the judge are loaded with the teeth of young black men] (p. 28). The judge's mouth is constructed as an instrument of punishment that is now divorced from any legitimacy, the sentence uttered by a substitute apparatus ripped from the mouths of those excluded from and condemned by the very justice supposedly being articulated. Genet revels in the idea that these dentures draw attention loudly to the artifice of their judgement as he evokes a 'mécanisme presque médiéval, en tout cas bruyant et toujours sur le point de se détraquer' [an almost medieval mechanism, noisy and always about to go haywire] (p. 28); Derrida's 'matrice dentée' here prefigured as a primitive mechanism that comes off its hinges to reveal the gaps in speech.

Genet's architecture of the *palais* not only unites the constructed nature of the court with the manufactured mouthpiece; but it also evokes the language of judgement, of moralising discourse, as a substitute that covers over the cracks and crevices that do not fit into a judicial logic. The false teeth of legal speech are no more than props in a ceremony of puppets whose totalising convictions are fractured by Genet's gaping presentation of language. Consider his mouth metaphor as a triple matrix. Visibly, Genet dramatises the image via a gridded *mise-en-page*, his metaphor slipping from a black square to a red square in an uncontainable process of textual filtration. Symbolically, the false teeth offer a metonym for the fallacy of any totalising condemnation. Ontologically, Genet seems to use the *palais* as a site of condemnation to pivot into a discussion around his own birth. Even before he was born, he toys with the idea that his fate was already sealed and gestating in the mouth-womb of the judge: 'condamné de toute éternité, étais-je de toute éternité complice de la sentence, prononcée ou grongnée, puis écrite?' [condemned for all eternity, was I eternally complicit with the sentence that was delivered or grunted, then written down?] (*S*, p. 28). Amidst this image of predestination, Genet figures himself as born in order to fulfil the sentence that is imposed upon him, his embryonic selfhood burgeoning not in the maternal matrix, but inside the judge's mechanised 'toothed matrix'.

Genet gets carried away by the metaphor, and, just as Derrida does, starts to turn the possibility of any totalising discourse entirely on its head. In a rhetorical question, he asks:

> Venu ici pourquoi? 'Afin d'y être condamné pour avoir fait main basse...', répond la voix multiple — c'est la voix d'une multitude cherchant à m'en imposer. Ma foi, c'est un bel organe! [...] saut de carpe à la retournée [...] l'oreille qui rencontre la langue poreuse [...]. Nuit: jour de perme et de sperme [...] cul qui roule n'amasse pas zob, n'entasse pas l'herbe... Derche à la recherche d'une colonne en marche — en marche ou en repos? ...J'oublie ce qui m'a défini et qui remonte à la surface de ma page. (*S*, p. 28)

> [Come here for what? 'In order to be condemned for theft...' responds the multiple voice, the voice of the multitude seeking to make that decree. My word, what a beautiful voice/ penis [...] let's flip this over [...] the ear that gleans this porous language [...]. At night: on duty, on heat [...] the rolling arse gathers no pricks, picks up no moss [...]. Backside looking for an erect penis — erect or flaccid? — I forget what has defined me and what rises up to the surface of my page.]

The stale, diagnostic language of the verdict is evacuated of any supposed objectivity to transform into an erotic site of reverie. Words and idioms are reorganised so that they tickle the visceral underworld of Genet's punitive imagination. The vocal 'organe' that condemns and moralises to the masses now transforms into the phallus that pleasures; the obedient expectations of the 'jour de perme' are subverted to form a night of illicit sex; the columnar pillars of the justice courts morph into the erect penis looking to satisfy anal desire; even the crime itself, 'avoir fait main basse', plays on the sexual innuendo of grabbing the nether regions. The social discourse of judgement is porous to Genet: words become a gauze-like mechanism of law and order that filters out the prurient and the visceral, which only allows Genet to bring both more easily to the surface of his texts. Indeed, his wanton puns seem to be produced by the very geometric strictures that try to contain them. As the rhythms of his words pick up pace, the 'derche' slipping to 'recherche' and then to 'marche', we bear witness to a geometry of sound that skims over the imprisonment of the symbolic and evacuates the socially-agreed codes of meaning recited by 'la voix d'une multitude'. After all, that 'bel organe' only serves to further satisfy Genet's homosexual desire as he uses the language of transgression against itself. Like the original idiom 'a rolling stone gathers no moss', so we tumble through Genet's double entendres to find ourselves liberated from any judgement that might stick. Thus, his penitentiary discourse does not only destabilise the dialectical power structures that allow for vice to be cleaved from virtue. Rather, it draws attention to the architecture of the verdict as itself a grid whose bars can but *frame* the convict, containing them only partially, and never able to essentialise the criminal *as such* given that the palate (*palais*) of justice is itself founded on artifice.

In a gesture of radical re-appropriation, Genet substitutes the institutionalised *palais de justice* for a different *palais*: the palate, or voice, of the criminal holding court within their own prison cell. He wonders what would happen to the justice system if the prisoner did not corroborate the dialectics of crime and punishment on which it is based, asking 'donc, si [...] LE CONDAMNÉ NE L'AVAIT ÉCRITE [LA SENTENCE], JOUR APRÈS JOUR ET À CHAQUE SECONDE, DANS LES DISPOSITIONS RECTANGULAIRES DE CELLULES, DES COURS, DES CORRIDORS, DE BEAUCOUP DE PRISONS? [so, what if [...] THE CONVICT HADN'T KEPT REWRITING THEIR SENTENCE, DAY IN DAY OUT, EVERY SINGLE SECOND, IN THE RECTANGULAR SPACE OF THE CELLS, THE COURTYARDS, THE CORRIDORS, OF MANY PRISONS?] (S, p. 18). Inside the rigid geometry of the prison, Genet wonders whether the convict who is forced to countersign their own prison sentence is also able to free themselves from its injunction by frustrating the dialectics of submission and co-opting the space of exclusion as one of belonging. If transgression only reinforces the rules sanctioned by the social order, then the convict will always be enslaved. Genet must imagine the prisoner indulging in their social exile to the extent that they intensify that transgression to a point of irreversibility. The sentence is no brittle binary Genet has any interest in breaking. Rather, he claims that 'alors qu'il [le condamné] croyait casser l'écriture de la sentence, elle n'était qu'un délié permettant un plein plus noir dans les seules limites de sa cellule' [while [the convict] thought he was going to break away from the verdict, it actually released an even blacker fullness within the confines of the cell] (p. 24). Sinking further into the black box of imprisonment releases a feeling of fullness that defies the language of 'lack' that society imposes upon the delinquent. By reconfiguring the rectangular cell, courtyard and corridor once intended for subjugation and control as sites of fulfilment, Genet uses spaces of domination to collapse the language of power.

Perhaps, as Claire Boyle has argued in relation to *Miracle de la rose*, this is how Genet 'claims for himself and his protagonists the potential to exceed the strictures imposed by a social system based on the surveillance-knowledge-power economy'.[18] In *La Sentence*, he skews a logic in which the convict falls victim to the judge's rule to locate them as the irritant that then constitutes the law: refusing to re-enact the servitude of their original sentence, his criminals gestate within the womb-like borders of the cell 'envoyant assez de sang dans toute la magistrature pour que soient dites de nouvelles sentences' [sending enough blood to the bench that they pass new sentences] (S, p. 24). The uniform geometry of the disciplinary space is thus provocatively embodied as Genet conjures up the body politic of the penal system, playing with the polyvalence of the term 'cell' to arouse the judiciary body into ejaculating more edicts. In Genet's *palais de justice*, the language of punishment is hollowed out as an empty frame whose square regulations give rise to an acutely erotic space of freedom.

My argument, then, is that the stylistic geometries of the circle and the grid in Sartre and Derrida's interpretations of Genet's language — which afford him the freedom to escape from the totalising dialectic — give rise to a spatial form of becoming in Genet's carceral imagination. This is not incidental: the dialectic is a form of linguistic imprisonment that runs counter to Genet's desire to break from the violent dichotomies of judicial sentencing that arbitrate between right and wrong. Like Foucault's long-standing invective against the fickle discursive codes of disciplinary systems and how 'une société *définit* le bien et le mal, le permis et le pas permis, le légal et l'illégal' [a society *defines* good and bad, permissible and not, legal and illegal], so Genet contests the binding judgements of the *palais de justice* by repossessing the postures, choreographies and geometries intended to stymie the individual in prison and locating these at the very origin of the criminal's purpose and self-understanding.[19] The revolutionaries in *Un captif amoureux* who look to start 'un incendie sautant [...] de prison en palais de justice' [a conflagration leaping [...] from prison to lawcourt] (*CA*, pp. 359; 306), find solidarity in Genet's own explosion of the hegemonic temporalities of rehabilitation and structures of reform directed outwards towards the health of society.[20] Instead, he poetically turns the experience of being behind bars into a formative geometry where the subject finds meaning beyond socially regulated forms of existence. The circuits he obsessively describes in the square spaces of Mettray and Fontevrault, and in the dramatic prisons of *Pour la belle* (the first version of *Haute surveillance*, written in 1942), *Haute surveillance* and *Le Bagne*, are far less nihilistic than Sartre's *tourniquets* may make us believe. Rather, throughout the rest of this chapter, I argue that they produce what Bachelard calls 'une géometrie intime' [an intimate geometry], or a gestational matrix to use Derrida's terms, that produces new forms of sodality and subjectivity.[21] Little attention has been paid to the cellular dynamics of Genet's prison as a space of gestation that creates subjects who cannot be totalised.[22] Thus, by focusing on the *ronde*, or circuit, around which the inmates process, I explore Genet's creation of a synecdoche that threatens the wholeness of the subjects that move within it. This partiality challenges the hard geometries of the prison aimed at forcing the individual into compliance, to reveal a maternal circularity in Genet's carceral imaginary. Through the insistent circular signifiers of the sun and the moon, I explore how geometry is connected to time in Genet's prison texts: his criminals destined to live from womb to tomb in what he calls in the screenplay of *Le Bagne* the country of crime. As a territory rooted in 'le mal' [evil], rather than in the nations of 'la France, ni l'Autriche, ni Pigalle, ni Marseille' [France, Austria, nor Pigalle, nor Marseille]', he constructs a citizen in perennial exile, orphans to their own motherland, since 'on ne peut pas faire le mal, [parce qu'] on est dans le mal' [we cannot do evil, since we are in it] (*B*, p. 226). Genet's prison undoes the oppositional language of transgression itself, his square and circular geometries forcing the dialectic to break apart and create a new form of social relation.

Ce cube clos et sa vie monotone': Prison Geometry[23]

Throughout the early 1970s, intellectuals, writers and activists in France mobilised against the injustices of the prison system. After Sartre launched a tribunal against the state in 1970 following the death of miners at Fouquières-lez-Lens, Daniel Defert and Michel Foucault founded the Groupe d'information sur les prisons (GIP) as 'a social movement whose aim was to let the prisoners speak, to give truth to the discourse and experience of the incarcerated, to create a field in which a certain truth of the prison could emerge'.[24] Although Foucault disbanded the group in 1973 (believing that the objective 'la parole aux détenus!' [Let the prisoners speak!] had been achieved), the GIP played an important role in Genet's own, albeit non-domestic, crusade against the penitentiary in his campaigns for the Black Panthers. White tells us of Genet's mercurial involvement with that group: first accompanying Foucault in the trial for George Jackson's prison rights; then, following his assassination on 21 August, writing the introduction to GIP's brochure, *Intolérable*, published on 10 November 1971, alongside unsigned essays by Deleuze, Foucault, Defert and Catherine von Bülow.[25] Genet was keen to assert his difference from his contemporaries bent on punitive reform, and when asked by Defert why he had not, at that point,[26] published a political text about prison, Genet explained that:

> On m'a dit que ça sera l'enfer. J'ai répondu que j'en ferai le paradis [...] si je publie quelque chose sur la France, je passerai pour un intellectuel. Je suis un poète. Pour moi, défendre les Panthères et les Palestiniens s'accord avec ma fonction de poète.

> [People have told me that would be hell. I answered that I would make a paradise out of it [...] If I publish something about France, I'll strike a pose as an intellectual. I am a poet. For me to defend the Panthers and the Palestinians fits in with my function as a poet].[27]

Despite seeming to divorce a political posture from a poetic one, Genet nevertheless politicises his poetic imaginary by asserting his anti-patriotic dissidence. He differentiates himself from the intellectual who speaks as an authority on social issues, and who seeks to effect change in the real world, seemingly because France is already imbricated in a legacy of domination which renders its struggles for justice at best obsolete, and at worst, hypocritical. As a poet, Genet is more interested in the prison as a space of a more abstract and universal exclusion, personified by the Black Panthers and the Palestinians as the constitutively dispossessed, marginalised and subaltern. Rather than fetishising the alterity of these two groups, Genet here uses poetry to contribute a new politics within the 1970s context of prison reform. He transforms the 'hell' of a punitive system that is imposed upon the criminal and that renders them a social pariah, into the 'paradise' of being free from the power structures that are institutionalised by any space of belonging. Only language has the capacity to recalibrate imprisonment. As such, the captivity that haunts his poetic imaginary from 'Un condamné à mort' in 1942 (a linguistic nod to Victor Hugo's own literary legacy of vilified criminality in *Le Dernier Jour d'un condamné*) to *Un captif amoureux* in 1986 is steeped in an idealised and hermetic abstraction that removes it from the tired master-slave logic tackled by the GIP.

In his posthumously-published epic on the penal colony, *Le Bagne*, which he never completed and wrote in spurts between 1949 and 1964, Genet insists on precisely the detached self-sufficiency of his prison:

> Une fois de plus je répète que ce récit veut être un poème. C'est-à-dire qu'il s'efforce de rendre sensible, apparente un certain complexe subjectif. Son but n'est pas de rendre compte du monde extérieur, de décrire un bagne réel, existant vraiment dans un lieu géographique précis et peuplé de forçats vivant encore, ayant vécu, ou de personnages copiés, calqués sur des êtres criminels réels. L'imagination de l'auteur crée donc, à partir de sa seule sensibilité, un univers arbitraire. Qu'on ne s'attende pas à découvrir entre les forçats ou entre les gardiens et les forçats, les rapports psychologiques habituels. Un univers

arbitraire, dis-je. Mais non incohérent. C'est d'ailleurs cette cohérence, cette logique dans chacun des rapports entre les éléments constituant ce récit qui donnera à l'œuvre sa vie. (*B*, p. 232)

[I repeat once more that this story is intended to be a poem. It strives to highlight a certain subjective complex. Its purpose is not to report on the outside world, to describe a real prison that really exists in a precise geographical place and populated by convicts who are still alive, or did historically, or characters modelled on real criminals. From his sensibility alone, the author's imagination creates an arbitrary universe. One does not expect to discover the usual psychological relationships between the convicts or between guards and convicts. This is an arbitrary universe. But not inconsistent. It is, moreover, this coherence, this logic in each of the relationships between the elements constituting this narrative that will bring the work to life.]

Closed off from the outside world spatially, historically and psychologically, Genet crafts the prison space as auto-telic and anti-mimetic. By uprooting it from any social realism, he cuts us off from the possibility of a moralising narrative to invite us to look inwards at new relations and subjectivities made possible by the networks of the prison space. Without external reference, Genet's 'univers arbitraire' plays around with the etymology of arbitration as a form of judgement or decision to locate him in the position of judge, allowing him to govern the space of his own prison imaginary rather than subject it to a (similarly arbitrary) rule of law. Liberated from the surveillance of a societal superego, Genet's poetic prison draws on the bars of its square architecture to withdraw from the world in a way that recalls the liberation described by art historian Rosalind Krauss's definition of the grid:

Flattened, geometricized, ordered, it is anti-natural, anti-mimetic, anti-real. It is what art looks like when it turns its back on nature. In the flatness that results from its coordinates, the grid is the means of crowding out the dimensions of the real and replacing them with the lateral spread of a single surface [...] its order is that of pure relationship [...] the grid declares the space of art to be at once autonomous and autotelic [...for] Mondrian and Malevich [...] the grid is a stairway to the Universal, they are not interested in what happens below in the Concrete.[28]

As a persistent figure of modern art, the grid signals a stepping away from a representational mode that directs us back towards the natural, inhabited world, towards an abstract space of contemplation of far more universal questions. The grid rejects any essentialising depth, or any of the 'rapports psychologiques' that Genet forbids in his imagined penal colony, to reposition us at the surface of networks and relations that interact with themselves in an aesthetic economy of meaning. The grid does not have to engage in the concrete political sphere of governance and ethics, but can propose a way to focus on internal relations freed up from the systems of oppression that aim to totalise them. Crucially, the grid is all boundary, simultaneously drawing attention to itself as well as its own, ungraspable outside.

Genet fixates on the gridded *mise en scène* of *Le Bagne*, paying strict attention to the form of the prison:

Carré, le bagne est entouré d'un mur de ronde très épais et très haut. Aux quatre coins, quatre miradors. Les murs sont très blancs. Les ombres projetées s'y découperont avec une parfaite netteté [...]. Il y a une série de bâtiments blancs, réguliers, rectangulaires, avec, quelquefois, une voûte et même une colonnade. Ils sont disposés autour d'une cour centrale dans laquelle il n'y a rigoureusement rien. [...] Le dortoir est une immense salle, divisée, sur tout un des grands côtés, en de nombreux box cloisonnés, très étroits. Dans chaque box, un lit de fer. Chaque box est séparé du couloir, par une grille de fer. (*B*, pp. 99, 131)

[As a square, the penal colony is surrounded by a very thick and very high perimeter wall. At the four corners, four watchtowers. The walls are very white. The projected shadows will be cut out with perfect clarity [...]. There are a series of white, regular, rectangular buildings, sometimes with a vault and even a colonnade. They are arranged around a central courtyard in which there is absolutely nothing. [...] The dormitory is a huge room, divided, on one of the long sides, into many partitioned boxes, very narrow. In each box, an iron bed. Each box is separated from the corridor by an iron grid.]

From the outer frame to the neatly apportioned network of square compartments, even the shadows that cut through the central courtyard of the penal colony create a grid. The hard-edged corners of the prison produce a network of ephemeral lines whose geometric precision generate the aspect of additional bars that force the individual into submission. The parade of repeated, rectangular blocks vertically barricade entry, while the curved 'voûte' cuts off any lateral access. In the square fortress of Genet's penal colony, an inexorable repetition seems to oppress the convict from every angle, as though space itself breeds the same patterns of endless sameness. As Krauss reminds us, 'structurally, logically, axiomatically, the grid *can only be repeated*'.[29] In this Russian doll architecture where squares sit within squares, Genet explores how the convict internalises their imprisonment such that they no longer seek a way out of the grid that obstructs them. In *La Sentence*, he explains that although:

La prison peut multiplier les ressources de l'espaces: les cours, les cellules, les corridors, les escaliers, les barreaux, malgré ces ruses, le condamné vertigineusement revient dans sa cellule [...]. Immobile dans sa cellule, elle était peut-être au centre de la prison puisqu'il avait accepté, peut-être voulu ce cube clos et sa vie monotone. Il faut parler de lui comme on le ferait d'une montre, suisse ou non, d'une boussole, d'un cadran solaire à l'ombre. 'Il marquerait midi' dans le langage des prisons signifie qu'il bande. (*B*, p. 24).

[The prison can multiply its use of space: the courtyards, the cells, the corridors, the staircases, the bars, but despite these tricks, the convict dizzyingly returns to his cell [...]. Stationary in his cell, this was perhaps the centre of the prison because he had accepted, perhaps even desired this closed cube and his monotonous life. We must speak of him as we might do a watch, Swiss or otherwise, a compass, or a sundial in the shade. In prison speak, 'he points to midday' means to have an erection.]

It is tempting to read this through Foucault's interpretation of 'la géométrie simple et économique' [simple, economic geometry] of the panopticon, where the threat of perennial visibility causes the prisoners to self-regulate and comply voluntarily.[30] But, Genet's take feels much more radical. Here the convict wills the prison's square architecture for its hermetic closure, transforming social scrutiny into a site of individual fulfilment. Not only is 'ce cube clos' a metonym for the wider prison, but it becomes its intimate centre, governed not by guard but by inmate. The grid that locks up the convict becomes a space of erotic sanctuary that locks out the social world, Genet overturning the power dynamics that Foucault ascribes to the panopticon by reversing the roles of this 'assujettissement réel naît mécaniquement d'une relation fictive' [real subjection born mechanically from a fictitious relation].[31] In Genet's imagined penal colony, we, the social gaze seeking compliance and dominance, are subjected to the whim of the prisoner who re-appropriates disciplinary geometries to fashion a space of self-love. As such, the bondage of the cubed space is fetishised as a form of masochistic pleasure, as though the physical restrictions of the cell, coupled with the social sanctions that sent the convict there, give rise to an implicit freedom. Genet teases us in *La Sentence* with the polyvalence of the 'voleur', to mean both thief and flyer, who imagines that their 'cellule cubique [est] emportée plus vite que l'avion le plus vite' [cubic cell gets carried away quicker than the quickest airplane] (*S*, p. 14). Internment is thus transformed into a vehicle of flight, as Genet recasts the static and stifling geometry of the prison that was intended as control into a space of freedom with the convict at its heart.

Genet figures the prisoner as a compass or a sundial around which the prison turns: its purpose, cardinal points and temporality all dependent on the convict who is apparently subordinated. As compass, Genet's prisoner becomes the geometric tool that draws out the circumference of their own confinement; they become the author of that restriction, using the deprivation of freedom inside the penitentiary to afford them new-found agency. Where Foucault claims the prison produces docile subjects within a disciplinary culture, Genet disrupts those master-slave relations by eroticising docility and turning compliance into arousal.[32] Indeed, the compass point is imagined as the erect phallus of the convict masturbating in his cell, the shadows made by his body producing a new semiotics of time and space that locates him as the dominant centre of the prison. His 'sexe dressé vers son nombril [qui] marquerait l'heure ou le nord [...] autour de lui et de son sexe, l'univers s'engendre et tourne mais selon des axes différents' [his phallus erect up towards his navel to tell the time or point North [...] around him and his phallus, the universe still turns but on a different axis] (*S*, p. 14). The phallic compass allows the prisoner to dominate his own domination; imprisonment generates a sexual stimulation that usurps the hard-edged geometry that Foucault attributes to the punitive apparatus to render it instead a site of visceral solipsism. Foucault explains that the architectural order of the prison 'impose sur le sol ses règles et sa géométrie aux hommes disciplinés' [the order of the architecture [...] imposes its rules and its geometry on the disciplined men on the ground], but Genet co-opts that prison geometry and makes it play to his own tune, collapsing the universalised patterns of time, power and even astrology that govern on the outside to form a new order that is beholden to the condemned.[33] Once a pariah, Genet's convict as compass now disorientates the poles of centre and margin so that we as reader, spectator, enemy, find ourselves absolutely lost.

Perhaps this is what is behind Genet's visceral thrill when, in the prologue to *Pour 'La Belle'*, he recounts that 'à me souvenir ce que fut ce cube d'air noir en moi quelque viscère se crispe' [to remember what this cube of black air meant to me my insides tense up].[34] Oppression is lent geometric form here, Genet transforming the cube from an abstract shape into a sensation of pestilent closure. Yet, that affect operates on and in the body of the prisoner, such that this square box becomes impervious to outside coercion. The cube that represses the individual, also generates a singular, visceral experience that cannot be universalised through any generic form of comprehension. The cube reveals the tension between torment and protection: an escape from social tyranny, albeit a claustrophobic one. If Genet demands in 'L'Enfant criminel' that 'le bagne [...] soit féroce' [the penal colony [...] is brutal] (*OC*, v, 385), perhaps it is to intensify that acute, ungraspable subjectivity that is vilifed in a social context. If we return to Krauss's analysis of the grid as that which 'does not reveal the surface, laying it bare at last; rather it veils it through repetition', we might argue that Genet's square geometries are far from incidental but re-enforce an idealised closure that will not lay bare his criminals to any ethical or psychological subordination.[35] He defies that social recuperation and instead aestheticises the penal colony as the apotheosis of his artistic vision: 'mon attitude devant l'œuvre d'art, que je veux close, monolithique, sans prolongement dans l'univers social, morte enfin. On ne saurait donc, ici, chercher une résonance sociale — soit une revendication, soit une justification' [My approach to art is something sealed off, monolithic, and with no repercussions in the social world. This is not where we'd look for a social response — be it a responsibility, or justification].[36]

The *marche en rond*: Geometry in Movement

In *Surveiller et punir*, Foucault famously argues that subjectivation is best achieved through highly ritualised corporal practice: 'des formes de coercition, des schémas de contrainte appliqués et répétés. Des exercices, non des signes: horaires, emplois du temps, mouvements obligatoires, activités régulières' [forms of coercion, schemata of constraint applied and repeated. Exercises, not signs: time-tables, compulsory movements, regular activities].[37] In performing these uniform rites and serialised movements, prisoners are regimented into a martial conformity that quells any autonomy. The language of linear formation that dominates such drills — line units, line-up, line personnel, line supervision — wards off recalcitrance, to the extent that Foucault characterises discipline as 'l'art du rang et technique pour la transformation des arrangements. Elle individualise les corps par une localisation qui ne les implante pas, mais les distribue et les fait circuler dans un réseau de relations' [the art of rank, a technique for the transformation of arrangements. It individualises bodies by a location that does not give them a fixed position, but distributes them and circulates them in a network of relations].[38] Stripped of subjectivity, the prisoner is controlled by being reduced to an ambulant body on a conveyor belt of repetitive movement. They are differentiated according to position, not character; their individuality commodified as an anonymous good in a wider logistics of power determined by the disciplinary authority. These measured steps serve no other purpose than the Sisyphean futility of walking around in circles, moving around the prison in calculated gestures that by definition go nowhere. For both Boyle and Amin, in two excellent articles on the intersections between Foucault's and Genet's writing on Mettray, the dehumanising effects of such repetitive disciplinary routines are either flouted or side-stepped completely by Genet. Either because he registers these routine techniques, but situates himself and his characters outside their laws of subjectification;[39] or because he defies their numbed, forward-marching time, what Amin calls the prison's 'chrononormative technologies', by 'giv[ing] way to automatism, and thence to dreaming'.[40] However, I believe that Genet intensifies these geometric choreographies in his prison writing, over-ritualising such cyclical gestures in a performance of solidarity and irreverent, non-totalisable subjectivity. Rather than being subordinated by corporal formation, Genet tempts us to see what formative, subjective possibilities are available within the most totalitarian methods of constraint.

Consider the embodied geometries strewn throughout his prison works. The rigorously empty, square courtyards of Mettray and the penal colony, which are intended for maximal surveillance, are produced in Genet's imagination by the bodies that mark their angles: in *Le Bagne*, 'quatre Noirs [...] forment un carré dont ils sont les angles' [four Black guards form the corners of a square] (*B*, p. 211); while in *Miracle de la rose*, the 'Grand Carré', is embodied by ten prison families such that 'cinq forment l'un des côtés du carré en face des cinq autres formant l'autre côté' [five of them form one side of the square, the other five form the side opposite] (*MR*, pp. 289; 81). Genet anthropomorphises the repressive architectures of the prison by allowing his subjects to embody its topography. The square — like the shadows criss-crossing the penal colony — cannot exist as a fixed barrier but must be implied negatively by those who demarcate it; its corners constituted by bodies who are geometricised, made 'anti-natural' in Krauss's terms, or de-essentialised so that their only function is to form the posts of an abstract quadrangle they guard. This symbiosis between the 'Grand Carré' and the subjects that partially inhabit and create it is reinforced through their measured movements in *Le Bagne*:

> La cour je l'ai dit est un grand espace vide, crépitant de soleil. Aucun bagnard, aucune corvée ne la traverse d'une façon libre et fantaisiste. On doit, pour aller d'un point à un autre, longer le bâtiment que l'on quitte, aller jusqu'à un de ses angles, faire un quart de tour, soit à droite, soit à gauche, et franchir l'espace vide en perpendiculaire. (*B*, p. 100)

> [I have already said that the courtyard is a big empty space, scorched by the sun. No convict nor chore may be traversed in a free and whimsical manner. To go from one side to the other, prisoners must walk along the building they are leaving, go to one of its corners, make a right angle, either to the right or to the left, and cross the empty space at a perpendicular angle.]

By tracing the square at right angles, Genet's prisoners mimetically re-enforce not only the limitations of its borders but the emptiness of its centre. Any movement that might deviate from this perpendicular route is forbidden, such that to traverse the central void, to 'franchir l'espace vide', is not to cross through but to walk around: *franchir* notably deriving from *affranchir*, to 'rendre libre' such that circumnavigation of the empty space also liberates it. Insisting on this ritualistic choreography around a centre that cannot be crossed, Genet appears less focused on the oppressive exercise of coercion, and more on the performance of a reverence, or fear, of a centre that escapes any such control. The prisoners' orbit brings that central emptiness into relief; their gait positioned in ritualistic homage to a radically inhospitable 'espace vide' that defies the totalitarian authority of the prison. No role nor task can encroach on the aesthetic freedom housed by this negative space, such that Genet demands his prisoners sink into their subjugated postures to produce an emptiness that becomes their territory alone.

This geometric ballet has none of the automatism or monotony that subdues the prisoner in Foucault's analysis. Rather, it calls to mind the much more self-conscious circuits that Beckett experiments with in his 1982 television play, *Quad*, during which four hooded performers repetitively navigate a square circuit that is divided into four triangles via two diagonal movements. As Beckett's performers obsessively complete their 75 cycles and 4800 steps around an imaginary quad, actively avoiding one another and a central void called 'E: supposé zone de danger. D'où déviation' [E: supposed danger zone. Hence deviation], their bodies deviate to produce a central gap is of their own making.[41] The square is set up as a site of potential: the spectator expects something to happen within it, that an event or encounter may bring it to fulfilment. In Deleuze's interpretation of the play in 'L'Épuisé', it is precisely this dual possibility that 'quelque chose *se* réalise et [...] que quelque part *le* réalise' [something realises *itself* and some place realises it] that is thwarted by the quadratic movements of the performers whose only action is one of avoiding any such happening.[42] Critics including Minako Okamuro and Steven Connor have read the geometry of *Quad* as plotting a course of 'increasing entropy, tending towards eventual lack', while Brett Stevens suggests that the mathematical patterns of the play lead to zero.[43] But, Beckett codifies this empty centre not as unfulfillment, nor sheer vacuity, but rather as a 'taboo [...]. Gradually one realised they were avoiding the center. There was something terrifying about it. . . it was danger'.[44] The void is thus made act; its 'supposed danger' deriving from the terrifyingly emancipatory possibility that this is a site that refuses any event, any system, any routine, a site that Deleuze perceives as exhausting space entirely:

> La potentialité du carré, c'est la possibilité que les quatre corps en mouvement qui le peuplent se rencontrent [...]. Épuiser l'espace, c'est en exténuer la potentialité, en rendant toute rencontre impossible [...] chacun se déhanche en solo pour éviter le centre. Ce qui est dépotentialisé, c'est l'espace.

> [The potentiality of the square is the possibility that the four moving bodies that inhabit it will collide [...]. To exhaust space is to extenuate its potentiality through rendering any meeting impossible [...] each sidesteps in solitude to avoid the centre. It is the space that is depotentialised.][45]

As the four performers move mechanically around the square, they, like Genet's prisoners in *Le Bagne*, exhaust the productivity of space. The taboo of this central void is perhaps its resistance to any kind of progress: it is anathema to the onward futurity and rehabilitation of penitentiary logic. Avoiding the centre offers a subversive gesture of resisting activity itself, such that when the prisoner Laurenti in *Le Bagne* barks 'contourne les bâtiments,... ne coupe pas les cours en diagonale, mais fais avec les murs un angle droit [...] file' [skirt round the buildings... but don't cut the corner at a diagonal, make a right angle with the walls... go!] (*B*, p. 48), Genet dramatises the remaining autonomy that the prisoners have left: only their perpendicular ballet can reinforce the dangerous centre that depotentialises space, collapses purpose and defies totalitarianism.

Derrida reads the 'Grand Carré' in *Miracle de la rose* not as a site of inactivity, but of disarticulation. For him, this totemic, empty square is a space that refuses exegesis: 'qu'est-ce qui bande ce texte, séduit et trouble le discours doctoral, introduit un écart (un "Grand Carré") dans la pièce où le patient se déshabille, se couche, ne dit finalement rien, fait en revanche bégayer le maître' [what bands this text erect, seduces and troubles doctoral discourse, introduces a gap (a 'Big Square') into the room where the patient is undressed, beds down, finally says nothing, makes the master stutter in return] (*G*, pp. 242b; 216b). The prison square transforms into the privileged gap in discourse that Derrida uses to destabilise any presumption of critical authority. Once again, the 'Grand Carré' disavows fulfilment: just as Beckett's performers or Genet's prisoners spatially circumnavigate this central gap, so too is Derrida's 'master' left stuttering, circling the words attempting to pin down what troubles any fixed thesis. Derrida's metaphor evokes the diagnostic set up of the psychoanalytic couch in which the patient transfers his inarticulacy, his gap in speech, to a master who attempts to cure or fill in, explain and totalise the missing link. Such terms endorse Derrida's earlier reproach to Lacan who, without any reference to Genet throughout his *Écrits*, presents the phallus as the 'clé universelle glissant dans toutes les lacunes signifiantes' [the universal key sliding into all the signifiying lacunae] (*G*, pp. 37b; 29b).No such phallic presence can unlock a prison square that has no keyhole, Derrida reading this 'écart (un "Grand Carré")' as the destabilisation of a hermeneutics of completion that seeks a transcendental key to fill in the gaps. Genet's 'Grand Carré' not only makes action stutter and vacillate undecidably; but it draws our attention to the periphery as a site of meaning that defies spatial or exegetical wholeness.

Turning from centre to margin, we might note that both Deleuze in 'L'Épuisé' and Foucault in *Surveiller et punir* warn that these marginal marches tend to sacrifice identity to form: 'determinés que spatialement' [only determined spatially], the individual is abstracted as no more than a coordinate in a series of anonymised positions that all defer to a higher authority.[46] However, Genet argues that it is along the perimeter that the subject expresses themself most fully. Genet is a writer of borders: limited by them in prison; liberated by them in his nomadic drift away from any notion of 'home'. He claims to live not just at the borderline in *Miracle de la rose*, embodying the geometric frame of the prison to the extent that 'son activité se limite à son cadre' [his activity is limited by its framework], but he extends the

metaphor so that his prisoners are exiled 'aux confins du cercle polaire arctique]
[the confines of the Arctic polar circle] (*MR*, pp. 247; 32). This latitudinal line
marks a frontier of habitation, such that Genet's prison, this 'univers restraint,
mesuré' [confined, measured universe] (pp. 246; 32), is imagined as a topography
of the contours that border the living. The prison is abstracted to no more than its
linear coordinates; the universe thinned out to map the outline of territory that can
only be lived in relief, never wholly. Although residency is uncompromising and
austere, Genet's 'cercle polaire arctique' conditions the figure of the *ronde* around
which his prisoners march, as a harsh border where he argues the self expresses itself
most fully. Indeed, it is in *Un captif amoureux*, when he extols 'la marche — ou la
marge frontalière — [comme] l'endroit où la totalité d'une personne humaine, en
accord et en contradiction avec elle-même s'exprime le plus amplement' [a border
is where human personality expresses itself most fully, whether in harmony or in
contradiction with itself] (*CA*, pp. 203; 170). Only when displaced and estranged
from the dominance of a homeland or national identity, can the subject confront
the otherness that coexists within and alongside us. By choosing to be marginalised,
Genet suggests that the individual is able to realise themselves totally because
they no longer bear allegiance to an abstract or external notion of belonging.
The paranomasia of *marche* and *marge* here reunites walking with its etymology
of marking a border: as though mobility encourages the individual to cross over
into a new frontier to thwart the yoke of a motherland and its limits. Certainly,
for Laroche, this *marche-marge* cuts to the core of the politics of Genet, who hunts
out the liminal as a space of freedom from 'une définition capitale eu égard à la
patrie' [the definition of homeland].[47] However, as Mairéad Hanrahan points out,
'la marche est à la fois endroit et mouvement, stabilité et changement' [walking/ the
step is both a place and a movement, stability and change], such that embedded into
Genet's language itself is a contradiction that defies the very totality of which he
speaks.[48] It seems that the marginal march he vaunts as a site of full self-expression
is one which also protects the individual from being imprisoned by any binding
identity or concrete placement. Rather, the totality of the subject resides in the
symbolic and syntactic gap that Genet exacts between 'la marche' and 'la marge',
a sense of self wrought as a liminality that jolts the stability of both centre and
margin.

The prison courtyard around which the inmates turn in *Le Bagne* dramatises
this insubordinate, slippery logic of the *marche-marge*. As the prisoners tread the
perimeter of the 'espace vide', their steps defy allegiance to the hegemony of fixed
territory. Rather, Genet exploits their status as outsiders to convert their *marche en
rond* into a form of social mobility that forges new alliances and sodalities across
borders. The self becomes a composite made up of encounters with marginal others
along a border that is not totalisable by any dominant authority. Consider the scene
in *Miracle de la rose* when Genet explores the power of these circular circuits in the
prison:

> La journée fut pénible, la marche harassante. Elle m'apporta pourtant la paix
> grâce à la puissance magique de la ronde. Car, outre cette paix d'être enfin en
> nous-mêmes par notre attitude penchée, nos bras croisés, la régularité de notre

pas, nous éprouvions le bonheur d'être dans une danse solennelle confondus par l'inconscient où dodelinait notre tête. Le réconfort de nous sentir unis, que l'on connait dans toutes les bandes en cercle ou en lignes, quand on se tient par la main, dans la farandole ou le kolo... nous tirions cette force de nous savoir marcher liés aux autres, dans la ronde. Nous éprouvions encore un sentiment de puissance, parce que nous étions vaincus. Et notre corps était fort parce qu'il bénéficiait de la force de quarante musculatures.

[The day was painful, the drill harassing. Yet it brought me peace, thanks to the magical power of the circular march. For, in addition to the peace of being within ourselves at last (by virtue of our stooping posture, our folded arms and the regularity of our pace), we knew the happiness of being merged in a solemn dance by the unconsciousness in which our heads dangled, and the comforting sense of unity that one feels in all round dances and other groups dances when people hold each other's hands, as in the farandole or the Kolo... We drew this force from the knowledge that we were bound to each other as we marched round and round. We also felt a sense of power, because we were conquered. And our bodies were strong because each profited from the strength of forty sets of muscles.] (*MR*, pp. 460; 280)

The *ronde* here replaces the angular march around the square courtyard. Genet embraces the geometric regularity of the drill and the trance-like motion of its linear patterns which overwhelm any idiosyncrasy, turning the single bodies into the shared union of 'notre corps'. It is the power of formation, of homogeny along this circular 'kolo' that is exalted here, Genet presenting the 'puissance magique de la ronde' as a self-governing circuit that evokes Krauss's grid as itself 'a world apart [...] both prior and final [...] autonomous and autotelic'.[49] Genet's *ronde* is also both prior to and beyond the subjects that follow its sequence as he references the 'kolo' and the 'farandole' as traditional dances that exceed the world of the prison. The *ronde* is vital to Genet's articulation of selfhood as it lulls the subject into a meditative self-assurance, being 'enfin *en* nous-mêmes'. However, the status of the self in 'ourselves' is troubled as the *ronde* is constitutively multiple: a synecdoche constituted by subjects, parts, which imply a unified whole. Walking in unison, Genet's subjects form a chain of parts in which they are bolstered by their participation in the whole — 'nous tirions cette force de nous savoir marcher liés aux autres, dans la ronde' — and through this unification they simultaneously suppress individuality and withdraw into themselves as though protecting their selfhood. The prisoners are empowered in their ligature to others in this concatenation, expressing themselves fully in their partiality within a chain constituted by gaps. For Derrida, this circular march partakes of a logic of substitution in which 'la "ronde des punis" qui se tiennent strictement debout, se ressemblant et se substituant l'un à l'autre en silence comme des lettres sur la page, l'une à la place de l'autre, l'une comptant pour l'autre' [the 'circle of inmates' who stand up straight, resembling one another and substituting for one another in silence like letters on the page, one in place of another, one counting for another] (*G*, pp. 47b; 38b). Derrida perceives the inmates' chain as producing a subjectivity that sacrifices its individuality to the series of which it is part, a plural singularity in which Genet creates a symbiosis through atomistic parts which can never entirely cohere. The subject is imagined as a plural singular 'corps [qui] était fort parce qu'il bénéficiait de la force de quarante musculatures'. The prisoners are strengthened by their uniformity, eschewing the individuation that Foucault finds at play in these subjugating corporal practices. Instead, Derrida reads Genet's *marche en rond* as 'un détachement en chaînes. Les Colonies, les Bagnes, les Centrales forment cette chaîne de chaînes qui sont toutes détachées' [a detachment in chains. The Colonies, the Prisons, the State jails form that chain of chains that are all detached] (G, pp. 154b; 136b), wherein the subjects are inextricable from the prisons they inhabit, those prisons themselves inextricable from one another. Genet persists in unifying his subjects along a chain from which they can be untied, their detachment in chains imbued with the 'reconfort de [...] sentir unis, que l'on connait dans toutes les bandes en cercles ou en lignes'. Not only does Genet attribute a sense of self specifically to circular geometry of this procession, but in so doing, he also aligns the subject with the *marge* of the *marche* which yokes the subject to a gap that cannot be expressed. Genet's subjects define themselves as much through the links (thus breaks) in the chain as on the 'réconfort' afforded by the 'pas' (a term itself implying both an affirmative step forward and a negative) that forges its connection: 'un détachement en chaînes'.

Like the solidarity experienced in these circular dances — where the individual abandons themself to the collective unity of form — Genet's visual language of gyration is similarly present in the opening scene of *Un chant d'amour*.[50] Here, the prisoners' circular movements produce a non-verbal semiotics of relation. Watch as the younger man restlessly paces in his cell and then begins a slow, circular dance (0.33). His movement offers an alternative form of communication, it is a way of making his presence known in the silent solitude of the space. His body harbours its own narrative power too (2.54) as his macro rotations in the cell forge a unilateral relation with the prisoner on the other side of the wall, which in turn catalyses smaller micro circular gestures that evoke their own story that is etched onto his body. In this geometric body language, we find a complex network of relations: the circular movements form a semiotic code that intertwines the prisoners. Through varying degrees of the same circular gesture (7.10, 7.51, 9.18), we move across the surface of individual bodies by indulging in common circulations. The prisoners are connected by visual gesture, not touch. In these erotically charged cycles, each inmate is tied to another through circular geometries — even the voyeuristic guard who moves from cell to cell and salaciously peers through the round hole in the wall — to establish a symbolic connectivity that brings subjects together in a shared solitude. In the privacy of their cell, the prisoners *do* dance across the centre, their movement more 'fantaisiste' or trivial than the *marche en rond* in the outer courtyard. Yet, the 'espace vide' is still in circulation since any voyeurism is predicated on a gap, here framed by the square aperture through which the guard gazes. Such is Genet's refusal to privilege one signifier over another that the 'espace vide' is not solely a consequence of a rectangular choreography nor is it only the product of a square frame; rather it is a question of Genet's impetus to insist upon the spatial construction, and liberation, of a void which cannot be breached.

The semiotic value of the circular chain thus rests on how it both affirms and compromises the singularity of Genet's prisoners. Grafted into and as the perimeter, the *marche en rond* becomes a way of effacing difference by promulgating the symbiosis of the inmates with the space they inhabit:

> La Salle est une sorte de grand hangar dont le parquet est admirablement ciré — et je ne sais s'il le fut avec des brosses et encaustiques ou par les chaussons de drap des générations de punis qui tournent l'un derrière l'autre, espacés de façon à garnir tout le périmètre de cette salle, sans qu'on puisse distinguer un premier d'un dernier, et tournant ainsi de la même manière que les colons punis, à Mettray, tournaient dans la cour du quartier.

> [The Cell is kind of a big shed, the floor of which has a high polish — I don't know whether it's polished by brushes and floor-wax or by the canvas slippers of generations of punished men who walk in a circle and are so spaced as to occupy the entire perimeter of the hall without anyone's being first or last, and who walk in circles the way punished colonists at Mettray walked round and round the yard.] (*MR*, pp. 252; 38)

As generations of down-trodden men tread literally into the floor of the prison, so Genet counters this vertical oppression by associating the circular march with a profoundly horizontal ethics of equality. A 'bonheur d'être' derives from the fact that the first subject cannot be differentiated from the last, just as the colonist in another prison performs the same movement in an act of deterritorialised sodality. Genet's language turns around itself in the lulling repetitions of 'tournant' and 'tournaient', as our eyes walk round and round the page of a whole heritage of subjugation that is smoothed over by the high shine of a floor that leaves no traces of its own violence. Individualism gives way to the camaraderie of resemblance, as Genet finds solace in the drudgery of this circular chain where rank, the ordering of 'un premier d'un dernier', loses any meaning. Instead, Genet vaunts the ethical possibilities of a 'marche *vers* l'homme' [march towards maleness] (*MR*, pp. 241; 26). Frechtman's translation equates this walking towards with a homosexual desire, whereas I wonder if there is a more intangible universality at play, one which echoes Giacometti's walking figures who reach for an ephemeral community that escapes their grasp. But Genet's vision of community becomes almost cannibalistic in this geometric 'marche vers l'homme', as he muses that:

> Durant ces années de mollesse, que ma personnalité prenait toutes sortes de formes, n'importe quel mâle pouvait de ses parois serrer mes flancs, me contenir. Ma substance morale (et physique qui en est la forme visible avec ma peau blanche, mes os faibles, mes muscles mous, la lenteur de mes gestes et leur indécision) était sans netteté, sans contour. J'aspirais alors [...] à me laisser étreindre par la splendide et paisible stature d'un homme de pierre aux angles nets. Et je *n'avais tout à fait* le repos *que* si je pouvais *tout à fait* prendre sa place, prendre ses qualités, ses vertus *lorsque* je m'imaginais être lui, que je faisais ses gestes, prononçais ses mots: *lorsque* j'étais lui.

> [During those years of softness when my personality took all sorts of forms, any male could squeeze my sides with his walls, could contain me. My moral substance (and physical substance, which is its visible form, what with my white skin, weak bones, slack muscles, my slow gestures and their uncertainty) was without sharpness, without contour. I longed at the time [...] to be embraced by

the calm, splendid stature of a man of stone with sharp angles. And I was not completely at ease unless I could completely take his place, take on his qualities, his virtues. When I imagined I was he, making his gestures, uttering his words: when I was he.] (*MR*, pp. 241–42; 26)

Genet stakes his pursuit of subjectivity on a geometry that exceeds the square *salle* and the circularity of the *ronde*, but which rests on the geometric contours of the inmates whose 'angles nets' lend form to his amorphous selfhood. The other becomes an implacable building whose hard-edged 'parois' offer a site of sanctuary in which Genet's inchoate body looks not only to be housed, but to gestate and become fortified. The other is further reified as a sort of Greek caryatid who upholds the *salle*, a pillar that Genet looks up to for an embrace based more on coercion than reciprocity. Indeed, Genet transforms relation here into an assimilation by his own desires. There can be no hospitality in the Levinasian sense, where the radical alterity of the other is respected through an infinite separation, rather than a desire for mastery; instead, Genet projects himself into the other convicts, assuming their dehumanised, angular stone features in a process where the self is formalised through erasure.[51] By chiselling himself into this sculptural 'homme de pierre aux angles nets', Genet abstracts his own individuality into a form of imitation: he too becomes more statue than man, more icon than subject, more outline than whole. As such, the anaesthetised language of shape — 'netteté', 'contour', 'angles nets', 'forme visible' — allows Genet to modify the dynamics of domination that subordinates the convict to the penal system; they are subordinated instead to his own imaginary, 'prisonniers de cet univers clos: ma rêverie et ce bagne' [prisoners of this hermetic universe: my dream and this penal colony] (*B*, p. 233). Yet, Genet's power play is more complex than simply exercising authorial sovereignty. In fantasising that he might find himself inside 'la splendide et paisible stature' of the exalted convict, he exploits the abstraction of form to other himself, and then make himself indomitable.

In a play of anaphora, Genet holds part of himself back from the assimilative encounters he seems to promote in the *ronde*: 'tout à fait' twice repeated as he grasps for a wholeness that is never reached; self-completion mired in the contingency of 'ne... que' and 'lorsque' as he propels the self into the imaginary realms of possibility and performance. When Genet takes the place of the other, inhabiting their words, gestures and actions, he is fashioning himself inside a simulacrum; the convict is stylised as a symbol of virility, standing, an image not a reality. Like the anecdote in 'L'Enfance criminel' when he describes how a blunted tin-knife that can exert no actual violence is nonetheless extolled by the child criminal as the emblem of power, because an idea is stronger than an object (*OC*, v, 386), so Genet safeguards himself, and his fellow convict, through an abstraction that cannot be appropriated by external authority.

A complex vision of solidarity thus emerges, where Genet exploits the politics of form and formation to protect the self and defy the system. Despite monumentalising his fellow prisoners in the *ronde*, Genet also stresses the abjection that unites them in a notorious scene from *Miracle de la rose* when he describes orbiting the latrine:

Au centre du cercle, il y a la tinette, où l'on va chier. C'est un récipient haut
d'un mètre, en forme de cône tronqué. Ses flancs sont munis de deux oreilles
sur lesquelles on pose les pieds après s'être assis sur le sommet, où un très court
dossier, pareil à celui d'une selle arabe, donne à celui qui débourre la majesté
d'un roi barbare sur un trône de métal [...] les punis continuent leur ronde
silencieuse, et l'on entend la merde tomber dans l'urine qui gicle jusqu'à ses
fesses nues. Il pisse et descend. L'odeur monte. Quand j'entrai dans la salle, je
fus surtout frappé par le silence des trente gars et tout de suite, par la tinette,
solitaire, impériale, centre du cercle mobile.

[At the centre of the circle, the can into which the men shit, a recipient three
feet high in the form of a truncated cone. It has two ears, one on each side,
on which you place your feet after sitting down, and a very low back-rest, like
that of an Arab saddle, so that when you drop a load you have the majesty of
a barbaric king on a metal throne [...] the others continue their silent round,
perhaps without noticing you. They hear your shit drop into the urine, which
splashes your bare behind. You piss and get off. The odour rises up. When I
entered the room, what struck me most was the silence of the thirty inmates,
and, immediately, the solitary, imperial can, centre of the moving circle.] (*MR*,
pp. 253; 39)

The scene is darkly subversive. Genet plays with direction, ennobling the most
debased of objects to fashion a sovereign totem around which the prisoners
rotate. Unlike the homophonous 'cellule', the 'selle' provides a space of release as
Genet exalts the excrement that falls through this conical throne, momentarily
deterritorialising the prisoners to relocate them in the Arab world as savage kings.
The metaphor is dangerously orientalist, associating Arabic power with atavism
and degradation. Yet, look closer at the body politic: the head of state becomes the
convict's behind; the French criminal becomes the rival Arab leader. The scene
reorganises the social hierarchy itself, and for Derrida, this trivialisation of the
pecking order that categorises up, down, in, out, are a signature of Genet's 'glossaire
mobile [... un] trou érigé que l'on monte comme un cheval, un trône, le cône d'un
volcan. L'érection en abime' [mobile glossary [...] an erected hole that we mount like
a horse, a throne, a cone of a volcano. The erection in abyss] (*G*, pp. 46b–47b; 37b).
The sunken or sullied is sublimated by Genet's penitentiary imagination, as Derrida
pictures Genet gloriously straddling an abjection that, quite literally, reigns supreme.
However, Genet does not strictly reverse positions. Consider his attention to form:
the truncated cone ruptures the 'cercle ininterrompu' [uninterrupted circle] (*MR*,
pp. 368; 176) of the *ronde*, collapsing this disciplinary *rang* to migrate to a site of loss,
of a remainder that cannot be reintegrated back into the perimeter. As a funnel, the
'tinette' cannot fully contain the waste it houses; rather, it becomes a filter where
the remainder falls down in a *katabasis* that never reaches any fixed ground, splashes
back up, and is diffused around the circle of thirty men in uncontrollable abjection.
The imperious cone thus becomes an altar on which remanence is enshrined; the
ronde a ritualistic salute that unites the prisoners in abject defiance of the totalitarian
regimes of their oppressor.
     When Derrida puns on how '[il] reste — à savoir — ce qui fait chier' [remain(s)
— to (be) know(n) — what causes shitting] in Genet's texts (*G*, pp. 46b; 37b), he

highlights how the 'tinette' that glorifies the 'reste', while never entrapping it, also generates a discourse of resistance. The expletive *faire chier* is a cry of revolt that operates both as action and metaphor: the prisoners' ablutions pierce the silent *salle* in what Derrida reads as a post-structuralist excoriation of totalising language. He draws our attention to how 'le glaviau qui résonne en cadence contre les parois de la grotte comme un glas guttural et mouille, dur et enduit la gloire de l'excrément solide qui s'élève dans le chant incorporel de l'odeur alors que tout "descend"' [the glob that resounds in cadence off the walls of the grotto like a moiled, guttural, hard and coated *glas*, the glory of solid excrement raised in the incorporeal song of the odor while everything 'drops'] (*G*, pp. 48b; 38b). That glottal, hollow sound echoes around Genet's conical 'tinette', resounding in the 'gicle' which splashes as the remains fall, and recalling the 'gl' that tolls the death knell of signification throughout *Glas*. Notably this is a sound Genet aims for both in the 'voix gutturale' [the guttural voice] of the 'Un... deux! Un... deux!' [One... two! One... two!] (*MR*, pp. 253; 242) that governs the *ronde* in *Miracle de la rose*, and in his film script for *Le Bagne*, as he demands his actors 's'expriment, s'il se peut, dans la langue africaine la plus gutturale. Dans ce film il semble que tous ignorent le français' [speak, if they are able, in the most guttural African language. In this film, no one speaks French] (*B*, p. 116). It is curious that Derrida's privileged motif of glottal (in)articulation is actively invoked in Genet's only text unknown to him at the time of writing. For Genet, that glottal sound evacuates what can be codified through a commonly understood symbolic order ('le français') and similarly for Derrida, the very purpose of 'gl' is its uniquely uncodifiable meaning: 'je ne dis pas le signifiant GL, ni le phonème GL, ni le graphème GL [...]. Cela n'a pas d'identité, de sexe, de genre, ne fait pas de sens, ce n'est ni un trou défini ni la partie détachée d'un tout. gl reste gl' [I do not say either the signifier GL, or the phoneme GL, or the grapheme GL [...]. That has no identity, no sex, gender, makes no sense, is neither a definite whole nor a part detached from a whole. gl remains gl] (*G*, pp. 137b; 119b). 'Gl' sticks in the throat, making signification stutter and reach for a fixed meaning that it cannot identify. 'Gl' defies the taxonomies we seek to make sense of; it has no place within them and thus becomes a remainder in any system that tries to channel it. Genet's faecal remainders are neither 'un trou' nor a 'partie détachée d'un tout'; rather they are a residual echo that reverberates in the 'tinette' (itself both a 'trou' and a part that entices a detachment away from the whole chain). Derrida breathes signification into the resonances produced by the hollow shape of the 'tinette', and so does Genet, who, 'frappé par le silence de trente gars', is then affected by the imposing majesty of the sounds that fall, rise and rebound within the cone. This scatological remainder mutes language to inspire an effect that circulates ineffably around the mobile *ronde*: remainders which descend and ascend in a guttural sonority that cries out against the totalitarian regimes of meaning, instruction and order in the prison.

'L'Être est rond': Cycles, Spheres, and the Circular *enceinte*

In the final chapter of *La Poétique de l'espace*, Bachelard explores the poetic and philosophical value of images of circularity in art. Citing artists from Van Gogh to Rilke, La Fontaine to Bousquet, he draws the conclusion that roundness appeals to an intimate expression of being. The circle holds neither a symbolic nor ornamental role that stands outside the individual for Bachelard, who contests those that argue that the comparison between ontology and geometry is incongruous: 'la vie, objecteront-ils, n'est certainement pas sphérique. Ils s'étonneront que cet être qu'on veut caractériser dans sa verité intime, on le livre aussi ingénument au géomètre, à ce penseur de l'extérieur' [they will object that life itself is certainly not spherical. They will express surprise that this being we seek to characterise in its intimate truth, should be so ingenuously handed over to geometricians, whose thinking is exterior thinking]. Rather than providing a way to map being in a spatial form, Bachelard contends that roundness is instrumental to the way we understand ontological notions of completion, wholeness and self-integration. He argues that 'vécu du dedans, sans extériorité, l'être ne saurait être que rond' [when it is experienced from the inside, devoid of all exterior features, being cannot be otherwise than round], as though constructing a model of being that is like one of Plato's forms, abstracted from the real world to exist in the imaginary space of selfhood as a perfected, indivisible whole.[52] Such is Carl Jung's psychoanalytic reading of 'the circle [which] always points to the single most vital aspect of life — its ultimate wholeness'.[53] There can be no room here for the empty circumference carved out by the disembodied hands of the compass; being for Bachelard is tied to 'la rondeur pleine' [full roundness] that is anathema to 'la sphère vide du géomètre [qui] est [...] essentiellement vide' [geometrician's sphere is an empty one, essentially empty].[54]

But for Genet, it is this precisely around this sparse geometric sphere that the subject finds their inner meaning, without being bound to any ontologising wholeness. Consider how the inmates' daily practice of the *ronde* mutates as a series of circular images in Genet's carceral imagination. In a passage in *Notre-Dame-des-Fleurs*, he describes how

> Les habitudes des prisonniers, ces habitudes qui font d'eux des hommes en marge des vivants [...] tourner en rond dans la cellule [...]. Les cercles et les globes me hantent: oranges, boules de billard japonais, lanternes vénitiennes, cerceaux de jongleur, ballon rond du garde-but en maillot.
>
> [The practices of prisoners, the practices that make of them men on the margin of the living [...] walking round and round the cell, and so on [...]. Circles and globes haunt me: oranges, Japanese billiard balls, Venetian lanterns, jugglers' hoops, the round ball of the goalkeeper who wears a jersey.] (*NDF*, pp. 115; 241)

Genet uses the routine orbit around the cell to transport us into an internal orgy of circular shapes, which far from mapping an idealised sense of self-completion, haunt his imaginary as hollow objects from whose grip he cannot escape. Most of these orbs enclose a space inside: the football is buoyant, while the Venetian lantern and the jugglers' hoops both allow light to pass through in a translucence that defies Bachelard's 'rondeur pleine'. These spheres roll randomly into one another in Genet's imagination; an inexorable poetry of movement where whole spheres transform into discrete, portable and banal entities. The unassuming randomness of an orange, a hoop, a ball, feels at odds with Bachelard's more grandiose desire for the circle to create an essentialising narrative of inner unification. In this spherical orgy, we travel from Japan to Venice to the goalkeeper's jersey, sliding over the surface of globes so that the very idea of the world is internalised by Genet as something accessible and mundane. In other words, Genet uses these round forms to transport himself out of the prison; out of the *ronde*, not further into it. We skate over these circles in a manner that recalls Barthes's reading of Bataille's circular metaphors throughout *L'Histoire de l'œil*, where 'tout y est donné en surface et sans hiérarchie, la métaphore est étalée dans son entier; circulaire et explicite, elle ne renvoie à aucun secret' [everything is given on the surface and without hierarchy, the metaphor is displayed in its entirety; circular and explicit].[55] Presenting these objects to us as endlessly changing surfaces that contain nothing, but are contained by his own imagination, Genet, like Bataille before him, refashions the image of the round as a shape that is non-essentialisable. It neither offers us the satisfaction of ontological completion, nor the symbolic value of wholeness; in Genet's world, it rolls around acrobatically trivialising the codes that force men to exist at the margins of the living.

The *ronde* is thus liberated from a purely mechanical movement inside the prison, or a lofty signifier of existential unity. Instead, it performs what Sartre calls a 'poetry of transmutation' that brings about Genet's salvation.[56] Genet uses language to catapult himself out of the reality of lived subjugation, charging his perception with square and circular forms that gambol around a spatial imaginary looking for freedom. In his hallucinatory 'word-poem' twenty pages later in *Notre-Dame-des-Fleurs*, Genet rhapsodises on Culafroy's wanderlust for Brazil, which he then superimposes with a premonition of Lou in prison. The temporality thrusts us into an imaginary future that whirls around confinement to produce creative modes of escape:

> Pour le boiteux, le Brésil était une île par-delà les mers et les soleils, ou des hommes aux carrures d'athlètes, aux visages frustres, s'accroupissent le soir autour de feux géants comme les bordes de la Saint-Jean, pour peler en lanières fines et frisées des oranges énormes, qu'ils tiennent dans une main, avec dans l'autre leur coutelas, comme les anciens empereurs des images tiennent le globe d'or et le sceptre. Cette vision l'obsédait au point qu'il dit '...des soleils...'. C'était le mot-poème qui tombait de cette vision et commençait à la pétrifier; le cube de nuit de la cellule, où tournoyaient comme des soleils (confondus dans une mêlée avec les jambes d'un acrobate en maillot d'azur exécutant un grand soleil autour d'une barre fixe) les oranges attirés par le mot 'Brésil'.

> [To the cripple, Brazil was an island beyond the sun and seas, where men with rugged faces and the builds of athletes squatted in the evening around huge fires like the bonfires of Midsummer Night, peeling in fine curling strips enormous oranges, with the fruit in one hand and a broad-bladed knife in the other, as, in old pictures, emperors hold the scepter and the golden globe. This vision so obsessed him that he said: '...suns.' It was the word-poem that fell from the

vision and began to petrify it; the night-cube of the cell, where the oranges attracted by the word 'Brazil' whirled about like suns (which mingled with the legs of an acrobat in light blue tights executing the giant circle on the horizontal bar).] (*NDF*, pp. 131; 266)

Genet names this sequence a 'mot-poème', in which a single word ('Brésil') conjures a chain reaction of signifiers: the squares — 'boîte-eux', 'carrures', 'cube', 'cellule', 'bordes' — contrasting with the rounded 'oranges', 'globe', 'soleil', 'tournoyaient', 'autour' in a complex geometry that casts Genet's imagination into an obsessive spatiality. What falls from this vision is the cubed cell around which the round sun turns: the square and circle *petrifiés*, fossilised, as two forms which sow the seeds of the metaphors that follow. The black box of the cell is illuminated by a mercurial sun that is not a sun, but an orange, then a globe. The sun is othered by its geometric slippage into adjacent circular forms, which collide with the 'carrures' of the prisoners who evoke the image of an acrobat rotating around the axis of a 'barre fixe'. These kinetic rotations trick the physics of space to allow Genet to defy the gravitational pull of the prison; his geometric shapes transforming the static, imperial insignia of the sovereign's globe and sceptre into the creative postures of an acrobat that uplift entrenched forms of power. We might think of Picasso's Harlequin whose supple movements reject the passive reception of the world to reconfigure a new visual language that multiplies perspectives of the world it describes.[57] Here, embedded in the signifier of the sun, is a whole new globe, protected from the outside world in the fertile astronomy of Genet's mind.

However, Sartre argues that Genet's 'mot-poème' is not generative but substitutive: the circle reproduces new metaphors that are no more than forms of absence. Genet's geometry thus formalises his failure to grasp at the freedom he constructs, as Sartre reads that:

> *Les* oranges se sont transformées en plusieurs soleils; le mot soleil laisse échapper un acrobate qui tourne et qui s'est imprégné du ciel sous forme d'un maillot d'azur. Le ciel tourne dans le soleil, les soleils tournent dans le ciel, le soleil est homme, l'orange est soleil, le soleil est couleur d'azur, le ciel est couleur de soleil, l'homme tourne, l'homme fait tourner dans sa main des oranges pareilles à des globes terrestres, à des soleils. Tout est donné dans les mots mais *comme absence*: quel œil humain pourrait voir à la fois, dans l'unité d'une même image, ces splendeurs contradictoires? Mais l'image est *à voir* et c'est son absence criante qui révèle l'Autre dans sa sollicitude.

> [The oranges have been transformed into several suns; the word 'sun' emits an acrobat whose body describes a circle and who has been saturated with the sky in the form of light blue tights. The sky turns in the sun, the sun turns in the sky, the sun is man, the orange is sun, the sun is azure-colored, the sky is sun-colored, the man turns, the man turns in his hand oranges similar to terrestrial globes, to suns. Everything is given in the words, but as an absence: what human eye could see these contradictory splendors simultaneously in the unity of a single image? But the image is to be seen, and it is its flagrant absence that reveals the Other in his solitude.] (*SG*, pp. 335–36; 299–300)

These symbolic mutations just reinforce Genet's absolute solitude for Sartre, his words circulating around images that stand in for impossible worlds or invisible relations. Holding the possibility of a new world like an orange in his hand, Genet cannot bring his imagined world to fruition in any logical way. Rather, the more he writes, the more his geometric language lends form to an abstract universe that is constitutively out of reach. For Sartre, that privation extends to mankind itself, as if 'le soleil est homme' is not a master metaphor but simply another permutation in a long line of symbolic images, such that all relation becomes as phantasmatic as the image of an orange-sun-acrobatic-Brazilian globe that Genet conjures. Rather than using metaphors to avoid and replace an absent alterity, Sartre argues that the circular signifiers in Genet's texts gesture to an alterity far beyond Genet's onanist imaginary.

However, arguably, this solar geometry is not as divorced from the embodied, social world of Genet's prison as Sartre's oneiric interpretation first implies. In *Miracle de la rose*, Genet's sun collapses the contours of the square and circular shapes it evokes in the 'mot-poème' to formalise instead those prisoners that blossom in its rays:

> En prison à ces instants où le soleil qui pénétrait par la fenêtre dispersait la cellule, chacun de nous devenait de plus en plus, vivait de sa propre vie, et la vivait d'une façon si aiguë que nous en avions mal, étant isolés, et conscients de notre emprisonnement par les éclats de cette fête qui éblouissait le reste du monde, mais les jours de pluie, au contraire, la cellule n'était plus qu'une masse informe d'avant la naissance, avec une âme unique où la conscience individuelle se perdait.

> [In prison, when the sun that streamed through the window scattered the cell, each of us became more and more himself, lived his own life, and lived it so acutely that we ached, for we were isolated and were made conscious of our imprisonment by the brilliance of the fête that dazzled the rest of the world, but on rainy days it was otherwise and the cell was merely a shapeless, pre-natal mass with a single soul in which the individual consciousness was lost.] (*MR*, pp. 318; 116)

By deforming the square outline of the 'cube de nuit de cellule', the sunlight disperses the rigid contours of the cell that limit the prisoners to galvanise a 'becoming' that renders them conscious of their imprisonment. The prisoners are vitalised by this solar radiance since it illuminates a universe beyond the cell, the universality of the sun enabling them to consider 'le reste du monde' and their isolated position within it. Here, to become is to form an individuality that is acutely solitary and lived in the full boundlessness of that isolation, since, although the sun 'dispersait la cellule', disseminating the hard surfaces of its walls, as the prisoners 'vivait de sa propre vie', they are captured in their own solitude, aware of the incarceration implied by their acute singularity. The sun does not shape-shift in this scene as it did in the 'mot-poème', but the image it illuminates does generate a similarly ungraspable alterity: the dazzling otherness of 'le reste du monde' from which the prisoners are withheld, the absence of their relation when they become undivided as an individual. Such individuality is 'aiguë', needle sharp, which, like the *punctum*, forges the subject in the unique wound of its singularity. Without the sun, the individual falls into quite literal obscurity as the pathetic fallacy of the murky 'jours de pluie' return the cell to a 'pre-natal mass' which deforms them. The prisoners are returned to an inchoate state as Genet foregoes their individual consciousness to depict the shapeless mass of the cell.

The image recalls the insistently embryonic representation of Genet's prisoners who live 'mollement' [limply] in the 'ventre sûr qu'est le bagne' [secure womb/belly which is the penal colony] (*B*, p. 111); foetuses looking for nurture in the maternal world of Mettray that Genet personifies as '"La vieille" puis "la sévère"' ['The Old Lady' then 'The Dreadnaught'] (*MR*, pp. 253; 195). As a womb in which his subjects gestate, Genet forces his prisoners to renounce their agency in regressive formlessness so that they are fully shaped by the shapes and structures of the prison. Even those subjects outside the cell who 'formaient un cercle ininterrompu de chair dure, bosselée, par où passait un courant assez puissant pour foudroyer l'imprudent' [formed an unbroken circle of hard, bulging flesh through which passed a current powerful enough to blast anyone] (*MR*, pp. 368; 173), whose hardened virility seems to defy any such nascence, awaken a chain of signifiers that nonetheless return us to the womb. As Elizabeth Stephens comments, in this 'entwined wreath of phallic bodies [...] virility surges like [...] an electric current'.[58] Yet that current recalls the circularity in *Le Bagne* when Genet insists that a 'courant électrique circule dans les fils qui ferment l'enceinte' [an electric current circulates around the wires that seal off the surrounding wall/pregnancy] (*B*, p. 94): these 'fils' (or sons) of the 'enceinte' (or pregnant womb) carry a current that seals off the prison just as it renders the circle of bodies intangible in *Miracle de la rose*. This 'cercle ininterrompu' thus becomes radically untouchable (albeit governed by touch), as Genet re-routes the current that guards the prison into the bodies of the prisoners who are now the ones not to be crossed. Such intangibility is both eroticised by Genet, who exalts the electric thrill he experiences in bearing witness to the ritualistic dance of the lawbreaker, and infantilised by him, as he folds this carousel of bodies into the uterine signifiers of his carceral imagination. Exploiting the abstract geometry of the circle, he abstracts the chain of prisoners so that the 'enceinte' and the 'ventre' around which they circulate creates an enclosure pregnant with 'fils', live wires and sons who are grafted into the peripheral 'enceinte' and who fill the pregnant prison with an orbit around vacuity.

Circulating as much around incubation as nothingness, Genet's *ronde* is intimately tied to a distorted kind of life-cycle that does not conform to the linear values of evolution, growth and progress that condition teleological notions of time. Part of what is most transgressive about Genet's circular space is how it refuses such developmental narratives. We might recall Bataille's definition of the *informe* as a process of aesthetic, moral and physical degradation, a bringing of 'things down in the world', such that the spheres of the *enceinte*, the *ronde*, the sun, or the unbroken ring of virile flesh that all return the individual to an inchoate state, collapse the productive narratives that govern our habitual understanding of a life-cycle.[59] As Amin points out, Genet crafts a circular temporality in *Miracle de la rose* when describing how 'à Fontevrault il me semble avoir grandi sans m'arrêter dans ma ronde' [at Fontevrault it seemed to me I had grown up without stopping in my round] (*MR*, pp. 252; 52). For Amin, Genet constructs an anti-developmental narrative as he walks around the *ronde* insofar as he 'grows and ages without maturing or making progress', while for Elizabeth Freeman, the *ronde* is static since 'the circular time of the march in the prison yard [...] is incommensurable with the cyclical rhythms of renewal associated with the seasons, the emotions, and the reproduction of life'.[60] Both critics read the circular space of the *ronde* as a form of queer time, where masculine solidarity and being bound to the ritualistic repetitions of ones ancestors supersedes personal growth.

While these readings are logical, I would argue that there is something even more nihilistic about Genet's penitentiary life-cycles. White questions whether Genet was ever a prisoner at Fontevrault since 'there is no notation of it in his prisoner record. Did he visit the prison, part of which was open to tourists, in order to correct his descriptions of it?'.[61] Growing up in the *ronde* at Fontevrault is thus far from autobiographical, far from tied to his actual life; it is *willed*. He conjures up these circular signifiers to lull him into the ever-infantilising safety promised by the protective poetics of the circle, seeking no egress from the imagined womb of the prison. Indeed, he figures the prison as the wheel of life: moving from the pre-natal 'ventre' to the *ronde* in which Genet 'semble avoir grandi', Genet then composes a *rondeau*, a musical round, in *Miracle de la rose* whose repeated refrain sings out:

> Le bagne a changé de place
> son nom a disparu
> mais on l'a remplacé par une prison immense
> Son nom est Fontevrault
> ce qui veut dire tombeau.

> [The colony has gone elsewhere
> Its name has disappeared
> And instead there's a big prison
> Whose name is Fontevrault
> which means grave.] (*MR*, pp. 343; 194)

In this facile prison ditty, Genet imagines the prison carrying its inmates from conception to delivery; and yet, the prisoners are held in Fontevrault as a grave. The womb of the prison thus entombs life: preventing its subjects from coming to full term by atrophying their progress and sealing it into 'les murs [qui] conservaient [...] la forme meme du futur' [the walls preserved [...] the very shape of the future] (*MR*, pp. 223; 7). The childhood sanctuary offered by Mettray formalises a future that is entombed by the walls of the cell, this square coffin mirrored by the *ronde* of the inmates that only accelerates the cycle of birth to death. We might recall Gayatri Chakravorty Spivak's analysis of the womb as intimately bound to the tomb, since 'the time of gestation *for* the mother [...] is a peculiarly contaminated exile from herself as a subject [...] human beings pregnant with nothing but their own death, always alive and dying until the completed "life" is delivered at death'.[62] Troubling the dialectical relationship between birth and death, Spivak's reading suggests that it is the maternal subject who is both forged and lost in this incubation, as she sacrifices her autonomous subjectivity to the mother she becomes. But for Genet in the *rondeau*, Fontevrault sacrifices the foetal inmates themselves, whose endless circuits around the prison shape their formation so that they travel from life to death without ever leaving the womb-tomb of the penitentiary.

Genet delights in the sterile sanctuary afforded by his maternal prison. In an interlude in *Le Bagne*, during which he stages an abstract discussion between the sun and the moon, he modulates the locus of the womb-tomb so that it is now housed by the moon that orbits the colony. The moon regales us with the lines:

> Je suis toute la féminité absente, laissée sur les anciens rivages, dit la nuit. Les forçats se coulent dans mon ventre noir, creux, plein, blême. Chaque nuit est engrossée. Les forçats oublient leur âge et leur agonie s'accélère [...] la nuit ouvre son cul immense où vient s'enfouir le jour oublié. (*B*, pp. 95–96)

> [I am all the absent femininity, left on the old shores, said the night. The convicts flow into my black belly, hollow, full, pale. Each night is impregnated. The convicts forget their age and their agony accelerates [...] the night opens its immense arsehole where the forgotten day is buried.]

Stripped of its folkloric fertility, Genet's moon is constructed as a barren womb full of emptiness, washed up on/as the peripheral *enceinte* of the prison and sheltering all those outcast from 'productive' society. The prisoner is constructed as a refugee housed by this atemporal cavern that collapses day and night, in a cycle that recalls Genet's *rondeau* as the subject is formed in an endless cyclicality that goes nowhere. Yet Genet's lunar *ventre-cul* is more radical than another incantation of the *ronde* in which the prisoners turn; rather, it equates the anus as a site of excretion with the production and eviction of the womb. The foetuses that gestate in the womb become equivalent to waste in this substitution of 'ventre' and 'cul', a comparison which recalls Bersani's famed reading of the scene in *Pompes funèbres* when Genet imagines rimming Jean: 'tout entier je pénétrais en rampant pour m'endormir sur la mousse, dans l'ombre, y mourir' [a cool bower which I crawled to and entered with my entire body, to sleep on the moss there, in the shade, to die there] (*PF*, pp. 161; 253). A sensation of ontological presence is afforded by Jean's anus into which Genet fully incorporates himself. The anus is described as a fecund woodland rather than a wasteland, its fertility gesturing to a pre-natal security in which Genet finds solace. Genet reverses the life-cycle by re-inserting himself as waste into his lover's anus as a (fertile womb-) tomb in which he dies. Such is Bersani's interpretation as:

> Genet's fantasized ascent into Jean through his anus is a savage reversal of this coming back to a life-nourishing site in the mother's body. The 'return' is now staged as reproductively sterile; from another man's body Genet can only emerge, or re-emerge, as waste [...] a parodistic reprise of the ecstatically sated infant slumbering at its mother's breast, as a lovely death within the 'cool bower' of Jean's rectum.[63]

Without referencing Genet's womb-tomb in *Le Bagne*, Bersani interprets this dualism as Genet's eroticised evacuation of the reproductive process. The cycle from birth to death is reversed so the life-giving womb delivers only death. The subjectivity that is granted by this other as a lover-mother, a womb-tomb, is thus figured as a remainder that falls from that space of otherness, which, in turn, falls from stable binaries. Perhaps what Genet is eroticising is in fact the evacuation of dialectical stability when conceptualising the subject. Genet's 'forçats [qui] se coulent dans [un] ventre noir, creux, plein, blême' are subjected to the non-dialectisable oppositions of a moon that cannibalises its own definitions. Both 'plein' and 'creux', 'noir' and 'blême', the moon that carries the subject is intimately bound up with the creation of a subject that sits nowhere. Instead, the subject slips ('se coule') into a moon which is itself a site of symbolic slippage.

The moon that cannot be appropriated into a stable linguistic schema is notably a signifier that Genet associates with the mother. The infamous scene in *Journal du voleur* sums this up when Genet believes he has encountered his unknown mother

> Dans une rue de la ville où j'écris, le visage blafard d'une petite vieille, un visage plat et rond comme la lune, très pale [...] la douceur de ce visage de poisson-lune me renseigna tout de suite: la vieille sortait de prison [...] si c'était elle [...] j'irais pleurer de tendresse sur les yeux de ce poisson-lune, sur cette face ronde et sotte!

> [In a street of the city where I am writing, the pallid face of a little old woman, a round, flat little face, like the moon, very pale [...]. The gentleness of that moon-fish face told me at once: the old woman had just got out of prison [...]. If it were her [...] I would weep with tenderness over those moon-fish eyes, over that round, foolish face!] (*JV*, pp. 22; 26)

The *ronde* returns as a signifier for Genet's maternal construct. Her imagined round, flattened moon-face recalls the pallid lunar sphere of the prison, but here she is not transcendentalised as the authoritarian prison itself, but the foetal prisoner subject to its whims. The master-slave dialectic is thus collapsed as Genet's rounded geometries rotate around any essentialisable position. When juxtaposed, Genet's metaphors constantly shift her position: in *Le Bagne*, 'La Lune' is a maternal substitute whose barren womb engulfs the prison; in *Miracle de la rose*, she is the colony itself; in *Journal du voleur*, she becomes an inmate in a prison she once embodied, leaving that space to assume the rounded image of a moon that stands contiguous to it. Genet's metaphors are made interchangeable: 'la vieille' a multiple cipher for prison and mother, inmate and moon; while the rounded light of the moon in *Le Bagne* bounces off the 'réverbère' that illuminates the lunar mother in *Journal du voleur*. When read intertextually, these maternal metaphors which circulate around the absent mother herself are, themselves, in circulation. As signifiers in constant flux, their circularity evokes the *ronde* to which Genet continually returns and yet, as a symbol of unfixed mobility, can never signify one single, thus totalisable, idea. The mother that inhabits this mobile circularity is rendered inaccessible precisely because Genet casts her into substitute images that are in endless circulation. She is everywhere Genet looks, and yet absent in any one single form.

To come full circle, it seems that the geometric prisms of the square and the circle that Sartre and Derrida apply to Genet's writing *post facto*, actually jostle throughout his carceral imagination from his earliest texts. These square and circular planes allow Genet to travel across the surface of his own imprisonment, as he instrumentalises the aesthetic possibilities of these shapes to defy the entrenchment that is willed by a penitentiary geometry looking to dominate the subject through containment, compliance and regulation. In the transformative potential of Genet's poetics, those patterns of docility are recuperated into a socially relevant politics (dramatising what Guattari later describes as Genet's use of the creative process, of 'fabulation' as a political re-engagement with the penitentiary condition).[64] The subject becomes in their abject circulation around the square prison; finds succour in the cubic enclosures that metamorphose into the maternal imago; and stages new ethical possibilities with those other inmates looking for a non-redemptive kind of relation. Genet's geometric imaginary is anathema to the psychologising effects of the disciplinary mode, which produces subjects through submission to power. Rather, it brings Genet's subjects to a symbolic surface of perennial movement, circulating as inchoate, dissident forms who bid their own abjection, their own incompletion, to radically resist the social, juridical and familial narratives that forever dominate the individual.

Notes to Chapter 4

1. Gaston Bachelard, *La Poétique de l'espace* (Paris: Quadrige, 2012), p. 196; *The Poetics of Space*, trans. by Maria Jolas (London: Penguin, 2014), p. 233.
2. G, pp. 350a; 251a.
3. See Christina Howells, *Derrida: Deconstruction from Phenomenology to Ethics*, Key Contemporary Thinkers (Cambridge: Polity Press, 1999), pp. 86–87, and 'Conclusion: Sartre and the Deconstruction of the Subject', in *The Cambridge Companion to Sartre*, ed. by Christina Howells (Cambridge: Cambridge University Press, 1992), pp. 318–52 (p. 349).
4. Albert Dichy and Michel Dumoulin, 'Entretien avec Jacques Derrida pour le film *Jean Genet l'écrivain*', 1992, IMEC, fonds Jean Genet, cited in Benoit Peeters, *Derrida* (Paris: Flammarion, 2010), p. 326, n. 683.
5. For a close reading of the differences between Sartre's and Derrida's texts see: Victor Kocay, 'Language and Truth: Sartre, Bataille, Derrida on Genet', *Dalhousie French Studies*, 48 (Fall 1999), 127–45; Robert Harvey, 'Genet's Open Enemies: Sartre and Derrida', in *Genet: In the Language of the Enemy*, ed. by Scott Durham (= *Yale French Studies*, 91 (1997)), 103–16; Howells, *Derrida*; Mairéad Hanrahan, 'Derrida hériter de Genet', *Méthode!*, 19 (Spring 2011), 53–59. Howells explains that '*Glas* may be read as an unacknowledged response to Sartre's work, whether by opposing it, striking off obliquely from it, expanding it, or even imitating it. Of course, *Glas* and *Saint Genet* remain radically different in many vitally important respects. Derrida's elaborate treatment of death or flowers, for example, Sartre's exploration of the "themes" of sainthood, evil or the medusa-like star of the other undeniably establish the specificity of their respective works' (*Derrida*, p. 87).
6. White, *Genet*, p. 651.
7. Peeters, *Derrida*, p. 326.
8. Harvey: 'By envisioning Genet as a mad botanist, Derrida is not far at all from Sartre who, in crediting Genet with creating himself from nothingness, reconstructs him as something of a do-it-yourself geneticist' ('Genet's Open Enemies: Sartre and Derrida', p. 110). Howells, *Derrida*, p. 91.
9. Howells, *Derrida*, pp. 91–94.
10. Aristotle, *Rhetorica*, in *The Works of Aristotle*, ed. by W. D. Ross, 12 vols (Oxford: Clarendon Press, 1908–52), XI, 1–6.
11. Jean Cocteau, *Le Passé défini*, ed. by Pierre Chanel (Paris: Gallimard, 1983), pp. 311–17; *Past Tense: The Cocteau Diaries Volume One*, trans. by Richard Howard (San Diego: Harcourt Brace Jovanovitch, 1987), pp. 263–70.

12. See Hazel E. Barnes, 'Sartre's Ontology: The Revealing and Making of Being', in *The Cambridge Companion to Sartre*, ed. by Howells, pp. 13–38 (p. 13).

13. Contemporaries Pierre Bourdieu, Louis Althusser and Geoffrey Hartman enthused about Derrida's rhetorical transgressions in this 'symphilosophy' or symbiosis of art and philosophy (Peeters, *Derrida*, p. 261), while Derrida also vaunted the epistemological possibilities of 'cette contamination d'un grand discours philosophique par un texte littéraire qui passe pour scandaleux ou obscène [...] elle rejoignait ou réveillait une tradition bien ancienne [...] une autre pratique de la lecture, de l'écriture, de l'exégèse' [this contamination of great philosophical discourse by a literary text that is reputedly scandalous or obscene', reawakening 'an old tradition [...] of another space, another practice of reading, of writing, of exegesis] (*Points de suspension*, pp. 360–61; 350).

14. Jean Genet, *La Sentence, suivi de J'étais et je n'étais pas* (Paris: Gallimard, 2010), p. 28 (hereafter referenced in main text as *S*). (Lane uses the term *canevas* in 'Trois mille ans d'histoire à treize mille mètres d'altitude', p. 45.)

15. Lane argues against Laurent Nunez's off-handed certainty of the 'évidence' of a connection to *Glas*, highlighting the temporal discrepancy between the 'vol à Tokyo dont il y est question ayant eu lieu dès 1967' and the fact that *Glas* was explicitly inspired by both *Ce qui est resté* and *Fragments* ('Trois mille ans d'histoire à treize mille mètres d'altitude', p. 47).

16. As Mairéad Hanrahan has argued, because Genet 'signs in the place of a loss, a loss with specifically maternal connotations [...] the Genet column [of *Glas*] thus invites reading as an exploration of what it might mean to sign 'in the name of the mother': 'Double Signature', *Paragraph*, 39.2 (2016), 165–86 (p. 169).

17. Barbara Creed, *The Monstrous-feminine: Film, Feminism, Psychoanalysis* (Oxford: Routledge, 2001), p. 106. Derrida also plays on the term *se méduser*, both to astound and to become a medusa, a figure whose head of snakes mythologically evoked the *vagina dentata*.

18. Claire Boyle, 'Autobiography, the Dangers of Knowledge and Genet's Suspect Reader', *French Studies*, 59.2 (2005), 189–202 (p. 195).

19. Foucault, *Dits et écrits*, II, 206, n. 95.

20. On the reform of aberrant or delinquent behaviour, see Foucault, *Surveiller et punir: naissance de la prison* (Paris: Gallimard, 1975); *The Punitive Society: Lectures at the Collège de France 1972–1973*, ed. by Bernard E. Harcourt, trans. by Graham Burchell, (London: Palgrave Macmillan, 2015).

21. Bachelard, *La Poétique de l'espace*, p.196.

22. Several critics have analysed Genet's prison texts to discuss the ethical dimension of his penitentiary imagination: Frieda Ekotto, *L'Ecriture carcérale et le discours juridique* (Paris: L'Harmattan, 2001); Laforgue *Notre-Dame-des-Fleurs*; Aicha El Basri, *L'Imaginaire carcéral de Jean Genet* (Paris: L'Harmattan, 1999); Suguru Minemura, *Jean Genet et la poétique du bagne (de la cellule pénitentiaire au bagne intime)* (Villeneuve d'Ascq: Atelier National de Reproduction des Thèses, 2001); Andrew Sobanet, 'A Pariah's Paradise', in *Jail Sentences: Representing Prison in Twentieth-century French Fiction* (Lincoln & London: University of Nebraska Press, 2008), pp. 63–100; Roland A. Champagne, 'Jean Genet in the Delinquent Colony of Mettray: The Development of an Ethical Rite of Passage', *French Forum*, 26.3 (Fall 2001), 71–90. However, few have launched a reading of the cell as a space of self-discovery, other than Boyle's 'Autobiography, the Dangers of Knowledge and Genet's Suspect Reader' that adopts a Foucauldian reading of Genet's autobiographical prison texts, and Kadji Amin's exploration of delinquency and criminality as modes of self-understanding in 'Anachronizing the Penitentiary: Queering the History of Sexuality', *GLQ*, 19.3 (2013), 301–40.

23. [This enclosed cube and its monotonous life] (*S*, p. 14).

24. Michel Foucault, 'Les Intellectuels et le pouvoir', interview with Gilles Deleuze, *L'Arc*, 49.2 (1972), 3–10, p.3: 'Deleuze: Quand vous avez organisé le groupe information prisons, ça a été sur cette base: instaurer les conditions où les prisonniers pourraient eux-mêmes parler' (cited in *Dits et écrits*, II, 106); *The Punitive Society*, p. 79, n. 32.

25. White, *Genet*, p. 652. See 'Préface à l'Assassinat de George Jackson' (*ED*, p. 111).

26. *La Sentence* was still unpublished. 'L'Enfant criminel', intended for broadcast on national French radio in 1949 was rejected, and now resides in *OC*, V, 377–93 (1979).

27. Cited by White, *Genet*, p. 259. Original citation from an interview with Defert in 1990.
28. Rosalind Krauss, *The Originality of the Avant-garde and Other Modernist Myths* (Cambridge, MA, & London: MIT Press, 1985), p. 9.
29. Krauss, *The Originality of the Avant-garde and Other Modernist Myths*, p. 160.
30. Foucault, *Surveiller et punir*, pp. 204; 202.
31. Ibid.
32. See Amin, 'Anachronizing the Penitentiary', for an exploration of how Genet uses queer temporality to resist compliance.
33. Foucault, *Surveiller et punir*, pp. 190; 200.
34. Jean Genet, *Pour la belle*, in *TC*, pp. 33–81 (p. 35).
35. Krauss, *The Originality of the Avant-garde and Other Modernist Myths*, pp. 160–61.
36. Cited in ibid., p. 111.
37. Foucault, *Surveiller et punir*, pp. 131; 128.
38. Ibid. pp. 147; 144–45.
39. Boyle argues that Genet refuses the processes of individuation by subjecting the scopic regime to its own controlling gaze, and by preventing the knowledge-gathering of punitive regimes by crafting an autobiographical genre that 'refutes the notion of a fixed identity' ('Autobiography, the Dangers of Knowledge and Genet's Suspect Reader', p. 199).
40. Amin, 'Anachronizing the Penitentiary', p. 320.
41. Samuel Beckett, *Quad*, in *Quad, et Trio du fantôme, ... que nuages ..., Nacht und Träume, traduit de l'anglais par Edith Fournier. Suivi de 'L'Épuisé' par Gilles Deleuze* (Paris: Minuit, 1992), pp. 8–15 (p. 12).
42. Gilles Deleuze, 'L'Épuisé', in Beckett, *Quad*, pp. 57–106 (p. 82); 'The Exhausted', trans. by Anthony Uhlmann, *Substance*, 24.3 (1995), 3–28 (p. 13).
43. See Minako Okamuro, '*Quad* and the Jungian Mandala', in *Samuel Beckett: Crossroads and Borderline, l'œuvre carrefour/ l'œuvre limite*, ed. by Emmanuel Jacquart (London: Rodopi, 1997), pp. 125–36 (p. 126); Steven Connor, *Samuel Beckett: Repetition, Theory and Text* (Oxford: Basil Blackwell, 1988), p. 94; Brett Stevens, 'Beckett's Mathematics in *Quad*', in *A Companion to Samuel Beckett*, ed. by S. E. Gonstarksi (Chichester: Wiley-Blackwell, 2010), pp. 164–81 (p. 170); Joanne Brueton, *Le Compas et la lyre* (Paris: Calvage & Mounet, 2018), pp. 140–48.
44. Samuel Beckett, RUL, ms 2100, quoted in Mary Bryden, '*Quad*: Dancing Genders', *Samuel Beckett Today/ Aujourd'hui*, 4 (1995), 109–22 (p. 111).
45. Deleuze, 'L'Epuisé', pp. 82; 13.
46. Ibid., pp. 80; 12.
47. Laroche, *Le Dernier Genet*, pp. 322; 369.
48. Mairéad Hanrahan, 'Silence et narration dans l'écriture de Genet', in *Cahier Genet*, ed. by Albert Dichy (Paris: Cahiers de l'Herne, 2018), pp. 1–21 (p. 9).
49. Krauss, *The Originality of the Avant-garde and Other Modernist Myths*, p. 10.
50. *Un chant d'amour*, dir. by Jean Genet (Connoisseur Video, 1950).
51. See Levinas, *Totalité et infinité*, and Derrida's elaboration in *Adieu à Emmanuel Levinas* (Paris: Galilée, 1997), p. 88; *Adieu to Emmanuel Levinas*, trans. by Pascale-Anne Brault and Michael Naas (Stanford, CA: Stanford University Press, 1999), p. 46: 'l'hospitalité suppose la "separation radicale" come l'expérience de l'alterité de l'autre, comme relation à l'autre' [hospitality assumes radical separation as experience of the alterity of the other, as relation to the other].
52. Bachelard, *La Poétique de l'espace*, pp. 209, 210; 233.
53. Carl Jung and Marie-Louise von Franz, *Man and His Symbols* (New York: Doubleday, 1964), p. 266.
54. Bachelard, *La Poétique de l'espace*, pp. 211; 235.
55. Roland Barthes, 'La Métaphore de l'œil', in *Œuvres complètes*, II, 88–95 (p. 91); 'The Metaphor of the Eye', in *Critical Essays*, trans. by Richard Howard (Evanston, IL: Northwestern University Press, 1972), p. 242.
56. Sartre: 'sa poésie n'est pas un art littéraire, c'est un moyen de salut' [his poetry is not a literary art, it is a means of salvation] (*SG*, pp. 337; 301).
57. For further exploration of Picasso's Harlequins, see Timothy Mathews, *Reading Apollinaire:*

Theories of Poetic Language (Manchester: Manchester University Press, 1990), p. 103: 'Apollinaire discovers in Picasso's work a space and a language that oppose the passive recording of the external world with a new access to creativity and to hitherto unexplored configurations of human experience'.

58. Stephens, *Queer Writing*, p. 135.
59. Georges Bataille, *Visions of Excess: Selected Writings, 1927–1939* (Manchester: Manchester University Press, 1985), p. 31.
60. Amin, 'Anachronizing the Penitentiary', p. 327. Elizabeth Freeman, *Time Binds: Queer Temporalities, Queer Histories* (Durham, NC: Duke University Press, 2010), p. 5.
61. White, *Genet*, pp. 288–89.
62. Gayatri Chakravorty Spivak, *Outside in the Teaching Machine* (New York: Routledge, 1993), p. 169.
63. Bersani, *Homos*, p. 159.
64. Guattari, *Cartographies schizoanalytiques*, p. 275.

CODA

❖

'Petits dessins géométriques'

Olga, j'ai repensé à votre plafond du salon. Il n'y a qu'un moyen pour faire disparaître cet affreux Sahara: trouvez une soie brochée rose très pale. De préférence broché à petits dessins géométriques. Pas de volutes ni de fleurs.

[Olga, I've thought about the ceiling in your lounge again. There's only one way to get rid of that awful, barren Sahara: find a very pale pink brocade silk preferably embroidered with little geometric drawings. No swirls or flowers.]

— Jean Genet[1]

From the ubiquity of shapes that emerge in Genet's writing to the conceptual significance they evoke around ontological singularity, non-familial lineage, the strange intimacy of displacement and non-metric spaces of becoming, this book has shown how productive Genet found geometry to be in articulating an idiosyncratic, indeterminate subjectivity. The practice of surface reading that has made these forms matter, has also revealed a surprisingly shared discursive field within the literature and theory of twentieth-century French thought. Genet's geometry renders him a thinker of his time, as his attention to forms and shapes stages unanticipated dialogues with post-structuralist thinkers also drawn to the poetics of space for configuring the fluidity of self and meaning. Just as Genet's geometric figures offer a configuration of becoming, rather than being, so Barthes, Derrida, Cixous, Nancy, Deleuze, Guattari, Foucault, overwhelmingly find inspiration in the mutability of points, lines, diagonals, grids, circles, whose forms never lead to formalisation.[2] Genet's geometric forms seem to anticipate several such theoretical postures: Deleuze and Guattari's notion of the rhizome; Barthes's *punctum*; Cixous's stigmata; Derrida's threads of filiation and the silkworm as a new kind of blood-line; Foucault's prison geometry and the oblique imaginary from which queer theory emerges. Yet, it diverges from a purely post-structuralist pull towards a spatialised reasoning, in which the tensions between representation and lack are perennially exposed.

Rather, Genet's uncertainty concerning the material dimensions of the *arpenteur*, the boundary, the science of navigation, the metrics of land, evokes some of the more phenomenological preoccupations of the existentialist moment in which his early works emerged. His attention to patterns, series, choreographies, contours, all reverberate in the desire to map and measure embodied space in the imaginaries of Beckett, Giacometti, Sartre, who, whether in direct relation to Genet, or as part of their own work, also seem to treat geometry democratically as a tool that enables the subject to navigate an incalculable, meaningless world. Geometry is never redemptive in this existential context; it does not provide a compass that leads the self to some form of enlightenment or self-discovery. It offers an aesthetic dramatisation of the urgent desire to orientate and anchor oneself in the world, and to re-examine the relations between the borders of space that force our bodies to walk blindly down the linear pathways of inherited norms, structures and systems that collapse any individual agency. Similarly, Genet's geometric shapes have intersected with non-francophone contemporaries such as Wassily Kandinsky, Louise Bourgeois, Walter Benjamin, who inscribe the geometric elements in their art as a way to fracture perspective and jolt the senses out of the (arbitrary) horizontal and vertical axes that render the world legible. It seems only by materialising abstraction through textual and artistic space can the individual think beyond codification.

Much as historicising Genet's metaphorical use of geometric figures helps to assimilate his work into the broader ontological concerns of twentieth-century France, there is a danger that this generalises the singularity of what geometry brings to constructions of the self. Genet never reifies his geometric surface into one essentialised concept from which we can plot a stable subjectivity. In a balletic resistance to the unity of form and meaning, his shapes operate both as signifiers and signifieds — rarely both at the same time — and thus geometry is never identical to itself in any of his texts. His *arpentage* holds the possibility for measurement, for mapping, for carving out a field of subjectivity in tension with a purely aesthetic image of an elsewhere that safeguards the subject from those metrics. This undertow of earthly tangibility that his geometry evokes, helps bring what otherwise remains ineffable and incalculable in the human into relief in his writing. The material and the imaginary can sit together, producing a geometric aesthetic that is profoundly emancipatory. The pursuit of axiomatic truth and a resistance to those axioms can be held together in Genet's work, liberating the subject from the closure of definition, identity, political category, teleology or ontological purpose to find material form in uprooted abstraction.

To close this book, I want to develop this aesthetic capacity of geometry to liberate the subject by reading four of Genet's geometric sketches that dramatise visually what I have been exploring textually. Borrowing a term that Genet casually uses in a letter to one of his editors, Olga Barbezat, here I present his 'petits dessins géométriques' as images that allow for subjects, space and even language to move within a dynamic of indeterminacy, discontinuity and ellipsis. Genet seems to use the idiom of geometric delineation, encirclement, limitation and circumscription against itself as he produces faces that modulate away from any logic or completion as we look. Except for one illuminating commentary in Fabrice Flahutez's chapter 'Jean Genet dessinateur' in *Toutes les images du langage*, later published as 'Les Multiples Pratiques du dessin chez Jean Genet', these images have been otherwise unexplored in Genet criticism.[3] As Flahutez remarks 'le statut "à part" de ce matériel graphique lui donne un intérêt certain car pour Jean Genet, il n'est pas fait pour être montré. Il est donc dénué de stratégies ou d'intentions précises' [that this graphic material has been set apart from Genet studies renders it worthy of analysis, precisely since it wasn't intended to be shown to anyone. It is thus devoid of any intentional strategy].[4] Studying these images vindicates the value I have found Genet to place in geometric figures as forms that instinctively drive his subjective representations. It is difficult to periodise the drawings, since as Flahutez points out, the only markers we have are the archival material on which they are produced: 'rapidement esquissés sur l'envers d'un bulletin d'abonnement pour *Les Temps modernes* ou sur des morceaux de papier déchirés, des cahiers d'écolier' [quickly sketched on the back of a subscription form for *Les Temps modernes* or on bits of scrap paper, or school books] (p. 81). Given that Sartre helped found the journal in September 1944, and Genet left prison in March 1944, it is fair to assume that they were sketched out of prison. However, a small note on top of the pile of sketches at the archive states 'carnet de prison de l'expo sur l'occupation' [prison notebook from the exhibition about the Occupation] implying that perhaps some date from his time in prison. The reason for trying to periodise Genet's images is to consider whether they were drawn in isolation or in relation to artworks made by his contemporaries, in particular Cocteau and Miró, who were responding much more overtly to geometric forms as ways of exploring representations of the subject. Indeed, Genet's sketches present four portraits whose abstract linearity evokes Cocteau's single line drawings of faces, while also resembling the detached lines and floating eyes of a Miró drawing. Across all three artists, there seems to be a common geometric inclination in the way in which faces are presented as a pure surface by one continuous line, all suspended in mid-air in an abstract formation that is ungrounded, disconnected and cut off from any external relation. Looking at Genet's four profiles, each face imposes a radical sense of isolation; their difference making it difficult to position them in relation to one another or indeed to us as we try to relate to them. The only element that unites them is a sovereign line that creates their contours, but which breaks off indeterminately on each one. For Flahutez, 'la ligne les caractérise, une ligne continue, enveloppante, pure silhouette comme un système de formes palpables' [the line characterises them, a continuous, enveloping, pure silhouette like a system of palpable forms] (p. 83). Although such linearity is dominant across all four, I find it to be disconcertingly so in Figure 1 of Genet's profiles in particular.

This is a profile of a man carved out by one unbroken line, reminiscent of the line drawings Picasso and Cocteau made famous. Genet's line expresses considerable profundity and visual understanding in distilling down an immense effect into one contour. The face he creates seems to resemble a mask of Ancient Greek theatre, fixed in one poignant expression of distress, or grief, with its angular brow hanging over eyes which are notably absent from the image. This is notable in relation to Genet's other sketches which dramatically emphasise the eyes, as he multiplies lines to create two eyes on stalks like periscopes straining awkwardly out of the heads in which they are held. Flahutez also notices these stalk-like, cylindrical eyes, which he compares to the Grebo dance masks that inspired Picasso's early sculptural take on Liberian masks (p. 85). Yet, Genet's mask-like image bears no gaze; it is blind, lacking any outward-looking perspective as the brow creates a protrusion that marks a gap where that gaze should be situated. The gaze is thus only negatively implied by the angle that obscures it, this jutting brow creating a crevice that suggests a downward looking gaze toward the indented mouth. The gaping mouth is poised to speak but is silenced by the artwork; its spatial opening marking a verbal closure since, as an image, it cannot articulate anything beyond what is fixed by its expression.

This mute guise thus lends the impression of a mask, which typically layers one emotion onto another. But Genet only draws one face, evoking a mask that does not appear to conceal anything, but which imposes itself in the full presence of its artifice. Genet inscribes the subject not behind the mask but *as* its façade, presenting the subject as a figure that is constituted by its own disguise. Just like the angle of the brow which implies a gaze that is nonetheless absent, Genet's mask-like geometric face figures the subject as a presence that implies an absence it conceals. The mask symbolically re-instigates the logic of substitution I explored through Genet's circular images; however, in this drawing, it is the line which replaces the *ronde* as its geometric abstraction creates the impression of a mask that constitutively acts as a substitute for something that cannot be revealed.

Flahutez's analysis of Genet's image translates a similar idea of substitution into a textual realm as he reads how 'la ligne ininterrompue s'apparente à une signature, à une arabesque' [the uninterrupted line resembles a sort of signature or arabesque] (p. 84). The flourish of Genet's line trails off indeterminately as might a hastily-scribbled signature, its geometric calligraphy of lines, semi-circles and angles producing a scripture that recalls Querelle's monogram in *Querelle de Brest* or the haunting angularity of Hebraic scripture in *Un captif amoureux*. A signature stands in place of a subject it identifies; it is his place-holder which marks a symbolic presence and a physical absence. The signature gestures to the constitutive absence of figuration which always points to an elsewhere it cannot contain. If this geometric flourish does evince a signature, then it brings the geometric figures I have explored throughout this book to bear on Derrida's remark in *Glas* that Genet 'a disposé ses signatures à la place de tous les objets manquants' [sets his signatures in place of all the missing objects] (G, pp. 58b; 41b). Like the mask that substitutes something missing, or the signature which replaces an absence, so Genet's geometric drawing signs in the place of a lack, a gap or wound, present throughout his work. The line of this arabesque dramatises that emptiness in the way it trails off discontinuously, getting gradually fainter as it hangs incompletely on the page. The line has no definite end, gesturing to a discontinuity that points to a gap that is not figured. The outer contour is brought across itself to inscribe a diagonal line through the centre of the image, carving it in two. This oblique line both helps to create the linear face and ruptures it, fracturing its wholeness by splitting it just like the text of 'Ce qui est resté d'un Rembrandt'. This image could be unravelled by pulling on the line that creates it, such that, in the same way as the thread I explored in Part Two/I 'Lines', Genet's geometry is a fragile construct that often points to its own undoing. Where Genet signs through the *pointillé* or through this semi-circular linearity, he also signs through geometric figures that gesture to an uncertainty, or a lack, that they cannot incorporate. In the discontinuity of its points or through an uninterrupted line that can also be unfurled, Genet's geometric signature signs in a way that highlights a partiality that makes what is absent all the more present. Across each drawing, Genet's lines gesture to that absence not through erasure, but by breaking down the image they have created into parts. As Flahutez notes 'Genet n'efface ni n'estompe pour soustraire, au contraire il ajoute hachures et rayures' [Genet does not erase or blur his lines, rather he scratches or crosses-out, adding rather than subtracting] (p. 83). Lines accumulate so that any homogeneity that he might lend to his subjects becomes fractured, palimpsestic, demanding that we understand his vision of the subject as a constellation of endlessly bifurcating traces. He destabilises his own inscription by engraving new lines on top of old ones, creating a geometric figuration in which parts replace each other to make it impossible to measure any fixed whole.

Perhaps this is why the image that Flahutez perceives as a signature is so salient to the way Genet signs his writing more generally, recalling the recurrent motifs of obliquity, circularity, boundaries, negative space we find throughout Genet's textual space. Mainly, this line drawing is striking because it affirms how any assertion Genet makes through his geometric representation gestures to its own undoing: both the verbal form of his geometric motifs and the lines that are drawn in this image figure the impossibility of circumscribing a stable meaning. As soon as they are inscribed, they gesture to an elsewhere, a gap, an absence that cannot be integrated into their own figures. There is a space of uncertainty that Genet cultivates through his geometric figures which cross out, venture in different directions and circulate around a negative space they cannot contain. Indeed, in Genet's three other angular drawings, each subject is figured in relation to an object that extends from them or toward which they reach, these objects themselves formed of curves and circles which only catalyse another chain of geometric replacements so that there is no comfortable place in which any subject or object might sit.

Genet's ubiquitous recourse to geometric figures takes the premise of measurement, of circumscribing his writing and being able to navigate his subjects, and systematically evacuates any such possibility. The presence of so many geometric figures in his texts certainly lends weight to the idea that Genet presents a geometric signature, or that he signs geometrically, but only if we are to consider that one of his signature methods is to trouble the basis on which a figure is typically used. In other words, it is only by exploiting the geometric figures of the point, the line, the oblique, the grid and the circle that Genet offers an example of how they figure a partiality that empties out the wholeness on which mathematic geometry is based. My argument has been that both Genet's geometric signifiers and their concepts of singularity, connection, indeterminacy and containment are highly unstable in his writing. This is either because the signifier shape-shifts and calls out to other adjacent terms that rupture any stable signification, or because Genet uses the concepts that he associates with these geometric motifs to highlight what they will not contain. Through each dynamic figure, I have explored how the subject might find form within Genet's variable, partial geometries, in an attempt to respond to his question of whether we can map our individuality 'en la mesurant, comme ferait un arpenteur'. To navigate requires fixed points to traverse; it demands an acceptance of the relation between those points. But Genet troubles our attempts to navigate his subjects by rejecting any such circumscription, challenging the idea that 'notre connaissance de nous-même se bornerait à des "rapports"' [our self-understanding is limited to 'relations'].[5] Rather than confining the subject to an external relation to which they would be bound, Genet's point, line, diagonal, square and circle all liberate the subject by revealing a common solitude that is only relational because it is discontinuous. The subject is not fully embedded in any relation, material or ethical, but is positioned in an internal space of uncertainty, masked by a geometric substitute that stands in place of its own inaccessibility.

To conclude, I return to the epigraph of this coda. Perhaps Genet's texts seek to fill the barren landscape of a Saharan ceiling, or a post-structuralist insistence on lack, by indulging in the shifting materiality of his 'petits dessins géométriques'. In his textual world, geometry is set aside both from the purely abstract and universal logic of Descartes, and from the humanist resistance towards essentialising metrics à la Césaire. Rather, it is embroidered into the fabric of his texts like an ornament whose forms and patterns help realise the sheer incommensurability of an anti-identitarian subject, who moves inconspicuously around the structures, systems, discourses and institutions primed to define and confine the self. Just as Genet cautions Olga that the geometric aesthetic should not be adorned by any symbolic frivolity — in his geometry there can be no room for the floral motifs or arabesques that Sartre had used to claim that Genet finds refuge in the unreal — so his shapes must testify to something both real and idealised, to a subject who is there but utterly irrecuperable. Geometry thus offers a prism through which the reader might map Genet's vision of subjectivity. But it also safeguards the subject by materialising them only onto the surface of the text, poised over an emptiness, and gesturing to the elsewhere of aesthetic space that denies the very navigation the science of geometry once promised.

Notes to the Coda

1. *LMOB*, p. 146.
2. See Michel Serres, 'The Geometry of the Incommunicable: Madness', in *Foucault and His Interlocutors*, ed. by Arnold Ira Davidson (Chicago: University of Chicago Press, 1997), pp. 36–56, for an exploration of the alliance between geometric spaces, knowledge production and the discursive creation of subjectivity.
3. See *Genet et les arts*, ed. by Vannouvong, pp. 85–96. The drawings to which I refer can be found on pp. 95 (Figure 1) and 94 (Figures 2, 3, 4).
4. Fabrice Flahutez, 'Jean Genet dessinateur', in *Toutes les images du langage*, ed. by Frieda Ekotto, Aurélie Renaud and Agnès Vannouvong (Fasano: Schena; Paris: A Baudry, 2008), pp. 81–89 (p. 83).
5. Jean Genet, *J'étais et je n'étais pas*, in *S*, pp. 35–42 (p. 42).

BIBLIOGRAPHY

❖

Primary Works by Jean Genet

Le Bagne (Paris: L'Arbalète, 1994)

The Criminal Child, trans. by Charlotte Mendell and Jeffrey Zuckerman (New York: New York Review of Books, 2020)

L'Ennemi déclaré: textes et entretiens, ed. by Albert Dichy (Paris: Gallimard, 1991)

The Declared Enemy: Texts and Interviews, ed. by Albert Dichy, trans. by Jeff Fort (Stanford, CA: Stanford University Press, 2004)

Fragments... et autres textes (Paris: Gallimard, 1990)

Fragments of the Artwork, trans. by Charlotte Mendell (Stanford, CA: Stanford University Press, 2003)

Funeral Rites, trans. by Bernard Frechtman (London: Grove Press, 1994)

'How to Play *The Maids*', trans. by Julie Rose, in *The Maids*, trans. by Benedict Andrews and Andrew Upton (London: Faber & Faber, 2016), pp. 9–15

Journal du voleur [1949] (Paris: Gallimard, 1986)

The Thief's Journal, trans. by Bernard Frechtman, preface by Jean-Paul Sartre (New York: Grove Press, 1964)

Lettres à Ibis (Décines: L'Arbalète/Gallimard, 2010)

Lettres à Olga et Marc Barbezat (Décines: L'Arbalète, 1988)

Lettres à Roger Blin (Paris: Gallimard, 1966)

'Letters to Roger Blin', in *Reflections on Theatre and Other Writings*, trans. by Richard Seaver (London: Faber & Faber, 1972), pp. 7–60

The Maids and Deathwatch, trans. by Bernard Frechtman (London: Faber & Faber, 1989)

Miracle of the Rose, trans. by Bernard Frechtman (New York: Grove Press, 1966)

Œuvres complètes, 6 vols (Paris: Gallimard, 1952–79)

Our Lady of the Flowers, trans. by Bernard Frechtman, intro. by Jean-Paul Sartre (New York: Grove Press, 1963)

'Les Palestiniens', in *Genet à Chatila*, ed. by Jérôme Hankins (Arles: Solin, 1992), pp. 87–150

Pour la belle, in *Théâtre complet*, ed. by Michel Corvin and Albert Dichy (Paris: Gallimard, 2002), pp. 33–81

Romans et poèmes, ed. by Emmanuelle Lambert and Gilles Philippe, with Albert Dichy (Paris: Gallimard, 2021)

La Sentence, suivi de J'étais et je n'étais pas (Paris: Gallimard, 2010)

'Something Which Seemed to Resemble Decay', trans. by Bernard Frechtman, *Art and Literature*, 1–3 (March 1964), 83–90

The Studio of Alberto Giacometti, trans. by Phil King (London: Grey Tiger Books, 2014)

'That Strange Word', in *Fragments of the Artwork*, trans. by Charlotte Mendell (Stanford, CA: Stanford Universty Press, 2003), pp. 103–12

Théâtre complet, ed. by Michel Corvin and Albert Dichy (Paris: Gallimard, 2002)

The Tightrope Walker, in *The Criminal Child*, trans. by Charlotte Mendell and Jeffrey Zuckerman (New York: New York Review of Books, 2020), pp. 98–117

'Towards a Lettrist Lexicon', trans. by Paul Hammond, in *Theory of the Dérive and Other Situationist Writings on the City*, ed. by Libero Andreotti and Xavier Costa (Barcelona: Museu d'Art Contemporani de Barcelona, ACTAR, 1996), pp. ★★–★★

Un captif amoureux (Paris: Gallimard, 1986)

Prisoner of Love, trans. by Barbara Bray, intro. by Ahdaf Soueif (New York: New York Review of Books, 1986)

Un chant d'amour, dir. by Jean Genet (Connoisseur Video, 1950)

Secondary Works

ACKERLEY, C. J., *Obscure Locks, Simple Keys: The Annotated 'Watt'* (Edinburgh: Edinburgh University Press, 2010)

ADAMS, PARVEEN, *The Emptiness of the image: Psychoanalysis and Sexual Differences* (London & New York: Routledge, 1996)

AHMED, SARA, *Queer Phenomenology: Orientations, Objects, Others* (Durham, NC, & London: Duke University Press, 2006)

AMIN, KADJI, 'Anachronizing the Penitentiary: Queering the History of Sexuality', *GLQ*, 19.3 (2013), 301–40

——*Disturbing Attachments: Genet, Modern Pederasty, and Queer History* (Durham, NC: Duke University Press, 2017)

ANDREOTTI, LIBRERO, and XAVIER COSTA, eds, *Theory of the Dérive and Other Situationist Writings on the City* (Barcelona: Museu d'Art Contemporani de Barcelona, 1996)

APOLLINAIRE, GUILLAUME, *Le Bestiaire, ou cortège d'Orphée* (Paris: La Sirène, 1919)

ARISTOTLE, *The Works of Aristotle*, ed. by W. D. Ross, 12 vols (Oxford: Clarendon Press, 1908–52)

BACHELARD, GASTON, *La Poétique de l'espace* (Paris: Quadridge, 2013)

——*The Poetics of Space*, trans. by Maria Jolas (London: Penguin, 2014)

BADIOU, ALAIN, *L'Être et l'évènement* (Paris: Seuil, 1988)

BALIBAR, ÉTIENNE, *Citoyen sujet et autres essais d'anthropologie philosophique* (Paris: Presses universitaires de France, 2011)

BARNES, HAZEL, E., 'Sartre's Ontology: The Revealing and Making of Being', in *The Cambridge Companion to Sartre*, ed. by Christina Howells (Cambridge: Cambridge University Press, 1992), pp. 13–38

——*La Chambre claire*, in *Œuvres complètes: 1962–1967*, ed. by Éric Marty, 5 vols (Paris: Seuil, 2002), V, 785–892

——*Camera Lucida*, trans. by Richard Howard (New York: Hill & Wang, 1982)

——*Le Degré zéro de l'écriture* (Paris: Seuil, 1953)

——*Writing Degree Zero*, trans. Annette Lavers & Colin Smith (London: Cape, 1984)

——'La Métaphore de l'œil', in *Œuvres complètes: 1962–1967*, ed. by Éric Marty, 5 vols (Paris: Seuil, 2002), II, 88–95

——'The Metaphor of the Eye', in *Critical Essays*, trans. by Richard Howard (Evanston, IL: Northwestern University Press, 1972)

——*Roland Barthes par Roland Barthes* (Paris: Seuil, 1975)

——*Roland Barthes by Roland Barthes*, trans. by Richard Howard, (London: University of California Press, 1994)

BATAILLE, GEORGES, *L'Expérience intérieure* (Paris: Gallimard, 1943)

——*Inner Experience*, trans. by Stuart Kendall (Albany: State University of New York Press, 2014)

——*La Littérature et le mal* (Paris: Flammarion/Folio, 1990)

——*Œuvres complètes*, 12 vols (Paris: Gallimard, 1970–88)

—— *Visions of Excess: Selected Writings, 1927–1939* (Manchester: Manchester University Press, 1985)

BAUDELAIRE, CHARLES, *Œuvres complètes II*, ed. by Claude Pichois (Paris: Gallimard/ Pléiade, 1990)

BEAUMONT, MATTHEW, *Nightwalking: A Nocturnal History of London, Chaucer to Dickens* (London: Verso, 2016)

BECKETT, SAMUEL, *Disjecta* (New York: Grove Press, 1984)

—— 'The Exhausted', trans. by Anthony Uhlmann, *Substance*, 24.3 (1995), 3–28

—— *Quad: et Trio du fantôme, ... que nuages ..., Nacht und Träume, traduit de l'anglais par Edith Fournier. Suivi de 'L'Épuisé' par Gilles Deleuze* (Paris: Minuit, 1992)

—— *Watt* (London: Faber & Faber, 2009)

BENJAMIN, WALTER, *Arcades Project*, trans. by Howard Eiland and Kevin McLaughlin (Cambridge, MA: Harvard University Press, 1999)

—— *Gesammelte Briefe*, ed. by Christoph Godde and Henri Lonitz, 6 vols (Frankfurt: Suhrkamp, 1995–2000)

—— 'Painting and the Graphic Arts', in *Selected Writings*, ed. by Marcus Bullock and Michael W. Jennings, 4 vols (Cambridge, MA, & London: Belknap Press of Harvard University Press, 1996–2003), ★★, ★★–★★

—— *The Work of Art in the Age of Its Technological Reproducibility, and Other Writings on Media*, ed. by Michael W. Jennings, Brigid Doherty and Thomas Y. Levin, trans. by Edmund Jephcott (Cambridge, MA: Harvard University Press, 2008)

BENNINGTON, GEOFFREY, *Not Half No End: Militantly Melancholic Essays of Jacques Derrida* (Paris & Edinburgh: Edinburgh University Press, 2010)

BERSANI, LEO, *Homos* (Cambridge, MA: Harvard University Press 1995)

BEST, STEPHEN, and SHARON MARCUS, 'Surface Reading: An Introduction', *Representations*, 108.1 (Fall 2009), 1–21

BIZET, FRANÇOIS, *Une communication sans échange: Georges Bataille critique de Jean Genet* (Geneva: Droz, 2007)

BOURGEOIS, LOUISE, *Destruction of the Father/ Reconstruction of the Father: Writings and Interviews, 1923–1997*, ed. by Marie-Laure Bernadac and Hans-Ulrich Obrist (London: Violette, 1998)

BOYLE, CLAIRE, 'Autobiography, the Dangers of Knowledge and Genet's Suspect Reader', *French Studies*, 59.2 (2005), 189–202

BRAIDOTTI, ROSI, *Patterns of Dissonance* (Cambridge: Polity Press, 1991)

—— *Transpositions: On Nomadic Ethics* (Cambridge: Polity Press, 2006)

BRADBY, DAVID, and CLARE FINBURGH, eds, *Jean Genet* (London: Routledge, 2012)

BRUETON, JOANNE, *Le Compas et la lyre* (Paris: Calvage & Mounet, 2018)

—— 'Drifting with Direction: Going Astray with Jean Genet', in *On Drifting*, ed. by Carl Lavery, Marielle Pelissero and David Pinder (= *Performance Research*, 23.7 (2018)), 81–88

BRYDEN, MARY, 'Deleuze and Anglo-American Literature: Water, Whales and Melville', in *An Introduction to the Philosophy of Gilles Deleuze*, ed. by Jean Khalfa (London & New York : Continuum, 2003), pp. 105–13

—— '*Quad*: Dancing Genders', *Samuel Beckett Today/ Aujourd'hui*, 4 (1995), 109–22

BUTLER, JUDITH, *Excitable Speech: A Politics of the Performative* (New York: Routledge, 1997)

—— *Undoing Gender* (New York: Routledge, 2004)

CAPUTO, JOHN D., *The Prayers and Tears of Jacques Derrida: Religion Without Religion* (Bloomington: Indiana University Press, 1997)

CERTEAU, MICHEL DE, *L'Invention du quotidien* (Paris: Gallimard, 1980)

CÉSAIRE, AIMÉ, 'Poésie et connaissance', *Tropiques*, 12 (January 1945), pp. 157–70

—— 'Poetry and Knowledge', in *Lyric and dramatic poetry 1942–82*, trans. by Clayton

Eshleman and Annette Smith (Charlottesville: University of Virginia Press, 1990), pp. xlii–lvi

CHAMPAGNE, ROLAND A., 'Jean Genet in the Delinquent Colony of Mettray: The Development of an Ethical Rite of Passage', *French Forum*, 26.3 (Fall 2001), 71–90

CHAOUAT, BRUNO, 'Out of Palestine', in *Israeli-Palestinian Conflict in the Francophone World*, ed. by Nathalie Debrauwere-Miller (London: Routledge, 2010), pp. pp. 141–62

CIXOUS, HÉLÈNE, *L'Entretien de la blessure* (Paris: Galilée, 2011)

——*Philippines: predelles* (Paris: Galilée, 2009)

——*Philippines*, trans. by Laurent Milesi (London: Polity, 2011)

——*Portrait de Jacques Derrida en jeune saint juif* (Paris: Galilée, 1991)

——*Portrait of Jacques Derrida as a Young Jewish Saint*, trans. by Beverley Bie Brahic (New York: Columbia University Press, 2004)

——*Stigmata: Escaping Texts*, trans. by Eric Prenowitz (London & New York: Routledge, 1998), pp. x–xiv

——'Stigmates', *Lectora*, 7 (2001), 195–202

COCTEAU, JEAN, *Le Passé défini*, ed. by Pierre Chanel (Paris: Gallimard, 1983)

——*Past Tense: The Cocteau Diaries Volume One*, trans. by Richard Howard (San Diego: Harcourt Brace Jovanovitch, 1987)

CONLEY, TOM, 'From Image to Event: Reading Genet through Deleuze', in *Genet: In the Language of the Enemy* (= *Yale French Studies*, 91 (1997)), 49–63

——'A Restive Word', *Genet*, ed. by Mairéad Hanrahan (= *Paragraph*, 27.2 (2004)), 77–84

CONNOR, STEVEN, *Samuel Beckett: Repetition, Theory and Text* (Oxford: Basil Blackwell, 1988)

CONSTANT, PIERRE, *Violon solo: la musique de Jean Genet* (Paris: L'Amandier, 2011)

CREED, BARBARA, *The Monstrous-feminine: Film, Feminism, Psychoanalysis* (Oxford: Routledge, 1993)

CRITCHLEY, SIMON, *The Ethics of Deconstruction* (Edinburgh: Edinburgh University Press, 1999)

——*Ethics, Politics, Subjectivity* (London: Verso, 1999)

DANTE ALIGHIERI, *The Banquet*, trans. by Christopher Ryan, Stanford French and Italian Studies, 61 (Saratoga, CA: Anma Libri, 1989)

DE LAURETIS, TERESA, 'The Essence of the Triangle, or, Taking the Risk of Essentialism Seriously: Feminist Theory in Italy, the U.S., and Britain', *Differences*, 1.6 (Summer 1989), 3–37

DEAN, TIM, 'Lacan and Queer Theory', in *The Cambridge Companion to Lacan*, ed. by Jean-Michel Rabaté (Cambridge: Cambridge University Press, 2003), pp. 238–52

DEBORD, GUY, *La Société du spectacle* (Paris: Buchet & Chastel, 1972)

——*The Society of the Spectacle*, trans. by Ken Knabb (London: AK Press, 2005)

——*The Society of the Spectacle*, trans. by Donald Nicholson-Smith (New York: Zone Books, 2006)

——'La Théorie de la dérive', *Les Lèvres nues*, 9 (December 1956), 6–10 (repr. *Internationale Situationniste*, 2 (December 1958), 19–23)

——'Theory of the *dérive*', in *Situationist International Anthology*, revised and expanded edn, ed. and trans. by Ken Knabb (Berkeley, CA: Bureau of Public Secrets, 2006), pp. 135–45

DELEUZE, GILLES, *Cinéma 1: l'image-mouvement* (Paris: Minuit, 1983)

——*Cinema 1: The Movement Image*, trans. by Hugh Tomlinson and Barbara Habberjam (London: Continuum, 1986)

——*Critique et clinique* (Paris: Minuit, 1993)

——*Essays Critical and Clinical*, trans. Daniel W. Smith and Michael A. Greco (London: Verso, 1998)

——'L'Épuisé', in *Quad: et Trio du fantôme, ... que nuages ..., Nacht und Träume, traduit de l'anglais par Edith Fournier. Suivi de 'L'Épuisé' par Gilles Deleuze* (Paris: Minuit, 1992), pp. 57–106

——'The Exhausted', *Substance*, 24.3 (1995), 3–28

——*Foucault* (Paris: Minuit, 1986)

——*Foucault*, trans. by Séan Hand (London: Continuum, 1999)

DELEUZE, GILLES, and FÉLIX GUATTARI, *Mille plateaux* (Paris: Minuit, 1980)

——*A Thousand Plateaus: Capitalism and Schizophrenia,* trans. by Brian Massumi (London: Continuum, 2004)

DELEUZE, GILLES, and CLAIRE PARNET, *Dialogues* (Paris: Flammarion, 1997)

——*Dialogues II*, trans. by Hugh Tomlinson and Barbara Habberjam (London: Continuum, 2002)

DERRIDA, JACQUES, *Adieu à Emmanuel Levinas* (Paris: Galilée, 1997)

——*Adieu to Emmanuel Levinas*, trans. by Pascale-Anne Brault and Michael Naas (Stanford, CA: Stanford University Press, 1999)

——'Circonfession', in Geoffrey Bennington and Jacques Derrida, *Jacques Derrida* (Paris: Seuil, 1991), pp. 7–291

——'Circumfession', in Geoffrey Bennington and Jacques Derrida, *Jacques Derrida*, trans. by Geoffrey Bennington (Chicago: University of Chicago Press, 1993), pp. 3–315

——'Countersignature', in *Genet*, ed. and trans. by Mairéad Hanrahan (= *Paragraph*, 27.2 (July 2004)), 7–42

——*De la grammatologie* (Paris: Minuit, 1976)

——*Of Grammatology*, trans. by Gayatri Chakravorty Spivak (Baltimore: John Hopkins University Press, 2016)

——*Derrida: Critical Reader,* ed. David Wood (Blackwell, 1992)

——*La Dissémination* (Paris: Seuil, 1972)

——*Dissemination*, trans. by Barbara Johnson (Chicago: University of Chicago Press, 1981)

——*Edmund Husserl's Origin of Geometry: An Introduction*, trans. by John. P. Leavey (Lincoln & London: University of Nebraska Press, 1989)

——'"Etre juste avec Freud": l'histoire de la folie à l'âge de la psychanalyse', in *Penser la folie: essais sur Michel Foucault* (Paris: Galilée, 1992), pp. 141–95

——'"To Do Justice to Freud": The History of Madness in the Age of Psychoanalysis', trans. by Pascale-Anne Brault and Michael Naas, *Critical Inquiry*, 20.2 (Winter 1994), 227–66

——*Glas* (Paris: Galilée, 1974)

——*Glas*, trans. by John P. Leavey, Jr. and Richard Rand (Lincoln & London: University of Nebraska Press, 1986)

——*H.C. pour la vie, c'est-à-dire...* (Paris: Galilée, 2002)

——*H.C. For Life, That's to Say...*, trans. by Lauren Milesi (Stanford, CA: Stanford University Press, 2006)

——*Marges de la philosophie* (Paris: Minuit, 1975)

——*Margins of Philosophy*, trans. by Alan Bass (Brighton: Harvester Press, 1982)

——*Mémoires d'aveugle: l'autoportrait et autres ruines* (Paris: Réunion des musées nationaux, 1990)

——*Memoirs of the Blind*, trans. by Pascale-Anne Brault and Michael Naas (Chicago & London: University of Chicago Press, 1993)

——*Passions* (Paris: Galilée, 1993)

——*On the Name*, ed. by Thomas Dutoit, trans. by David Wood and others (Stanford, CA: Stanford University Press, 1995)

——*Points de suspension: entretiens*, ed. by Elisabeth Weber (Paris: Galilée, 1992)

——*Points: Interviews 1974–1994*, trans. by Peggy Kamuf and others (Stanford, CA: Stanford University Press, 1995)

——*Positions: entretiens avec Henri Ronse, Julia Kristeva, Jean-Louis Houdebine, Guy Scarpetta* (Paris: Minuit, 1972)

——*Positions*, trans. by Alan Bass (Chicago: University of Chicago Press, 1986)

——*Psyché: inventions de l'autre*, 2 vols (Paris: Galilée, 1998–2003)

——*Pysche: Inventions of the Other*, ed. by Peggy Kamuf and Elizabeth Rottenberg, 2 vols (California: SUP, 2007–08)

——'Un ver à soie: points de vue piqués sur l'autre voile', in Hélène Cixous and Jacques Derrida, *Voiles* (Paris: Galilée, 1998), pp. 23–85

——'A Silkworm of One's Own, in Hélène Cixous and Jacques Derrida, *Veils*, trans. by Geoffrey Bennington (Stanford, CA: Stanford University Press, 2002), pp. 17–93

DESCARTES, RENÉ, *Discours de la methode; plus La dioptrique; Les météores; et La géometrie* (Paris: Fayard, 1986)

DICHY, ALBERT, *L'Échappée belle* (Paris: Gallimard, 2016)

——'Genet, écrivain?', *Europe*, 808–09 (August-September 1996), 4–5

DICHY, ALBERT, ed., *Les Valises de Jean Genet: rompre, dispaître, écrire*, exhibition catalogue (Saint-Germain-la-Blanche-Herbe: IMEC, 2020)

DICHY, ALBERT, and PASCAL FOUCHÉ, *Jean Genet: essai de chronologie 1910–1944* (Paris: Gallimard, 2010)

DONNE, JOHN, *The Complete English Poems*, ed. by A. J. Smith (London: Penguin, 1971)

EDDÉ, DOMINIQUE, *Le Crime de Jean Genet* (Paris: Seuil, 2007)

EDELMAN, LEE, *No Future* (Durham, NC: Duke University Press, 2004)

EKOTTO, FRIEDA, *L'Écriture carcérale et le discours juridique* (Paris: L'Harmattan, 2001)

EL BASRI, AÏCHA, *L'Imaginaire carcéral de Jean Genet* (Paris: L'Harmattan, 1999)

EUCLID, *The First Six Books of the Elements of Euclid: In Which Coloured Diagrams and Symbols are Used Instead of Letters for the Greater Ease of Learners*, ed. by Oliver Byrne (Cologne: Taschen, 2013)

——*The First Six Books of the Elements of Euclid, with a Commentary and Geometrical Exercises*, ed. by D. Lardner, 9th edn (London: Taylor & Walton, 1846)

FAEBER, JOHAN, 'L'Homme qui marchait dans la douleur', in *Jean Genet: rituels de l'exhibition*, ed. by Bernard Alazet et Marc Dambre (Dijon: Éditions universitaires de Dijon, 2009), pp. 91–102

FINBURGH, CLARE, 'The Anti-monumental Cemetery: Ghosts in Jean Genet's "Quatre heures à Chatila"', *French Studies*, 74.4 (October 2020), 587–604

FLAHUTEZ, FABRICE, 'Jean Genet dessinateur', in *Toutes les images du langage*, ed. by Frieda Ekotto, Aurélie Renaud and Agnès Vannouvong (Fasano: Schena; Paris: A Baudry, 2008), pp. 81–89

FOUCAULT, MICHEL, 'De l'amitié comme mode de vie', *Dits et écrits: 1954–1988*, 4 vols (Paris: Gallimard, 1994), II, 163–67

——'Friendship as a Way of Life', in *Ethics: Subjectivity and Truth. The Essential Works of Michael Foucault, 1954–1984*, ed. by Paul Rabinow, trans. by Robert Hurley and others (New York: New Press, 1997), pp. 135–40

——'Des espaces autres', *Architecture, Mouvement, Continuité*, 5 (October 1984), 46–49

——'Of Other Spaces', trans. by Jay Miskowiec, *Diacritics*, 16.1 (1986), 22–27

——'Les Intellectuels et le pouvoir', interview with Gilles Deleuze, *L'Arc*, 49.2 (1972), 3–10

——*Surveiller et punir: naissance de la prison* (Paris: Gallimard, 1975)

——*The Punitive Society, Lectures at the Collège de France 1972–1973*, ed. by Bernard E. Harcourt, trans. by Graham Burchell, (London: Palgrave Macmillan, 2015)

FREDETTE, NATHALIE, *Figures baroques de Jean Genet* (Montreal: XYZ; Saint-Denis: Presses universitaires de Vincennes, 2001)

FREEMAN, ELIZABETH, *Time Binds: Queer Temporalities, Queer Histories* (Durham, NC: Duke University Press, 2010)

FREUD, SIGMUND, 'Creative Writers and Day-dreaming', in *The Standard Edition of the Complete Psychological Works of Sigmund Freud*, ed. and trans. by James Strachey, 24 vols (London: Hogarth Press, 1953–74), ix (1959), 143–53

——*New Introductory Lectures on Psychoanalysis* (London: Penguin Freud Library 2, 1933)

GENETTE, GÉRARD, *Seuils* (Paris: Seuil, 1987)

——*Paratexts: Thresholds of Interpretation*, trans. by Jane E. Lewin (Cambridge: Cambridge University Press, 1997)

GIRARD, RENÉ, *La Violence et le sacré* (Paris: Grasset, 1972)

GOYTISOLO, JUAN, *Genet à Barcelone* (Paris: Fayard, 2009)

GROS, FRÉDÉRIC, *Marcher, une philosophie* (Paris: Carnets Nord, 2009)

GUATTARI, FÉLIX, *Cartographies schizoanalytiques* (Paris: Galilée, 1989)

——*Schizoanalytic Cartographies*, trans. Andrew Goffey (London: Bloomsbury, 2013)

HAND, SEÁN, *Emmanuel Levinas* (London: Routledge, 2012)

HANKINS, JÉRÔME, 'Entretien avec Leila Shahid', in *Genet à Chatila*, ed. by Jérôme Hankins (Arles: Solin, 1992), pp. 17–69

HANRAHAN, MAIRÉAD, 'Derrida héritier de Genet?', *Méthode!*, 19 (Spring 2011), 53–58

——'Double Signature', *Paragraph*, 39.2 (2016), 165–86

——'L'Exhibition du vide: la blessure indicible à l'origine de l'art', in *Jean Genet: rituels de l'exhibition*, ed. by Bernard Alazet and Marc Dambre (Dijon: Éditions universitaires de Dijon, 2009), pp. 13–24

——'Sculpting Time', *Genet*, ed. by Mairéad Hanrahan (= *Paragraph*, 27.2 (July 2004)), 43–58

——'Silence et narration dans l'écriture de Genet', *Cahier Genet*, ed. by Albert Dichy (Paris: Cahiers de l'Herne, 2018), pp. 1–21

HARAWAY, DONNA, *Simions, Cyborgs, and Women: The Reinvention of Nature* (New York: Routledge, 1991)

HARDT, MICHAEL, 'Prison Time', *Yale French Studies*, 91 (1997), 64–79

HARDT, MICHAEL, and ANTONIO NEGRI, *Empire* (Cambridge, MA: Harvard University Press, 2001)

HARVEY, ROBERT, 'Genet's Open Enemies: Sartre and Derrida', in *Genet: In the Language of the Enemy*, ed. by Scott Durham (= *Yale French Studies*, 91 (1996)), 103–16

HERODOTUS, *The Histories*, trans. by Aubrey de Sélincourt (London: Penguin, 1954)

HOWELLS, CHRISTINA, *Derrida: Deconstruction from Phenomenology to Ethics*, Key Contemporary Thinkers (Cambridge: Polity Press, 1999)

——*Sartre's Theory of Literature* (London: MHRA, 1979)

HOWELLS, CHRISTINA, ed., *The Cambridge Companion to Sartre* (Cambridge: Cambridge University Press, 1992)

HUGO, VICTOR, *Les Misérables*, 10 vols (Brussels: A. Lacroix, Verboeckhoven, 1862)

——*Les Misérables*, trans. by Julie Rose (London: Random House, 2008)

JABLONKA, IVAN, *Les Vérités inavouables de Jean Genet* (Paris: Seuil, 2004)

JAMESON, FREDERIC, *The Political Unconscious: Narrative as a Socially Symbolic Act* (London: Methuen, 1981)

JOMARD, EDME FRANÇOIS, *Mémoire sur le système métrique des anciens égyptiens* (Paris: Imprimerie royale, 1817)

JUNG, CARL, and MARIE-LOUISE VON FRANZ, *Man and His Symbols* (New York: Doubleday, 1964)

KANDINSKY, WASSILY, *Point and Line to Plane* (New York: Dover Publications, 1979)

KANT, IMMANUEL, *Critique of Judgement*, trans. by Werner S. Pluhar (Indianapolis, IN: Hackett, 1987)

KHÉLIL, HÉDI, *Figures de l'altérité dans le théâtre de Jean Genet: lecture des 'Nègres' et des 'Paravents'* (Paris: Harmattan, 2001)

KIM, ANNABEL, *Unbecoming Language: Anti-identitarian French Feminist Fictions* (Columbus: Ohio State University Press, 2018)

KLEE, PAUL, *The Diaries of Paul Klee, 1898–1918* (Berkeley & Los Angeles: University of California Press, 1964)

KHATIBI, ABDELKÉBIR, *Figures de l'étranger* (Paris: Denoel, 1987)

——*Jacques Derrida en effet* (Neuilly sur Seine: Al Manar, 2007)

KOCAY, VICTOR, 'Language and Truth: Sartre, Bataille, Derrida on Genet', *Dalhousie French Studies*, 48 (Fall 1999), 127–45

KRAUSS, ROSALIND, *The Originality of the Avant-garde and Other Modernist Myths* (Cambridge, MA, & London: MIT Press, 1985)

KRISTEVA, JULIA, *Pouvoirs de l'horreur* (Paris: Seuil, 1980)

——*Powers of Horror*, trans. by Leon S. Roudiez (New York: Columbia University Press, 1982)

LACAN, JACQUES, 'Le Stade du miroir comme formateur de la fonction du Je', in *Écrits I* (Paris: Seuil, 1949), pp. 93–100

——'The Mirror Stage as Formative of the Function as Revealed in Psychoanalytic Experience', in *Écrits*, trans. by Bruce Fink (New York: W. W. Norton, 2007), pp. 75–81

LAFORGUE, PIERRE. *Notre-Dame-des-Fleurs, ou La Symphonie carcérale* (Toulouse: Presses universitaires du Mirail, 2002)

LAMBERT, EMMANUELLE and ALBERT DICHY (eds.), *Jean Genet, l'échappée belle* (Paris: Albums Beaux Livres, Gallimard, 2016)

LANE, VÉRONIQUE, 'Trois mille ans d'histoire à treize mille mètres d'altitude', in *Jean Genet, toujours en fuite*, ed. by Véronique Lane (= *Spirale*, 240 (Spring 2012)), 45–47

LATOUR, BRUNO, 'Why Has Critique Run Out of Steam? From Matters of Fact to Matters of Concern', *Critical Inquiry*, 30.2 (Winter 2004), 225–48

LAROCHE, HADRIEN, *Le Dernier Genet: histoires des hommes infames* (Paris: Seuil, 1997)

——*The Last Genet*, trans. by David Homel (Vancouver: Arsenal Pulp Press, 2010)

LAVERY, CARL, 'A Panegyric for the Foot', *Performance Research*, 17.2 (January 2012), 3–10

——*The Politics of Jean Genet's Late Theatre: Spaces of Revolution* (Manchester: Manchester University Press, 2010)

——'To Perform Genet: Transversalité, Blessure, Pouvoir', in *Genet et les arts*, ed. by Agnès Vannouvong (Paris: Presses du réel, 2013), pp. 133–47

LAWRENCE, TIM, *Samuel Beckett's Critical Aesthetics* (Basingstoke: Palgrave Macmillan, 2018)

LEVINAS, EMMANUEL, *Difficile liberté* (Paris: Albin Michel, 1976)

——*Time and the Other*, trans. by Richard A. Cohen (Pittsburgh, PA: Duquesne University Press, 1987)

——, *Totalité et infinité* (The Hague: Martinus Nijhoff, 1961)

LORDE, AUDRE, *Sister Outsider: Essays and Speeches* (Trumansberg, NY: Crossing Press, 1984)

LYNCH, THOMAS, 'Euclid', in *The Walking Papers* (London: Jonathan Cape, 2010), pp. 3–4

LYOTARD, JEAN-FRANÇOIS, *Le Différend* (Paris: Minuit, 1983)

——*Les Transformateurs Duchamp* (Paris: Galilée, 1977)

——*Duchamp's TRANS/formers*, trans. by Ian McLeod (Leuven: Leuven University Press, 2010)

MACLACHLAN, IAN, 'A Hinge', in *Reading Derrida's 'Of Grammatology'*, ed. by Sean Gaston and Ian Maclachlan (London: Continuum, 2011), pp. 74–75

MAGEDERA, IAN HOLLIS, *Jean Genet: Les Bonnes*, Glasgow Introductory Guides to French Literature, 42 (Glasgow: University of Glasgow French and German Publications, 1998)

MARTIN, BILL, *Matrix and Line: Derrida and the Possibilities of Postmodern Social Theory* (Albany: State University of New York Press, 1992)

MARTY, ÉRIC, *Bref séjour à Jerusalem* (Paris: Gallimard, 2003)

——*Genet: Post-scriptum* (Paris: Verdier, 2006)

MATHEWS, TIMOTHY, *The Art of Relation* (London: I. B. Tauris, 2014)

——*Literature, Art and the Pursuit of Decay in Twentieth-century France* (Cambridge: Cambridge University Press, 2000)

——*Reading Apollinaire: Theories of Poetic Language* (Manchester: Manchester University Press, 1990)

MAY, TODD, *Gilles Deleuze: An Introduction* (Cambridge: Cambridge University Press, 2005)

MERLEAU-PONTY, MAURICE, *Phénoménologie de la perception* (Paris: Gallimard, 1945)

——*Phenomenology of Perception*, trans. by Colin Smith (London: Routledge, 1996)

MICHAUX, HENRI, *Emergences-résurgences* (Genève: Albert Skira, 1972)

——*Misérable miracle: la mescaline. Avec quarante-huit dessins et documents manuscrits originaux de l'auteur* (Paris: Gallimard, 1972)

——*Darkness Moves: An Henri Michaux Anthology, 1927–1984*, trans. by David Ball (Berkeley: University of California Press, 1997)

MINEMURA, SUGURU, *Jean Genet et la poétique du bagne (de la cellule pénitentiaire au bagne intime)* (Villeneuve d'Ascq: Atelier National de Reproduction des Thèses, 2001)

MORALY, JEAN-BERNARD, and OTHERS, *Les Nègres au port de la lune: Genet et les différences* (Paris: La Différence, 1988)

NANCY, JEAN-LUC, *Être singulier pluriel* (Paris: Galilée, 1996)

——*Being Singular Plural*, trans. by Robert D. Richardson and Anne E. O'Byrne (Stanford, CA: Stanford University Press, 2000)

——*Le Sens du monde* (Paris: Galilée, 1993)

——*The Sense of the World*, trans. by Jeffrey Librett (Minneapolis: University of Minnesota Press, 2008)

NIETZSCHE, FRIEDRICH, *Thus Spake Zarathustra* (Kent: Digireads, 2007)

NEUTRES, JÉRÔME, *Genet sur les routes du sud* (Paris: Fayard, 2002)

OKAMURO, MINAKO, 'Quad and the Jungian Mandala', in *Samuel Beckett: Crossroads and Borderline, l'œuvre carrefour/ l'œuvre limite*, ed. by Emmanuel Jacquard (London: Rodopi, 1997), pp. 125–36

PASCAL, BLAISE, *De l'esprit géométrique; entretien avec M. Sacy; Écrits sur la grâce et autres textes*, ed. by André Clair (Paris: Flammarion, 1985)

PEETERS, BENOÎT, *Derrida* (Paris: Flammarion, 2010)

PROCLUS, *A Commentary on the First Book of Euclid's Elements*, trans. by Glenn R. Morrow (Princeton, NJ: Princeton University Press, 1970)

PROVENCHER, DENIS, *Queer Maghrebi French: Language, Temporalities, Transfiliations* (Liverpool: Liverpool University Press, 2017)

RAWES, PEG, *Space, Geometry and Aesthetics: Through Kant and Towards Deleuze* (Basingstoke: Palgrave Macmillan, 2008)

RICH, ADRIENNE, *Blood, Bread, and Poetry: Selected Prose, 1979–1985* (New York: Norton, 1986)

SAID, EDWARD, 'On Genet's Late Work', in *Imperialism and Theatre*, ed. by J. Ellen Gainor (London: Routledge, 1995), pp. 230–42

——*On Late Style: Music and Literature Against the Grain* (London: Bloomsbury Academic, 2017)

SARTRE, JEAN-PAUL, *Saint Genet: comédien et martyr* (Paris: Gallimard, 1952)

——*Saint Genet: Actor & Martyr*, trans. by Bernard Frechtman (London: Heinemann, 1988)

SERRES, MICHEL, 'The Geometry of the Incommunicable: Madness', in *Foucault and His Interlocutors*, ed. by Arnold Ira Davidson (Chicago: University of Chicago Press, 1997), pp. 36–56

SIVITER, CLARE, *Tragedy and Nation in the Age of Napoleon* (Liverpool: Liverpool University Press, 2020)

SOBANET, ANDREW, *Jail Sentences: Representing Prison in Twentieth-century French Fiction* (Lincoln & London: University of Nebraska Press, 2008)

SPIVAK, GAYATRI CHAKRAVORTY, *Outside in the Teaching Machine* (New York: Routledge, 1993)

STEPHENS, ELIZABETH, 'Corporeographies: The Dancing Body in *'adame Miroir* and *Un chant d'amour*', in *Jean Genet: Performance and Politics*, ed. by Clare Finburgh, Carl Lavery and Maria Shevtsova (Basingstoke: Palgrave Macmillan, 2006), pp. 159–64

——*Queer Writing: Homoeroticism in Jean Genet's Fiction* (Basingstoke: Palgrave Macmillan, 2009)

STEVENS, BRETT, 'Beckett's Mathematics in *Quad*', in *A Companion to Samuel Beckett*, ed. by S. E. Gonstarksi (Chichester: Wiley-Blackwell, 2010), pp. 164–81

SONTAG, SUSAN, *Against Interpretation and Other Essays* (New York: Dell, 1966)

THODY, PHILIP, *Jean Genet* (London: Hamish Hamilton, 1968)

UVSLØKK, GEIR, *Jean Genet: une écriture des perversions* (Amsterdam & New York: Rodopi, 2011)

VÅGNES, ØYVIND, 'Working Through Contradiction Interminably? Towards a *Mathesis singularis*', *Nordic Journal of English Studies*, 2.2 (2003), 325–44

VANNOUVONG, AGNÈS, ed., *Genet et les arts* (Paris: Presses du réel, 2013)

VITRUVIUS, *On Architecture* (London: Penguin, 2009)

VOLTAIRE, *Questions sur l'Encyclopédie* (Paris: Stoupe, 1792)

WARNER, MICHAEL, *Fear of a Queer Planet* (Minneapolis & London: University of Minnesota Press, 1993)

WATSON, JANELL, 'Guattari's Black Holes and the Post-Media Era', in *Holes, Burrows, Lines of Flight: Media and Spatiality in Deleuze and Guattari*, ed. by Janelle Blankenship (= *Polygraph*, 14 (2001)), 23–54

WEBER, SAMUEL, *Theatricality as Medium* (New York: Fordham University Press, 2004)

WILLS, DAVID, 'La Techno-poétique de l'autre... en pointillé', in *Rêver, croire, penser autour d'Hélène Cixous*, ed. by Bruno Clément and Marta Segarra (Paris: Campagne première, 2010), pp. 115–27

WHITE, EDMUND, *The Burning Library: Essays* (London: Vintage, 1995)

——*Genet* (London: Chatto & Windus, 1993)

ŽIŽEK, SLAVOJ, *The Puppet and the Dwarf: The Perverse Core of Christianity* (Cambridge, MA, & London: MIT Press, 2003)

INDEX

❖